ABOUT THE COVER

The painting on the cover is an original computer graphic by Sabra Stein. It depicts the symbolic relationship between human and God.

In this painting, human is represented by the cogwheel containing twelve segments of color; whereas God is represented by a beam of divine light which is both outside the cogwheel, and yet at its very center.

A cogwheel was chosen to symbolize that a human is caught up in the restrictions of time when he/she functions as a part of this three-dimensional incarnation, just as a cogwheel is caught in the restrictions of time when it functions as a part of the inner workings of a mechanical watch. The twelve sections of color were added to the symbolic human to represent the Twelve Rays and the Twelve Chakras which have become so vital to the evolutionary progress of humankind.

A beam of divine light was chosen as the symbolic representation of God because in this way, God could be shown to be outside of time, and yet at the very center of human existence.

A swash of multicolored light spirals inward to join into oneness with the single beam of divine light symbolizing the Journey of the individual into oneness with God.

The fact that there is such a path, and that it is unique to each of us, is the major message of the book!

Cover illustrations and design by Sabra Stein

What a Few Previewers Have Said About This Book

* Excellent work which is well researched and presents cogent arguments! I agree that the role of corporate religion is decidedly not to proclaim itself to be the only place in which the Beloved can be found. You make that point repeatedly and effectively!

* The Journey back into God is, for each of us, an intensely personal and unique one. The moment of awakening to this truth is a fleeting touch of enlightmentment and a watershed experience along the Way. It is personal. The religious community can provide an environment of safety and encouragement in which the desire for the Beloved can be born and nurtured within us. That and that alone. Everything beyond that, all the rest, is our work on ourself. You present that conclusion often and well!

* Together with your personal experiences in Appendix C, Chapter 5 of *Part Two* stands out as some of the most powerful writing in your entire series of books. It is indeed a treat to nod in agreement with you as I resonate with what you have written.

Father John W. Groff, Jr., *Episcopal Priest*

* I have just finished reading your manuscript draft, and before I attempt to answer your questions, I must comment about my heart's feelings. *A Personal Pathway to God* is quite possibly the most visceral, heart moving and warm book of truths that I have ever read. Your presentation and the clarity of your words combined with your ability to talk to [not down to] me made the experience exciting and memorable.

* I would make no changes to this draft. I love it! I believe you have put together a loving, intellectually satisfying and well-written book on a subject matter integral to our happiness and success. Further, the introduction of your personal beliefs [and the reasons why] add charm, heart and life to an already detailed and insightful text.

Richard Fuller, Senior Editor, *Metaphysical Reviews*

* Again, you have written a book which simply <u>must</u> be published. In my opinion, if you could read only one book by Dr. L. David Moore, this is the one it should be!

* I mean this as a compliment. This book is not a manual, for it is not written in that manner. However, it is a marvelous Handbook on the practice of Buddhism for Christians!

Sabra Stein, founding co-editor of *Aquarius, A Sign of the Times*

* You have, as usual, done a wonderful job of clarifying basic premises which need changing. This is a beautiful, honest book which will delight any who truly seek God.

* I would like permission to use the explanation you give in the "Third Viewpoint of Reincarnation" in my new book *Gateway to the Dimensions*. This concept presents an explanation for something which has caused a struggle within me for some time.

Alice Bryant, Author of *The Message of the Crystal Skull*

* *A Personal Pathway to God* is a pathfinder and map-maker for the new paradigm of belief system being developed at The Center for New Beginnings. I will use it as a reference work and teaching aid in our new series of study and exploration called *Integrative Spirituality*.

Joseph Whitner, ordained Presbyterian minister and founder of The Center for New Beginnings

DEDICATION

Most books are dedicated by the author to a person or to persons who have helped along the way. As an example, I dedicated the first book of this series to all the members of the families to which I have belonged: to the family of blood; to the family of religion; and to the family of mankind.

I then dedicated the second book to a silent family whose names were unknown to me—to the family which consists of those who love, believe in and follow Jesus Christ, but who have left the Church which bears his name for reasons of conscience. There may have been times when they did not know why they felt they had to leave the Church with its doctrines and dogmas; but they did so because staying just did not seem right to them. I suggested that possibly through the pages of that book, they would start to understand why they felt they had to leave; and possibly they could find comfort in the hard and lonely decision which they made.

This book is dedicated to a family similar to that of the second book. However, it has been expanded in two ways. First, this book is dedicated to the family of all who have left the restrictive teachings of any established religion, whatever that religion might be. Secondly, this book is dedicated to "where we can go from here"; for the personal way into oneness with God is indeed preferable to the institutional one.

And finally, all three books are dedicated to the man who provided the quotation below; for it is in this quotation that the understanding of the major lessons of all three books can be found.

"I never told my own religion nor scrutinized that of another. I never attempted to make a convert, nor wished to change another's creed. I am satisfied that yours must be an excellent religion to have produced a life of such exemplary virtue and correctness. For it is in our lives, and not from our words, that our religion must be judged."
                    Thomas Jefferson, 1816

A

PERSONAL PATHWAY

TO GOD

OUR SONG

OF FREEDOM

DR. L. DAVID MOORE

PENDULUM
PLUS

PENDULUM PLUS PRESS
ATLANTA, GA

© Copyright 1995 by L. David Moore

All rights are reserved. No part of this book may be reproduced, stored in a retrieval system, or transmitted in any form by any means, whether electronic, mechanical, photocopying, recording, or otherwise, without prior written permission of the copyright holder. Queries regarding rights and permissions should be addressed to Pendulum Plus Press, 3232 Cobb Parkway, Suite 414, Atlanta, GA 30339 USA.

The author acknowledges the tremendous help and encouragement given by his wife Jan, his daughter Sherry, and those who gave their honest appraisals in the preview of this work: *viz.* Father John W. Groff, Jr., Alice Bryant, Sabra Stein, Joseph Whitner, Elias DeMohan, and Erik Myrmo. The author also acknowledges that he received a lot of help and guidance from his higher self and those "unseen ones" who are in his heart, unseen or not.

First Edition, 1995

ISBN 0-9635665-3-9

Library of Congress Catalog Card Number 95-69223

Published by
PENDULUM PLUS PRESS
3232 COBB PARKWAY
SUITE 414
ATLANTA, GA 30339

Printed in the United States of America
10 9 8 7 6 5 4 3 2 1

TABLE OF CONTENTS

PRELUDE   1

NOTES FROM THE AUTHOR   3
    A Prayer for the Second Reformation   8

INTRODUCTION   9

PART ONE
BACKGROUND INFORMATION

CHAPTER 1
SOME POSSIBLE DEFINITIONS OF GOD   17

CHAPTER 2
THE MESSENGERS SENT FROM GOD
    AND THEIR MESSAGES   25
        Melchizedek of Salem   26
        Moses   32
        Zoroaster   34
        Buddha   37
        Confucius and Lao Tze   39
        Jesus Christ   42
        Muhammad   44
        Other Messengers   47

CHAPTER 3
HOW THE MESSAGES SENT BY GOD
    HAVE BEEN ALTERED BY HUMANS   49
        There is Only One God   50
        God Advises Us on How to Live   55
        God Created All Things
            and They Are Good   56
        God Wants Us to Listen   59
        God Wants Us to Have Communion
            with Nature/Humans   61
        All Laws Can Be Replaced
            by Unconditional Love   63
        Some Esoteric Thoughts   65

CHAPTER 4
SOME THOUGHTS ABOUT REINCARNATION   71
    Time and Space   72
    Biblical Background   75
    General World Literature   79
    Two Viewpoints   84
    The Monadic-Influence Concept   86
    A Third Viewpoint   89
    The Universal Need   94

CHAPTER 5
ADDITIONAL BACKGROUND INFORMATION   97
    Dimensionality   97
    God's Thermodynamic Universe   103
    The Phenomenon of Coincidence   107
    The Chakra System   114
    Some Thoughts about Numbers   117
    The Presence of God   120

PART TWO
COSMIC CONCEPTS AND PERSONAL PATHWAYS

CHAPTER 1
THE FIRST COSMIC CONCEPT:
THE CREATION — 127
- Background Information — 127
- Analysis — 136
- Existence of Pain, Suffering and Evil — 141

CHAPTER 2
THE SECOND COSMIC CONCEPT:
UNCONDITIONAL LOVE — 145
- Background on Unconditional Love — 146
- Issues Concerning Unconditional Love — 168
- A Hymn for the Second Reformation — 178

CHAPTER 3
THE THIRD COSMIC CONCEPT:
ONENESS WITH GOD VIA FREE WILL — 179
- Oneness with God — 179
- Free Will — 184

CHAPTER 4
THE FOURTH COSMIC CONCEPT:
THE UNIQUE PATHWAY — 189

CHAPTER 5
PERSONAL PATHWAYS — 195
- The Worship of Material Things — 197

The Worship of God as Defined by Humans	201
The Worship of God as Defined by Spirit	209
The Absorption of Unconditional Love	213
The Absorption of Nothingness which is Everything	216
The Seven Seals	220

POSTLUDE:
A SUMMATION OF A FEW BELIEFS   229

REFERENCE INFORMATION

APPENDIX A: Additional Notes from the Author   239

APPENDIX B: Creation Myths from Around the World   244

APPENDIX C: Personal Steps Along the Pathway   251

BIBLIOGRAPHY   269

INDEX   271

PRELUDE

I BELIEVE THAT

In the beginning, the One God created *All* that ever has been;
And all which was created was good.
Nothing else was ever created,
Only transformed as needed to meet God's will.
One creation was made in Oneness with God's own image.
It is the creature known as *Human*.
God loved this human very much;
So much, in fact, that like a loving Father or Mother,
He/She sent human away from the loving Oneness,
So that human could experience all that existed,
Especially that which was *in* Nature and *in* other humans.
God did this in a sense of *Unconditional Love*,
A love so nurturing, fulfilling and joyful,
That it does not command or control.
When God looked at all of this, God felt that it was very good.
But in order to make human more completely like God
after human had experienced all that is,
He/She went one step further and gave human *Free Will*.
God did this so that human would choose
the experiences to be understood
By hearing God's Will, rather than by obeying God's Law.
For God is so encompassed by Unconditional Love,
That He/She creates nothing which must be obeyed,
Only that which the one being loved chooses to obey

As a means of returning God's love.
Now all was set for human to go out and experience all,
And to understand which experiences fit into God's will,
And which do not.
Human does this by listening,
And then by making his or her own, Free Will choice,
And not by following another's direction.
For each human is unique,
And only in this way can each unique human
Find his or her own, unique way
Into Oneness with God.

NOTES FROM THE AUTHOR

This book is the third book in a series. That series is described in the Introduction. The purpose for this segment is to present some thoughts about the author's feelings.

First, I would like to say that the Prelude which precedes this segment not only constitutes my belief system, it also represents an outline of this book. Next, despite my desire not to teach or preach, there may be parts of this work which may seem to present what I want you to think or believe. However, my real purpose is never to tell you *what* you should think or believe, but merely to convince you that you *should* think about what you do believe. I also want to state that by that thinking, you should not blindly follow the direction presented to you by another person, whether that other person directs his thoughts to you from the pulpit, or from the pages of a book—any book.

The major purpose for this book is to present the thought that the pathway into oneness with God is a personal pathway, unique for each individual being. This thought is based on two personal beliefs: [1] that the established religions are not the only place in which the Beloved One can be found, but instead are the places which provide encouragement and safety until the individual can strike out to find his/her own personal pathway; and [2] that God may have given us Four Cosmic Concepts in the beginning which the established religions neglected, thus creating unrest and disharmony between those created in the image of God. The Four Cosmic Concepts are presented in the Introduction, and described in detail in *Part Two*.

As this work developed, two things happened which changed its character. First, in an earlier draft of this work, the four "Cosmic Concepts" were called "Universal Truths." I later realized that by the term "Truths," I was saying that these were truths for all, rather than concepts which I have accepted for myself. Consequently, the term "Cosmic Concepts" was chosen as a substitute. Secondly, the original title for this book was *The Essence of Christ in the New Age*. In that concept, I was hoping to further the aims of the first two books which were to indicate to Christians that they should have no fear in leaving the restrictive thinking of the Church and broadening their spiritual horizons in order to find their way into oneness with God, a concept similar to the atonement ["at-one-ment"] taught by the established religions, particularly Christianity.

However, I started getting many letters and calls from the readers of the earlier books which stated that those books were wonderful background which had given them an understanding of the problem, and also had released many guilt feelings about having left the religion of their roots. However, many went on to say, "Where do we go from here?" Because I find that the person of Jesus Christ reflects the God who calls to me more than any other reflection that I can find, I answered by stating that the essence of Christ would take on a new meaning in the New Age, and that the restrictive teachings developed by the men of the early Church would be expanded to encompass a newer paradigm of belief. I went on to state that this could possibly lead to a second reformation of the Church.

It was with that intent that I started to write this book; but as it developed, I more and more accepted the belief that Jesus Christ was not the only representative of the Christ Consciousness who had been on this Earth. A personal experience which demonstrated this belief to me is presented in Appendix C [see pages 266-7]. This experience was especially important to me in that after more than fifty years in the Christian Church, I finally understood what Paul meant when he said, "it is no longer I who live, but Christ who lives in me" [Gal. 2:20].

As a result of that and other experiences which taught the meaning of Love, I came to understand that the restrictive teachings of the organized religions have kept many people from accepting the belief that Christ, and God, can live in them through Love. Consequently, instead of looking at *The Essence of Christ in the New Age* as I thought I would, I was examining the many personal pathways into oneness with God which were being practiced by people of good faith in all religious activities. In addition, I was made aware that the spiritual journey of each individual was accelerated when each was able to develop *A Personal Pathway to God* by singing the song of freedom which occurs when the restrictive teachings are removed. An example of *Our Song of Freedom* had entered into my being when I allowed the restrictive teachings of the Christian Church to be removed from me. This was an example of the freedom which is realized when all restrictive thinking is removed, as each individual accepts that becoming the "Christ Consciousness within" can develop *A Personal Pathway to God*. It is a song of freedom which leads to a closer relationship with a personal God, and even a closer understanding of the Love of the Christ. At least, that was my experience.

As a consequence of that experience, I was finding that the answer to the question of "where do we go from here" is not to be found solely in the Christian Bible and doctrines. In fact, it is possible that rich as that heritage is, those who are the farthest from finding their unique, personal pathway into oneness with God are to be found within the pews of the orthodox, doctrinaire Christian Churches. It was with this disturbing thought that I decided to address an audience which would be interested in more than merely the future essence of the Christ. Consequently, a new name and a new direction for this work were developed.

This book contains a Prelude which presents an outline of the entire book. The Prelude is followed by an Introduction which presents the entire book. This, in turn, is followed by *Part One* which presents the Background Information used to develop the thoughts presented in *Part Two*.

Part Two then presents the four Cosmic Concepts in greater detail than in the Introduction, and shows how these Concepts were altered by the humans of each religion. Finally, Chapter 5 of *Part Two* presents a possible definition of the milestones along a personal pathway into oneness with God. One previewer of this work, an

Episcopal Priest, said that Chapter 5 was the most powerful writing in the whole book, and stood out as some of the best religious writing of the entire series. The pathway presented in Chapter 5 is given with the full knowledge that it does not define anyone's pathway for them, because that must be done by each unique individual for his or her own unique self. However, there may be some understanding here which one might use in developing that unique pathway.

In the final part of this work, there are three short, independent Appendixes. Appendix A presents some additional Notes from the Author. Appendix B presents some Creation stories from around the world. In my opinion, these delightful stories are well worth reading. Appendix C relates some of my personal experiences along the pathway during this present physical incarnation. These experiences are very meaningful to me, for they have helped to generate some understanding about what was happening to me during this journey called life. They are presented here for the first time in print.

Unlike either of the previous books which were heavily footnoted, this book has no footnotes. In the few places where a reference was needed, I have included enough in the text to indicate the quality of the source. I have come to the conclusion that footnotes inhibit thought flow. It is hoped that by this elimination, the reader will think whether or not the thoughts being developed apply to him/her, and not need to break into those thoughts to see where the author got that particular idea or piece of information. If any reader wants to have the reference material for a particular point, I will supply it. The reference literature which was used in the development of this book is presented in the Bibliography.

Also, unlike the pronouns used in the previous books, I have used the acronym "S/He" as the pronoun for God. I do this to represent that God is neither a She nor a He, but is beyond such descriptions of mortality. In essence, I feel that God is an androgyny which is not adequately represented by terms of polarity or duality such as "Father," or "Mother," or "He," or "She." However, since I am writing in the English language, I have to use some sort of pronouns in the structuring of sentences, else the use of the word "God" would soon get monotonous.

Finally, I do feel I have something to offer as a religious writer, though none of my formal education was in a theological institution. Actually, I feel somewhat fortunate that is true; for my ability to think for myself has not been excessively inhibited by somebody else's knowledge. Throughout my life, I have been a deeply religious man in the original meaning of the word "religion." This word comes from the Latin word *religio* which means "bond between man and the gods." In turn, it is derived from two Latin words: *re* meaning "back" and *ligare* meaning "to bind." Consequently, I am religious in the sense of wanting to "tie back to God," but not necessarily religious in the presently accepted use of the word which is "a follower of organized doctrines."

Despite that, for fifty years of my life, I was a baptized, active member of mainstream Christianity, and I remember that experience with a great deal of fondness. I highly recommend that each individual spend a significant period of his/her life within the warm community of the established religion of his/her choice. My choice was Christianity, and for over twenty years, I was a highly respected teacher of mainstream Christianity to adult classes.

But that has recently changed. During my retirement, I have spent most of my time and energy trying to generate the understanding needed to continue on my pilgrimage as a follower of the Christ. Unfortunately, for many reasons which have been presented in all three books, I do not find the understanding I need within the Church; for I fear that the Church wants to dictate what and how I think in order to be accepted as a follower of the Christ.

Consequently, I have left the organized, doctrinaire Church; and I am writing these books to show how a lifelong Christian has been able to find a closer personal relationship with God, and to develop a stronger identity with the love of Christ, than I was able to find within the Church. Possibly from these writings, others can move closer to God and to the Christ or the Christ Consciousness, whether they stay within the Church or leave it. I sincerely hope that *you* can experience the closeness of a personal God, and the warmth of an Unconditional Love from the one who represents the Christ to you.

A Prayer for the Second Reformation

This Prayer was given to me in a dream when I was in retreat at The Center for New Beginnings in Northern Georgia. I share it with the belief that the Lord's Prayer was developed within a society which believed that the Earth was the center of the universe with a Heaven above and a Hell below. Since many people presently doubt that picture of God's Universe, it would seem as if an up-dating in words might be desired. I present this prayer as a shared gift, and with no offense intended for those who will continue to follow the beautiful and powerful words of the original Lord's Prayer.

LORD'S PRAYER	*PRAYER FOR THE SECOND REFORMATION*
Our Father who art in Heaven, Hallowed by thy name.	*Our Everything who is Everywhere, We love you unconditionally and unreservedly.*
Thy kingdom come, Thy will be done, On earth as it is in heaven.	*Open the Kingship within us all, And reconnect us to You, Both here and throughout the vastness of Your universe.*
Give us this day our daily bread; And forgive us our debts As we also have forgiven our debtors;	*Help us to radiate Love, the Bread of Life In order to show You rather than our own Ego to Others;*
And lead us not into temptation, But deliver us from evil.	*And to show that our activities are driven by Spirit, Rather than by Ego.*
For thine is the kingdom and the power and the glory, forever.	*For only in that way can our return to You be an everlasting one.*
AMEN	*SO BE IT*

INTRODUCTION

This series started with *Christianity and the New Age Religion*, published in the Summer of 1993. That book was intended to be "A Bridge Toward Mutual Understanding." For many people, it has been a bridge which has generated understanding. The second book was *The Christian Conspiracy*, published in the Fall of 1994. That book was intended to describe "How the Teachings of Christ Have Been Altered by Christians." It has been successful in defining today's Christian by presenting the story of how the orthodox teachings of today's Church got established. It is a fascinating story because most of those teachings did not come from the Christ!

This book describes the personal pathways which those who love and honor God may be taking in the future. It is not intended to present religious dogma [i.e. that which must be believed] or even religious doctrines [i.e. that which is taught as a part of a systematic religion]. Instead, it is intended to present *understanding* which the reader may accept or reject.

The major purpose for this book is to present an example of a personal pathway to God, using the premise that as God populated the universe with conscious beings created in the image of God, S/He blessed them with four Cosmic Concepts which were intended to create peace and harmony between all of them. Unfortunately, many of those beings have decided, as an act of Free Will, to ignore these Cosmic Concepts, or even to modify them in an attempt to control the followers of a particular religious sect. As a result of this activity, unrest and disharmony have continually existed between those created in the image of God.

The four Cosmic Concepts presented in this book are:

1. That there is One God who created *all things*, and all of the things which S/He created are *good*;

2. That God practices *Unconditional Love* for all which S/He created, and requests that all of God's creatures and other creations also practice Unconditional Love;

3. That it is the Supreme Will that all of God's creations find their way into *oneness* with Him/Her by their own *Free Will*, even though such an effort might take an eternity;

4. That the pathway which each creation uses to find the way into oneness with God, is a *unique* pathway unlike that used by any other unique act of creation.

These Cosmic Concepts and their use on an individual's personal pathway into oneness with God will be described more fully in the five chapters of *Part Two*.

It is probable that many will now ask for proof that these four thoughts were given by God in the beginning. However, it is no more possible to establish that these four thoughts are the correct emanations of God, then it is to prove that God exists. Many attempts have been made to prove that God exists, but such proofs have been indirect at best. Many have tried to prove that God exists because there is order in the universe, and that there would be no order without a Supreme Being who created order where there should be chaos. Such indirect proof has satisfied some, but if that is accepted as proof, then there is a similar proof that these Cosmic Concepts exist; for in neglecting them, mankind has created chaos where there should be order. I believe that mankind will continue to flounder around in its present chaotic state until these four Cosmic Concepts are followed by the Free Will choice of all, thus generating the peace and harmony between creatures which was originally intended. We will then truly be in oneness with God's essence and will participate in His/Her kingdom.

I feel certain that many who have heard the messages presented in a church, or in a synagogue, or in a mosque, or in whatever source the voice of man has proclaimed that his God, and *only* his God is the true God, will now want to pause and say, "Well, that isn't the way I heard it." I echo that statement. As I was growing up, that isn't the way I heard it either. I used to have pity for those who had not heard the word of Jesus Christ as it was presented to me from the pulpit. I now believe that at the same time, there was an Arabic, or Jewish, or Indian boy about my age who felt the same way about me.

But I challenge anyone to go back to the root sources of the major established religions and see if the messengers from God did not give us the Cosmic Concepts presented above, each in his own individual way. I would also challenge anyone to deny that these messages were later distorted by the followers of each messenger. The information which supports this stance is presented in Chapters 1-3 of *Part One*, and is repeated throughout *Part Two*.

A short summary of the four Cosmic Concepts is presented in the following paragraphs. As previously stated, a more complete discussion is presented in *Part Two*.

The first Cosmic Concept has to do with the fact that God created *all* things, and that *all* which S/He created was *good*. Later, many followers distorted this message by defining the physical body as an evil thing which entrapped the good soul; or by going further and defining all material things as being evil with only the spiritual things being good; or by going even further to claim that all things which have been defined as evil were created by man and thus were not from God; or by going even beyond that to state that since anything evil was not of God, then all who would commit any evil act were not of God, and were therefore to be condemned for eternity. These distortions were introduced by the follower, and not by the messenger. They were introduced by man, and not by the messenger sent from God.

The second Cosmic Concept describes the belief that God loves *everyone* and *everything* without any conditions being attached. This means that S/He loves *all*, and not just the Christian, or just the Muslim, or just the Jew, or just the Hindu, or just the Buddhist, or just the heterosexual, or just the Church-goer, or just the one who loudly beats on his chest to proclaim his devotion to God, or just the one who lives within the warmth of a conventional family, or just the deer, or just the dolphin, or just the eagle, or just the oak tree, or just the sandstone, or just any other single unit of creation. God loves them *all*, without conditions; for since God <u>created</u> them all, S/He <u>loves</u> them all. The distortions which the follower has introduced to the teachings of Unconditional Love presented by the messenger could fill many large volumes, for in order to organize and give special meaning to each established religion, all religious leaders have had to proclaim that they, and only they, know the *true way* back to God; and that you could get on this true pathway only if you met certain conditions which they would define for you. The followers have therefore forgotten about the law of Unconditional Love, despite the teachings of the messengers sent from God.

The third Cosmic Concept was concerned with the fact that *all* will be in oneness with God and be with Him/Her forever. This is the universalistic approach, so condemned by those who proclaim that Jesus Christ, or Mohammed, or Buddha, or Zoroaster, or some other messenger is the final Word of God; and that therefore, no additional truth will ever be presented from the ineffable God, even if one were to be so patient as to wait an eternity to hear it!

By these statements, I do not criticize those who accept one messenger to follow, for I do this myself. In addition, I do not criticize those who participate in an established religion, for I did that for many years myself and found it to be a truly wonderful experience. Instead of criticism, I applaud their commitment.

I follow Jesus the Christ; because his reflection of God represents the God who calls to me. But this acceptance of the Christ does not mean that I accept what the Church which bears his name has done to his message; for I feel that God loves *all* of us *unconditionally*, and not solely the practicing Christian.

Again, some reader may want to say, "Well, that isn't the way I heard it." And I would reply, "Please reflect, think and feel your own internal knowing."

As a part of that reflection, take a look at how the messenger I follow, Jesus the Christ, absorbed these Cosmic Concepts. I feel justified in calling Jesus Christ a "messenger" rather than the *only* son of God as the early Church Fathers declared, for neither Christ nor the scriptures in their original language had proclaimed this concept. The Church has been selective in their presentation of the prophecies about the Messiah from scripture. As a simple example, they proclaim that Jesus was born of a *virgin* to fulfill prophecy even though Isaiah 7:14 in its original language does not say that at all. The Hebrew word used in this verse is *almah* which means "young woman" and has absolutely no reference to her sexual experience. The Hebrew word for a "sexually inexperienced woman" is *betulah*, which does not appear in Isaiah 7:14. It is a mis-translation of prophecy to say that Jesus would be born of a "virgin," and yet it is often proclaimed by the men of the Church as evidence that Jesus fulfilled the ancient prophecies.

However, these same men never proclaim that Jesus would be a *messenger* from God, even though Isaiah predicts to Israel that they will be deaf to a messenger God will send [Isaiah 42:19]. This is no mis-translation; for Isaiah, <u>does</u> predict that God will send a messenger. For many reasons presented in the first two books of this series and emphasized later in this book, I see Jesus Christ as a very special, unique, one-of-a-kind messenger and teacher from God who is still available to me and whom I follow because he reflects the God who calls to me. I can follow him without accepting the theological theories of the early Church Fathers who proclaimed Jesus as *God*, some 300 years <u>after</u> the Resurrection.

As a messenger, Jesus followed the four Cosmic Concepts. First, he did not condemn material things as evil. Instead he expressed joy during festive occasions at which wine was served, and expressed joy as little children experienced the things of this Earth. In addition, as a carpenter he seemed to enjoy working with material things. Finally, he did not reject material things as he admonished us: *Render therefore to Caesar the things that are Caesar's, and to God the things that are God's* [Matt. 22:21]. Instead, he rejected the teachings of the Zealots who would condemn Rome's material demands as an evil thing.

Both here and in Matt. 6:32 where he says that the Father knows that people need material things, Jesus says that material things are not evil unless you would choose them instead of God. He therefore seemed to practice the belief that God created all things, and that the things which God had created were good, so long as he did not reject the divinity in them by using them to follow his will rather than that of his Father.

Next, he showed that he accepted people unconditionally. He did this when he dined with the many who were rejected by the Pharisees, such as tax collectors and sinners [Matt. 9:11]; and also when he accepted and enjoyed the company of the Samaritans who were hated by the society of his time; and finally when he tried to elevate the female of his time above the social status to which she had been assigned by her society. He therefore seemed to absorb the second Cosmic Concept as he accepted *all* people without placing any sort of condition on his acceptance of them.

In addition, there is his teaching that all which was needed to be with God was to accept His will. He knew that he and the Father were one [see John 10:30]. He even predicted that all would attain oneness with God when he declared that "Where I am you may be also" [John 14:3]. Consequently, he seemed to accept the third Cosmic Concept as he explained to his friends and followers how they could find oneness with God similar to that which he had found.

While doing all of this, Jesus the Christ showed that he participated in the fourth Cosmic Concept as he taught the world how to live if only they would do it. How did he demonstrate that participation? He did it by demonstrating that when there was a fork in the road which led to God, the path to be taken was God's will for your life and not your own will. When he personally came to this fork, he took the fork which was God's will rather than his own; and he did this so consistently that soon God's will and his will became identical and synchronous.

As he did this for himself, he followed a pathway which was unique for him, just as each of us follows a pathway which is unique for us. Getting back to Jesus, in my own mind I have absolutely no doubt that Jesus the Christ could have turned stone into bread; or could have levitated above the crowd beneath the high temple in Jerusalem; or could have run any Earthly kingdom he would choose. But to do this would not have been following his Father's will for his life; and so he turned his back on such temptations [Matthew, Chapter 4 and Luke, Chapter 4].

To me, these temptations of Jesus Christ have helped to define the temptations of evil and the reason that evil exists on Earth. God wants all to return to him, but only by the choices they make when they use their own Free Will. If there were no evil, then there would be no choice to make. When the fork in the road would come, there would be only one direction to go—that of God's will. But with the existence of evil [defined further in Chapters 1 and 2 of *Part Two*], then the fork in the road presents two choices—God's will or the will of the individual. As we will discuss in more detail in many parts of this book, particularly in Chapter 5 of *Part Two*, there are many forks in the eternal road which an eternal soul will follow. Each of these forks will eventually lead to God, although some will introduce a few detours. The lesson of life is to get into oneness with God by using the pathway which is meant for you, whatever that pathway might be.

Some may now want to ask why God did not simply pass a Law which had to be obeyed instead of expressing the wish that all would come into oneness with Him/Her. After all, if God is omnipotent [all-powerful], why not merely demand by Law that they all come into oneness, *immediately*. The simple answer is that God chose not to do it that way. Instead of *ordering* all to come into oneness with God, S/He wanted them to do it of their own *Free Will*. The word "will" is derived from the Latin verb *velle*, meaning "to wish"; whereas the word "law" is derived from the Old Norse verb *lag*, meaning "to lay down." Therefore, when God wills something, S/He wishes it to happen; whereas a Law from God would mean that the decision has already been laid down. In other words, if God were to have passed the Law, we would have had no say in the matter; and spiritual growth on the part of an individual would be a meaningless term. In order to encourage spiritual growth, God *willed* [i.e. wished] it to happen, rather than *ordering* it to happen by making it a requirement.

The message about God's *will* is the message presented by Her/His messengers. However, that did not prevent the leaders of those who followed the messengers from passing laws or legal requirements which had to be *obeyed*. They often did this to promote their own thoughts or careers. This happened frequently within the ranks of those who followed the Buddha, Zoroaster, the Christ, or Mohammed. But if God's will becomes a law which must be obeyed however you may feel about it, then what purpose is served in practicing Unconditional Love for all the other people of this Earth, especially those who do not follow the law which you must obey? In my opinion, this denial of Unconditional Love would prohibit a return to oneness with God. I feel that by letting God's will become your will, you will accept that all created things are good, and that all of His/Her creations are to be loved unconditionally. When God's will and your will coincide at all times, then the return to oneness with God is automatic. However, when God's will becomes a Law dictated to you by another, it becomes a tremendous blockage to the goal of freely accepting God's will for your life. This issue will be addressed frequently in this book, particularly in Chapter Five of *Part Two*.

The book which follows is a journey of thought and understanding—one which each person is invited to evaluate, and to accept or reject as he/she sees fit. These thoughts will not be accepted by all, but that is as it should be; for each individual is unique, and each unique individual has to experience his/her own personal pathway into oneness with God. The thoughts which are presented are some which have been useful for me.

I will close this Introduction by recalling that during the premier showing of the television show *Chicago Hope*, an episode came up which involved a very serious, "never-been-done" operation to separate Siamese twins. Just prior to starting on the operation, the leader of the surgical team made the following statement: "For those of you who have a God in their lives, please make contact now!"

In a paraphrase of that statement plus another statement attributed to the immortal Sherlock Holmes, I will say:

"Come, Dear Reader, if you realize that you have a God in your life, please make contact now, because the game is afoot!"

PART ONE
BACKGROUND INFORMATION

CHAPTER 1
SOME POSSIBLE
DEFINITIONS OF GOD

This chapter presents some thoughts about God. This background information has helped me on my personal pilgrimage. These thoughts do not represent dogma which has to be accepted, but are offered as suggestions which may help others to experience their personal pilgrimage.

Although this chapter suggests some definitions of God, no definition can possibly be totally adequate and consistently true for all; for to do this would require an understanding of God which is probably beyond the limits of human capabilities. However, some humans have defined God in such a way that something useful could be done with the definition; and some individuals have defined God in such a way that the definition could be used as a guideline for life, and as a definition for a personal pathway into oneness with God. In addition, some religions have defined God in such a way that many millions of followers have believed that they have been presented with the *only truth* about God.

But all of that falls by the wayside when it is realized and accepted that God is *ineffable*, and that all the great thinkers who have spent time thinking about God have come to the viewpoint that S/He is indeed ineffable. By doing so, they have stated that it is the ultimate folly for us to try to define the One who defines us.

Some definitions of "ineffable" are "beyond expression," or "indescribable," or "unspeakable." We speak of an ineffable delight when we have had an experience which we cannot describe to another person because they simply would not understand. We speak of an ineffable taste sensation when we believe that it is beyond the reach of language. We speak of an ineffable love when being with the specific person whom we love transcends mere words.

The word "ineffable" also means "not to be uttered; taboo." In using this definition, we speak of the "ineffable [i.e. "unspeakable"] name of the deity," and by doing so mean that His name is one which cannot be said. The basis for this is found in Exodus 3:13-16, which says:

Then Moses said To God, "If I come to the people of Israel and say to them, 'The God of your fathers has sent me to you,' and they ask me, 'What is his name?' what shall I say to them?" God said to Moses, "I AM WHO I AM." And he said, "Say this to the people of Israel, 'I AM has sent me to you.'"

This is the first time in the Bible that God has been asked to submit His name. The answer, "I AM WHO I AM," is a translation of a translation of a translation; and as such has "lost something in the translation." Most biblical scholars believe that the name which God said to Moses was the divine name, YHWH, a name which cannot be pronounced, although later, writers added vowels in order to pronounce the divine name as "Yahweh" or "Jehovah." But the Tetragrammaton of YHWH really is "the name which cannot be said," or the "ineffable [unspeakable] name of the deity." It ties into "I AM WHO I AM" through the Hebrew verb *hayah* meaning "to be."

Several pages which discuss the many names given to God are presented in *Christianity and the New Age Religion*, and will not be repeated in that depth here. However, those pages do support the point being made, which is that not only is God ineffable, so is His name; especially if one believes, as the ancients did, that the name and the essence of the one being named were not separate, but were the same. In our modern usage, we have tended to use the name "God"

Some Possible Definitions of God

to describe the One. The word "God" is merely a name which is more convenient to use than other names such as "the One," or "Beloved One," or "Supreme Being," or "El Shaddai," or "YHWH," or "Yahweh," or "Allah" or whatever other name we might use in reference to the one whose "name cannot be said," a phrase which states that even the <u>name</u> of God is beyond the comprehension of humans. If the understanding of the name of God is beyond us, then certainly the understanding of the character of God is even further beyond our comprehension.

Nevertheless, humans have tried to describe or characterize Him. Although it would be impossible to repeat all the descriptions or characterizations of God which have been generated through the years, a few pertinent ones will be presented.

The following descriptions are presented in the Fideler book [see the Bibliography]. In the sixth century BCE [see page 240], Heracleitus, a Greek philosopher, believed that both man and God exist in a world of change where, *"All is flow and it is impossible to step into the same river twice."* This implies that God does change; whereas the Christian Church speaks of God as being changeless. At about the same time as Heracleitus, Xenophanes, a Greek religious thinker, spoke of the *"one God, the greatest of gods and men, neither in form nor in mind like mortals."* This implies that God and Man are different, a philosophy espoused by Christianity which describes God as being the Creator, and Man as being the Created.

About the time of Jesus, Maximus of Tyre, another Greek philosopher, wrote that, *"The one doctrine upon which all the world is united is that one God is king of all and father, and that there are many gods, sons of God, who rule together with God. This is believed by both the Greek and the barbarian."* This, of course, differs from Christianity which has only the three persons of God in one substance, i.e. the Trinity. This also differs from Islam which has *only* one God.

The following additional descriptions from the Christian world are excerpts from *The New Catholic Encyclopedia*, Volume 6 pages 535-562 [see Bibliography for the edition].

"The early Church Fathers were content to describe God as having omnipotence, goodness and mercy. Other than that, there was no real definition of God developed by the ecumenical Church during its first millennium, just as there is no real definition of God in the Bible. Instead, the Bible just seems to take the existence of God for granted.

"Despite the lack of any ecumenical definition of God, several of the thinkers of the Church did try. In the early fifth century, St. Augustine wrote: *...perhaps it ought to be said that God alone is essence. For He alone truly is: because He is unchangeable, and it is this He declared to Moses, His servant, when He said, 'I am who I am.'* St. Augustine went on to say that this statement, 'I am who I am' merely postpones what man could not understand.

"A dogmatic statement of the twelfth Ecumenical Council [Fourth Lateran Council of 1215] says: *We firmly believe and profess without qualification that there is only one true God, eternal, immense, unchangeable, incomprehensible, omnipotent and indescribable, the Father the Son and the Holy Spirit; three Persons but one essence, substance or nature that is wholly simple.* In an appendix to the main report of the 1215 Council are these words: *...between Creator and creature there can be found no similarity in which an even greater dissimilarity cannot be found.*

"In the thirteenth century, St. Thomas Aquinas attested that although man, by his reason alone, can know *that* God is [a belief echoed in Romans 1:19-20], man's reason alone cannot grasp *what* He is. St. Thomas said, 'God's essence is therefore His act of being.' In this way, St. Thomas differed from St. Augustine. Augustine interpreted God's statement to Moses as, 'I am He who never changes,'; whereas Thomas understood it to be, 'I am the pure act of being.' In addition, St. Thomas states that since 'no effect can exist without a pre-existing cause,' then knowledge of the effect will infer the existence of its cause. Consequently, he states that the existence of God can be demonstrated from effects which are known to man. Since this can be done, then if it were to be done for all things, God would be seen as the ultimate cause of everything."

An interesting thought is presented on page 542 of the *New Catholic Encyclopedia,* where it is stated that none of man's concepts of God have univocal validity. However, man seems to have trouble accepting that God is, "He who *is*," without always wanting to ask, "He who *what*?"

In Vatican I, the twentieth Ecumenical Council in 1869, the following dogmatic statement appears:

"*The Holy Catholic Apostolic Roman Church believes and confesses that there is only one, true, living God, creator and Lord of heaven* and earth, almighty, eternal, immense, incomprehensible, infinite in intelligence, in will, and in all perfection, who, as being one, sole, absolutely simple and immutable spiritual substance, is to be declared as really and essentially distinct from the world, of supreme beatitude in and from Himself, and ineffably exalted above all things besides Himself which exist or are conceivable."

In my opinion, instead of generating a definition which all people could use for understanding God, the twentieth Ecumenical Council presented a definition which was designed by a committee of bureaucratic lawyers.

Thomas Erastus [nee Thomas Luber or Lieber], a Swiss physician and religious philosopher of the sixteenth century said, *"Try as we may, we cannot do without God."* This was presented in a time when men had despaired of ever defining God, and had even started to wonder if having a God were a worthwhile thing.

In 1932, Henri Louis Bergson, a leader of late 19th and early 20th century spiritualism, stated that man can know of God's existence only through a mystical experience with real philosophical value. As Divine attributes, he mentions several which are grasped intuitively: i.e. "God is Love," "He is personal and free," "He is the Creator and His creations are the labor of Love," etc.

As a recent example of an attempt to define God, on October 11, 1994, the *Atlanta Constitution-Journal* reported that the Mormon Church had censured a woman member for writing an article stating that God had a wife who lived with Him in heaven. The Church went on to state that having a Mother God was not a bad idea, but that in no way could Mother God be considered to be an equal to Father God. Isn't it interesting how we keep trying to define God by using terms of our daily life? It is almost as if we are trying to create God in our image!

And finally, there is 1 John 4:16 which says: *God is love, and he who abides in love abides in God and God abides in him.*

These definitions of God are rather cold; and to me, they do not describe the warmth of the God who calls to me. Despite all of these attempts, with the possible exception of the last statement which says that "God is love," these definitions of God leave us with the original feeling that God is ineffable in that S/He cannot be defined.

Possibly if we could define "love" we could then define God. However, who amongst us can present a definition of love which would be accepted by all?

For myself, I have come to the conclusion that we cannot define God other than by trying to define what S/He *is* by what S/He *does*. This is the reason for trying to address the "Functions of God" in *Christianity and the New Age Religion*, where I explained that defining God, or trying to locate Him/Her, was like applying the Heisenberg Uncertainty Principle. This principle of sub-atomic physics says that the closer you try to measure both the position and the velocity of a particle, the more uncertain you will be of the measurement of either one; for the exact velocity and the exact position together, in fact, have no meaning in the natural universe. In a similar manner, the exact definition and the exact location of God would have no meaning in the spiritual universe.

I accept that God is omnipotent [having all power], omniscient [having all knowledge] and omnipresent [being in all places]. I also accept that S/He is transcendent rather than immanent, in the fully accepted use of those definitions [see below]. In addition, I feel that God is unchanging, but only in one sense [see below]. Finally, I completely accept that God is ineffable in the sense that S/He is beyond our human comprehension. To fill out these beliefs, the following paragraphs will attempt to put three words about God into perspective. Those three words are *ineffable*, *transcendent*, and *unchanging*. Many major religions have used their interpretation of these words to define God.

Ineffable means that we cannot define Him/Her, for S/He is beyond our human comprehension, and therefore is indescribable or ineffable. It is the opposite of *effable* which means "capable of being expressed in words."

Transcendent is from the Latin, *transcendere* meaning "to climb over, to surpass, or to go beyond." It means that in a comparison, one is superior to another such as God is to the world and its occupants. Transcendent is opposed to being immanent which stresses remaining within or under. Thus, God is transcendent since S/He is above the world as the highest being and ultimate cause. However, as the Church states, God is also immanent by being present in the world through participation and through causality [i.e. causing things to happen] by His being and his presence in ALL that is.

If all of this is accepted, then I can accept that God is transcendent. However, it has been my experience that when most Christians hear that God is transcendent, they do not hear the next phrase, that S/He is also immanent. They thus believe that God is outside, when S/He must also be inside or within in order to participate. Possibly one of the best illustrations that Christians feel God is outside is the oft-told story of the Catholic priest in a large city in India. He saw a group of children playing together. Some of these children were Catholic, while others were Hindu. He went up to these children and asked, "Where is God?" Every Catholic child pointed to the sky; whereas every Hindu child pointed to his or her heart. The point of this story is that to each of us, God resides where we have been taught that S/He is. To most Christians, God is generally male and is outside; whereas to most Easterners, God is male/female and is inside.

In official documents, the Christian Church often refers to God as being both transcendent and immanent: transcendent in the sense of being superior but immanent in the sense of being a participant. In truth, one cannot accept one part without the other.

Unchanging is a common word, but in its application to God, it needs some additional understanding. I can accept that God is unchanging in the sense that from the beginning, S/He has been the *ALL*; and the ALL is always the ALL. Therefore, it is unchanging. However, the ALL can participate in transformational events which change its form without enlarging or diminishing the ALL in any way. As an example, if you or I can, through spiritual growth, participate in a transformational event, then in this act we have changed God, for we have changed the ALL. In this way, God has <u>changed</u> with our growth, while S/He has remained <u>unchanged</u> as the totality of the ALL. A further description of the impact of transformational events is presented in Chapter 5, in the section entitled "God's Thermodynamic Universe" [see pages 103-7].

In conclusion, we might say that God cannot be described by the human mind, is superior to anything else albeit a participative part of everything else, and comprises an ALL which is constantly changing.

This may be an adequate definition for some. However, it is highly likely that no adequate definition of God could ever be developed which would meet the needs of all the unique and individual members of humankind.

There is nothing wrong with this; for in reality, God needs to be experienced rather than defined.

CHAPTER 2
THE MESSENGERS SENT FROM GOD AND THEIR MESSAGES

I believe that there have been messengers sent from God. If this belief is accepted, then several questions immediately arise, such as: who were these messengers; how did they get here; how did they differ from the rest of us; and what messages did they deliver to the people of this planet?

In order to answer these questions and understand the messengers, it will be necessary to go back to the very beginning of creation when the first act was done by that ineffable entity which we presently call "God." Many philosophers who have thought about the beginning of creation have developed the thought that the first act was an emanation through which God could create that which was to be created. Many have called this emanation, the *Monad*, a term which will be used in this book. The generation of the Monad did not diminish God, for S/He was still One with ALL. From the Monad came all who were created in the image of God. This creation of the new forms did not diminish the ALL; for God still remained One with the wholeness that is the ALL.

After a significant period of time, God saw that in several planetary specks of dust throughout His/Her universe, those generated from the Monad were starting to forget the Source. In order to remind them of this Source, God sent them a messenger who did not pass through the Monadic experience and who was, therefore, a unique one, more nearly like God than those who had been created by the Monad. Through the experiment of sending the messenger, God hoped to create a remembrance of Him/Herself in the minds of those who were of God. Through this experiment, some remembered, but many did not; some learned how to live life, but many did not; some learned to love, but many did not; some developed their own unique, personal pathway into oneness with God, but many did not.

And so, God repeated the experiment. S/He sent another unique, God-like messenger to these small specks of planetary dust throughout His/Her universe. Again this unique one taught the people how to live if they just would do it. Again, some remembered their Source; some learned how to live; some learned to love; and some experienced their unique, pathway into oneness with God— but many did not.

The experiment was repeated many times on the many specks of dust onto which those generated in the image of God had been sent by the Monad. Earth was one such speck of dust. One day, those on Earth will meet their brothers, or sisters, or androgynies [i.e. those who contain all sexes in one body] of similar experiences. Those who have experienced the presence of God [see pages 120-4] will be ready for such a meeting.

The humans on Earth have received many messengers from God, all sent to generate a remembrance in those who were created in the image of God. Many of those messengers arrived in a time which has been lost in the pages of prehistory. Fortunately, there are eight whose messages have been preserved for our use. The first of these is Melchizedek of Salem; followed, in sequence, by Moses, Zarathustra [whose Greek name is Zoroaster], Buddha, Confucius, Lao Tze, Jesus Christ and Muhammad.

MELCHIZEDEK OF SALEM

Synopsis. According to the Bible, Melchizedek of Salem lived at the time of Abraham which was about 2,000 BCE, some 4,000 years ago. However, as to whether or not he "lived" in the same sense that we live is a real question; for *He is without father or mother or genealogy, and has neither beginning of days nor end of life, but resembling the Son of God he continues a priest for ever.* [Heb. 7:3]

Melchizedek is a singularly important messenger from God for three reasons. The first is that he is the oldest messenger recorded in our written history; the second is that Melchizedek had a great influence on Judaism, Christianity and Islam, because the father of each, Father Abraham, honored Melchizedek even before he received his covenant from God; and the third is that Melchizedek is honored by many of today's religious orders, among which are Judaism, Christianity, Islam, Mormonism, Freemasonry and the New Age.

References. References to the activities of Melchizedek can be found in the Bible, in *The Book of Mormon*, in the *Keys of Enoch*, in *The Urantia Book*, and in many other reference works which describe the world's great initiates, leaders or messengers from God. Because Melchizedek is so little known to the general public, this section will be longer than the same section for any other messenger.

Melchizedek is one of the mystery figures of the Judeo-Christian heritage. There are eleven references to Melchizedek in the Bible: one in Genesis [14:18]; one in Psalms [110:4]; and nine in Hebrews, most of which are similar to Hebrew 5:6 which says, *"Thou art a priest forever after the order of Melchizedek"* in which the "Thou" refers to Jesus Christ. The books of Genesis and Psalms are considered sacred scripture by both Judaism and Christianity. The Letter to the Hebrews is considered sacred scripture by Christianity.

In Genesis, Melchizedek is called, *"...king of Salem...and priest of God Most High."* Abram, before his name was changed to Abraham, honored Melchizedek and paid tithe to him. Thus, the Father of the Judeo-Christian-Islam heritage paid homage to Melchizedek, even before Abram had received his covenant from God. The name "Melchizedek" means "King of Righteousness" and the name "Salem" means "Peace." Therefore, Melchizedek of Salem is the first King of Peace and Righteousness mentioned in the Bible. In addition, as "king of Salem" he probably ruled in the place which later became known as Jerusalem, for Psalm 76:2 refers to Salem in a way which signifies it to be identical with Jerusalem, a name which was derived from the Semitic *Urusalim*, meaning "the foundation of peace." The homage which Abraham paid the King of Salem was part of the justification which King David used when he chose

Jerusalem as his headquarters, and as the home of his priesthood—almost 1,000 years after the time of Melchizedek and Abraham.

In Psalms 110, God mentions for the first time the "order of Melchizedek." This Psalm, attributed to David, mentions three great things that God can do, one of which is to make an entity "a priest for ever after the order of Melchizedek" a phrase often used in the Letter to the Hebrews.

The Book of Mormon is considered to be sacred scripture by those of the Mormon faith. In this book, in Alma 13:14-15, it is stated that you should:

"...humble yourselves even as people in the days of Melchizedek, who was also a high priest after this same order which I have spoken, who also took upon him the high priesthood forever. And it was this same Melchizedek to whom Abraham paid tithes: yea, even our father Abraham paid tithes of 'one-tenth part of all he possessed.' "

In Freemasonry, Melchizedek is considered to be the one who first used white lambskin as the source of its ceremonial aprons. In addition, many Freemasonry Lodges are said to be Melchizedek Lodges, while others are described as being a part of the "Order of Melchizedek."

In *The Urantia Book*, the Order of Melchizedek is mentioned often. *The Urantia Book* is a massive work, and a major source of universal information which goes beyond the doctrinaire religious references. In this work, several sections are devoted to one Melchizedek priest, Machiventa Melchizedek, who, according to the book, personalized on Earth as an emergency Son of world ministry. The activities of this Melchizedek, whose time of incarnation is identical with the Melchizedek mentioned in Genesis, are reported in depth in *The Urantia Book*. They will be described on page 31.

The Keys of Enoch is another source of information accepted by many who are searching for a new and expanded belief system. In this work, the Order of Melchizedek is mentioned often, primarily because this Order is considered to be a galactic Order of the White Brotherhood, having numerous priests and priestesses throughout the universe and having many orders of initiate levels. *The Keys of Enoch* consistently describes the importance of the Order of Melchizedek to the future of the Universe.

In *The Great Initiates*, another book which describes those who contributed greatly to the belief systems of this planet, it is said that Abraham treats Melchizedek: *as a superior, as a master, and communes with him using the elements of bread and wine in the name of the Most High God.* This ceremony was considered to be a sign of recognition between those who had been initiated in the great mysteries of God. It is echoed today when a Protestant Christian participates in communion; or a Catholic Christian receives the Holy Eucharist; or a Wiccan/Witch celebrates Feast.

Analysis. But who or what was Melchizedek and why was Jesus Christ, a man followed by almost one-third of the world's population, named by God to be a priest forever after the order of Melchizedek? In the Bible, The Letter to the Hebrews goes to great length to answer this question. The arguments are:

1. Melchizedek is greater than Father Abraham for three reasons. The first is the kingship of Melchizedek, which is that of righteousness and peace; again, the first in the Bible to be so designated. The second is the priesthood of Melchizedek. He is not simply named as being "a priest" but instead is designated as "priest of God Most High," and he is the first in the Bible to be so designated. The third is related to tithing. Abram gave Melchizedek a tenth of everything that he had, thus indicating his subservience;

2. Melchizedek is a symbol of timeless priesthood. The Old Testament usually identifies each of its great men by noting his birth and death; but Melchizedek appears on the scene with no introduction and equally disappears without note. He therefore symbolizes a priesthood which does not die; and

3. If Jesus were named by God to be "a priest for ever after the order of Melchizedek," then his priesthood would not die. Jesus is, therefore, a greater priest than any Earthly priest whom the Jews could follow.

For Christians, the argument presented by The Letter to the Hebrews would flow a little differently. In essence:

1. If Christ were to be a priest forever, then he would be eternally available to intercede on the behalf of his followers, not through earthly priests, but through the eternal priesthood of Jesus Christ in the Order of Melchizedek;

2. Although New Testament writers would often relate a present-day personage to one of the "men of Old" such as Moses or the like, the writer of The Letter to the Hebrews reverses this by having Melchizedek resembling the Son of God [Hebrews 7:3]. In this manner, he indicates that Christ was in existence before Melchizedek, and therefore is eternal; and

3. Since Jesus was of the tribe of Judah rather than the priestly tribe of Levi, he could never be a priest to the Jews. However, for Jesus to be named a "priest for ever, after the order of Melchizedek" means that he was made a priest in an order established before there were tribes. This means that not only could Jesus become a priest, so can anyone, whatever the tribal origin of his or her birth.

Dr. Charles R. Erdman has written many outstanding commentaries on the books of the New Testament. In his fine commentary on Hebrews, Dr. Erdman says:

"The majestic figure of Melchizedek stands for one short scene upon the stage of history and then disappears forever into the mystery from which it emerged. However, an unfading halo of glory surrounds his very name, for this royal priest is an accepted type of Christ."

This recognized Christian theologian thus makes the strong recommendation that the Christians of the Church should pay their respects to the memory of Melchizedek.

In addition to this homage which Christians in general are expected to pay to Melchizedek, Mormonism places great emphasis on their homage to him. The ecclesiastical organization of the Reorganized Church of Jesus Christ of Latter-day Saints is contained within two priesthoods: the Melchizedek, or higher and more spiritual priesthood; and the Aaronic, or lesser priesthood. In order to be an elder in the church and to be a part of the Standing High Council of 12 members, a Mormon has to be a part of the Melchizedek priesthood.

The Message. Based on the references and the analysis presented above, it should be obvious that if there is such a thing as a messenger from God, then Melchizedek is certainly one of them. But what was his message? His message was a simple one, but it is one of the most important messages ever presented to humankind. It was given when he stated that he is, "a priest of God Most High." Why is this message important? Because in stating that there is one

God above all the others [i.e. "Most High"], Melchizedek gives the message that there is only one creator God.

This statement predates the monotheistic message of Akhenaton who came along over 600 years later; it predates the message of Moses whose first commandment, *"Thou shall have no other gods before me."* [Exodus 20:3] came along over 700 years later; it predates the message of Jesus who gave the great commandment, *"You shall love the Lord your God with all your heart, and with all your soul, and with all your mind."* [Matt. 22:37] by about 2,000 years; and it predates the message of Muhammad who stated, *"There is no God but God."* by about 2600 years. In other words, in all of our written records, it is Melchizedek who first tells us that there is One Supreme Being!

The Urantia Book not only states that this message of one God was given by Machiventa Melchizedek, it presents in great detail how the message was transmitted by missionaries from Salem to all corners of the world; and how this missionary effort influenced major religious traditions such as the Vedic and Brahman cults in India [precursor to Hinduism and the basis for Buddhism], Taoism and Confucianism in China, early Egyptian practices [from which Moses received instruction], the practice of Mithraism [which extended from Persia to Rome and from which many Christian traditions came], etc. etc. In other words, *The Urantia Book* states that the presence of Machiventa Melchizedek influenced all of the world's present great religions.

Based on the Bible, Melchizedek has had a great message for Jews, Christians and Muslims. Based on *The Book of Mormon*, Melchizedek has a great message for the Mormon. Based on *The Urantia Book*, Melchizedek has influenced all of the great Eastern religions. Based on the *Keys of Enoch* and *The Urantia Book*, Melchizedek has had and still has a great influence on the practice of those of the New Age. It would seem that Melchizedek has brought a very important message to essentially every religious practice. It is the message that there is One Supreme Being, a message which has not been recorded in any presently existing document prior to the time of Melchizedek.

With all of this, it is a great wonder that Melchizedek is not honored today by all of the world's great religions. In particular, Christianity seems to have forgotten about him. It was, therefore, with great joy that I found a mosaic of Melchizedek outside the Church of the Beatitudes in Galilee, at the traditional spot where Jesus is thought to have given the Sermon on the Mount. There were other mosaics there, but the mosaic of Melchizedek was important to me; for this is the only time I have seen direct evidence of honor given to this great messenger of God at any Christian site.

MOSES

Synopsis. Moses is believed to have been born sometime in the period 1320-1240 BCE, but these dates are approximations which have not been confirmed by any historical evidence.

The relevance of Moses to Judaism is unquestioned; for without him, the Exodus of his people from bondage in Egypt, the Passover, the receiving of God's Ten Commandments on Mount Sinai, the generation of the Pentateuch [i.e. the first five books of the Bible in which Moses is the main human figure], and many other similar traditions would not have been introduced into Judaism and subsequently into Christianity and Islam. Moses is one of the major figures in the Judeo-Christian heritage, and is one of the major prophets of Islam. There is no question that if the concept of messengers from God is accepted, then among the established religions of the world, Moses is one of those significant messengers.

References. As mentioned above, Moses is the main human figure in the first five books of the Bible. Although he is not mentioned in Genesis, in the books of Exodus, Leviticus, Numbers and Deuteronomy, the name "Moses" is presented 649 times. In addition, the name "Moses" is used 199 times in the other books of the Bible. Anyone whose name is mentioned 848 times in the most-purchased and arguably most-read book of all time needs no other references.

However, two other works will be mentioned. *The Urantia Book* states that:

"Moses was an extraordinary combination of military leader, social organizer, and religious teacher... [and] was the most important individual world teacher and leader between the times of Machiventa

Melchizedek and Jesus."

That is indeed high praise. *The Urantia Book* also states that the monotheism presented to Egypt by the missionaries of Machiventa Melchizedek was developed into the Word of Light by Akhenaton, who could not share this message with the people because they would not understand him.

In *The Great Initiates*, it is stated that Moses brought these teachings out of Egypt in his golden ark and made them available for the later Christ who was to be the living torch for broadcasting these teachings to all people.

Other references to Moses could readily be presented, but these are sufficient to qualify Moses as one of the truly great messengers of God.

Analysis. Moses is so well known that there is almost no need to analyze his activities. Nevertheless, a summary of what the world would be like without those activities will be presented.

Without a messenger from God such as Moses, there would be no Judaism and no religious community such as Israel based on a covenant with God; for that religion and that community never could have existed within the confines of slavery and bondage as practiced by the Egyptians of that time. In addition, there would be no Ten Commandments with its resultant fostering of Western moral concerns and social ethics; no geographical site which would be available for the continuum of Judaism into Christianity; no Old Testament with its richness of stories and myths for our guidance; no tradition of monotheism to be absorbed by the Judeo-Christian-Islamic heritage; and no monotheistic concept of God which would be made available to all people and thus mitigate the development of a class or caste system in the West.

In other words, without Moses, our world would be quite different from the world we presently know. Although there may be some who do not like our world in its present state, I challenge them to imagine a world which had never known Moses. It arguably would not be nearly as close to God as it presently is.

The Message. The message which Moses presented was really quite simple, yet quite profound. It restated the message presented by Melchizedek, a message which stated that there was only one God Most High. Moses emphasized this message in the first of the Ten Commandments which stated that *"Thou shall have no other gods before me."* [Exodus 20:3]. But Moses went further when he accepted from God the next nine Commandments, and when he subsequently generated a social organization based on those rules of conduct. In essence, Moses said that it is not enough merely to recognize that there is only one God who is One with ALL; but that everyone must accept that there are certain rules of conduct which that One expects those who were created in His image to follow. That is a powerful and profound message which will become very important in developing a unique personal pathway into oneness with God.

ZOROASTER

Synopsis. Zoroaster is the Greek name for the Persian God, Zarathustra. Although some have reported a birth date as early as 1700 BCE, this is considered highly unlikely. Most historians place his birth date in the seventh century BCE, some as precisely as 628 BCE, based on a tradition which states that Zoroaster flourished "258 years before Alexander." It is the acceptance of this date which causes Zoroaster to be placed after Moses in the chronological presentation of the messengers from God.

This messenger from God, and the religion which he established, have had a profound effect on all of the world's major religions. The effect is especially notable on Judaism, Christianity and Islam. Despite this Western influence, Zoroasterism is presently practiced in any significant way only in India, where it is known as Pariism. Although little has been documented about the life of Zoroaster, his teachings are well known and widely respected by anyone who has spent any time studying the history of religion; and references to these teachings can be found in almost any legitimate work which describes the religions of the world. Zoroastrianism is considered to be one of the seven great religions developed during the recorded history of the world.

References. Zoroaster is not mentioned in the Bible. Instead, he is mentioned often in the holy book of the Persians [today's Iranians], the *Zend-Avesta*, in which he is said to be the first man to whom the living God spoke. Despite his non-mention in the Bible, it is likely that his followers had a great influence on many major events of the Bible. As one example, it is highly probable that the Magi, or the wise men from the East mentioned in the second chapter of Matthew, were followers of Zoroastrianism. As another example, Zoroastrianism strongly believed that saviors would periodically come into the world to present the "dawn of a new day." Zoroaster believed that he was one of these. This savior [or Messiah] influence was not in the beliefs of Judaism until after the Jewish exile in Babylon during the period ca. 586-526 BCE where they were exposed to the influences of Zoroastrianism. Other influences will be evident in the Special Comment section presented on page 36.

Analysis. The creation myth developed by Zoroastrianism is presented later [see pages 128-30]. In order to understand the message presented by this major personality in the history of the world's religions, that creation story should be reviewed, for it is in this story that the message of Zoroaster is presented.

Zoroaster presented this creation story in the form of conflict between Justice [or Order] and the Lie, because of his boyhood experiences. He was born into a modest family at Rhages, a town in Media near the location of Tehran in present-day Iran. At that time, Rhages was a pastoral village devoted to the raising of goats and sheep, and was not an urban village in any sense. Into areas such as this, the nomadic tribes would often come on raiding excursions during which they created chaos, suffering and pain. The natives considered such activities to be in violation of order and called the people who did such things "the followers of the Lie." Consequently, Zoroaster's religion was strongly influenced by the concept of a conflict between Order and the Lie.

The Message. Despite its characterization as a dualistic religion, Zoroastrianism strongly supported monotheism by stating that there was no other God except for *Ahura Mazda*, the Wise Lord. This is reminiscent of the teachings of Melchizedek. In addition, Zoroastrianism had a strong moral tone which asked its adherents to follow Order rather than the Lie in a manner reminiscent of the teachings of Moses. But Zoroaster added a third element to the teachings of the One God. As reported in Volume 24, page 707 of *The New*

Encyclopaedia Britannica:

"In a Hermitic treatise, for example, the existence of God was proved from the evident order of the world. This argument, which had first been formulated by Zoroaster, a 7th century [BCE] Iranian prophet, was expressed in the form of questions: Who could have created the heavens and the stars, the sun and the moon, except God? Who could have made wind, water, fire, and earth [the elements], the seasons of the year, the crops, the animals, and man, except God?"

I accept the statement made in *Britannica* that Zoroaster was the first to formulate the belief that God was the creator of all things. Consequently, the message which this messenger brings is that God is the creator of all things, and that the One God believed in by Zoroaster created only that which is good. This is a powerful message, and one which is required if the four Cosmic Concepts are to be understood, accepted and put into practice.

Special Comment. This raises the following question:

Since Judeo-Christian tradition has Moses writing the Pentateuch [i.e. the first five books of the Bible], and since the Judeo-Christian story of creation is presented therein, and since that story has God creating all things [see page 130], then why isn't Moses given credit for being the messenger from God who gave the message that God created all things?

The answer is simply that the Judeo-Christian tradition which has Moses writing the Pentateuch is not supported by historic fact. Very few legitimate biblical scholars believe that Moses was the author of the first five books of the Bible. Most, in fact, believe that these books were not written until after the Babylonian Exile, possibly about the time of the building of the Second Temple in 515 BCE. One of the reasons for this belief is that there is absolutely no documentation that many elements presented in the Pentateuch had been a part of Jewish thought until after the Exile in Babylon.

One thought which had not been in Judaism prior to that time is the belief that the Jews were God's "Chosen People." This belief was developed because of their need to survive such calamities as the destruction of Solomon's Temple by Nebuchadnezzar and the subsequent Exile in 586. In order to survive as a people, it was almost a necessity that these beings be declared the Chosen People to take God's message to the world.

Another concept which did not exist until after the Babylonian Exile was the thought that God created all that exists. In addition, as mentioned previously, there was no concept of a Messiah within Judaism until after the Exile. Finally, it could be argued that there were no hereditary Jews until after the Exile, for the only ones who retained their distinctive identity were those who had returned from Babylon. Of course, anyone who practices Judaism is considered to be a Jew today; but to be a hereditary Jew, it is necessary to be descended from those who returned from the Babylonian Exile, not the Egyptian one. This point is presented in detail in Volume 6, page 544 of *The New Encyclopaedia Britannica*.

The point being made in this Special Comment section is that there is much evidence to support the belief that the Judeo-Christian-Islamic heritage accepted a lot from Zoroastrianism, much of which was instigated during the Exile in Babylon. One of the concepts which was accepted was the belief that the One God created all which exists. That powerful message is a thought first expressed by Zoroaster, at least as far as our recorded history can document.

BUDDHA

Synopsis. The word "Buddha" generally means *"a sage who has achieved a state of perfect illumination in accordance with the teachings of Guatama Buddha."* The word comes from the Sanskrit word which means "awakened." A Buddha is therefore an "awakened one" or an "enlightened one."

The one generally acknowledged as the Buddha entered into his most recent incarnation in about 563 BCE. His parents were the rulers of the Sakyas of the Kosala Kingdom in the northeast corner of what is now the Bihar district of India. He was a member of the warrior caste of Ksatriya, and was consequently expected to live a life of ease and pleasure. His birth name was Siddhartha Gautama. At age 29, he left his life of married luxury to become a wandering ascetic. After six years he abandoned ascetic practices to seek his own, unique path to Enlightenment, a goal which he soon achieved. He spent the rest of his life teaching his principles to others. Despite the importance of this work to the followers of Buddhism, all

Buddhists recognize that there were Buddhas before and after Guatama Buddha, and that there will be additional Buddhas in the future.

One point to be emphasized is that the Buddha went to seek his own, unique pathway to Enlightenment. Although most Buddhists would consider it to be a an exaggeration to equate "Enlightenment" with "God," I would suggest that this is evidence that the Buddha looked for his own, unique personal pathway into oneness with <u>his</u> God. This suggests the possibility that each of us should do likewise, a major point of the fourth Cosmic Concept [see pages 189-94].

References. It is probable that more words have been written about the Buddha than have been written about any other entity who has ever walked on the face of the Earth with the exception of Jesus Christ. Consequently, references about him become an exercise beyond the scope of this book. However, it is of interest to note that *The Urantia Book* names Guatama Buddha as one of the great teachers of truth in the Orient who was a real prophet, but who had forgotten some of the teachings originated by Melchizedek.

Analysis. Although Buddhism is a religious practice of great diversity, most Buddhists practice the "Three Jewels" of: [1] I take my refuge in the Buddha [or leader]; [2] I take my refuge in the Doctrine [or the rules of the leader]; and [3] I take my refuge in the Brotherhood [or the community of adherents to the rules of the leader].

Most also follow the practice of some form of deep meditation such as the Buddha maintained despite the repeated attacks of Mara, the evil one, throughout the night which preceded the dawn of his great Enlightenment. He was able to do this because he was supported by the ten great virtues which he had perfected during his innumerable past lives. These ten great virtues were: charity, morality, renunciation, wisdom, effort, patience, truth, determination, universal love and equanimity.

Having thus defeated the evil one, Guatama Buddha spent the remaining time before the dawn of his Enlightenment in deep meditation, examining his past lives, acquiring the knowledge generated by the divine eye, and finally realizing the Four Noble Truths. These Truths were all concerned with how suffering exists and how it can be conquered by following the Eightfold Path of:

right views, aspirations, speech, conduct, livelihood, effort, mindfulness and contemplation. Later, Buddha established a strict moral code for his followers.

In order to understand Buddhism fully, one would probably have to make a full dedication for many lifetimes; and adherents to the subtleties of this religion have probably winced as I have tried to translate the esoteric Indian terms into acceptable English in the paragraph above. Suffice it to say that this religion has not been analyzed in the paragraph presented above. Instead, only enough insight has been presented to allow an interpretation of the message which the Buddha brought to us from God.

The Message. Unlike the previous messengers, Guatama Buddha did not build upon the messages which preceded him; for although he reinforced the need for a moral life while in this physical existence in much the same way that Moses did, he did so without having this morality done in reverent homage to the One God.

However, Buddha did introduce a major message from God when he brought deep meditation into the formula. It is often said that prayer is talking to God; whereas meditation is listening to God. It is important to listen, for as described in more detail in Chapter 5 of *Part Two*, when each unique individual experiences his/ her unique, personal pathway into oneness with God, the question becomes:

Which path shall I take, knowing that one is God's will for my life while the other is my will. What is God's will for my life? Which path is the one for me to take in generating my return to God?

Only by listening can we generate the answer.

Prior to Buddha, all the messengers had said, "Listen to me, because I have a message from God." The Buddha said, "Listen to God, because He has a message for you." And whether Buddha did this in recognition of the One God or not, his Enlightenment was the message of contemplation and listening to that which can give you the truth. That was a profound message for humankind.

CONFUCIUS AND LAO TZE

Special Comment. Some may object to presenting two messengers of God in the same segment. However, I feel justified in doing this because the ultimate goal of each is similar; merely the method of doing it is different. Each feels the need to be human, and in this human experience to find the Dao [older writings use Tao] which is the Way or the Path down which the universe is traveling. Each then tries to find how human life can best get in harmony with the movement of the universe. Confucianism tends to use the family unit of society as the basis for finding the Dao; whereas Taoism [the spelling which will be used in this work] feels that society is fundamentally artificial and corrupt, and consequently accepts nature as the basis for finding the Dao. Each religious philosophy is very diverse in its applications, and many do not consider either to be an organized religion in the sense of Judaism-Christianity-Islam.

In essence, Confucianism centers on humanity, emphasizing the active, external, official and rational side of the Chinese character; whereas Taoism centers on nature, emphasizing the passive, internal, mystical and private part of that character. Confucianism stresses cultivation; whereas Taoism stresses spontaneity and flowing. Confucianism is the yang, active and masculine; whereas Taoism is the yin, passive and feminine. But despite these different approaches to finding the Dao, each presents the same message.

Synopsis. Lao Tze and Confucius were contemporaries. Confucius, the younger, was born in 551 BCE.

Lao Tze built directly on the traditions presented by the earlier messengers when he taught that Tao was the One First Cause of all creation. In describing this "God," he said many things, one of which was: *The will of the Absolute God always benefits, never destroys; the purpose of the true believer is always to act but never coerce.* In regard to humans, Lao Tze said: *Goodness begets goodness, but to one who is truly good, evil also begets goodness.*

Confucius tended to ignore God in the sense that his major message had to do with moral living, and that by living the high moral life, one would find the Way of Heaven, which was the pattern of the Universe. In other words, Confucius tended to emphasize the journey rather than the goal.

References. There is much which has been written about each of these leaders of religious thought, and much of this can be readily found. Consequently, the reference section is not as important for these religious leaders as it was for the lesser-known messengers such as Melchizedek and Zoroaster. That will also be true for the segments on Jesus Christ and Muhammad which follow. However, it should be noted that *The Urantia Book* calls both Confucius and Lao Tze, "outstanding teachers."

Analysis. Lao Tze and Confucius tend to bring the human element into a more complete focus than any of the earlier messengers. Prior to the messages given by these two, the message seemed to be, "Live a proper life because God expects this of you." The messages presented by these two seems to be, "Live a proper life because nature and humanity expect this of you and because the harmony that results is the beauty and peace of life."

The approach offered by Lao Tze can best be summarized as:

While you are a human in this planet, become one with all elements of nature, honor them, and return anything given to you by them with goodness.

The message offered by Confucius would be:

While you are a human on this planet, become one with all elements of your human society, starting first with self, followed by family, community, country, world and finally that which is beyond the world.

These messages differ greatly from the messages delivered by the earlier messengers, all of whom had put God first.

What was developed by Lao Tze should not be confused with Nature Worship any more than what was developed by Confucius would be confused with the worship of your neighbor. Instead, each program is a communion directed toward oneness with nature or with society. When taken together, they would generate a oneness with all which exists, primarily oriented toward that which exists on Earth.

What was really developed by these two religions can possibly be expressed by the need for two words to greet another person. The first is "Namaste," an Indian greeting which is often accepted to mean, "My divinity honors your divinity." The other is "In-La-kish," an Inca word which has been phonetically spelled because it does not fit into our alphabet. It is often accepted to mean, "My humanity honors your humanity."

The point is that we are both human and divine [see pages 198-9]. Since earlier messengers emphasized the importance of God to such an extent that the importance of humanity and nature had become overlooked, these messengers were sent to emphasize the importance of our human nature, and of all other creations found on Earth. This resultant blend of divinity with humanity is a powerful message. Its need was emphasized about 950 years later when the Third and Fourth Ecumenical Councils of the Christian Church were required because Christians had so emphasized the divine nature of Jesus Christ, that they had started to forget about his human nature. This episode of history is presented in great detail in *The Christian Conspiracy.*

The Message. From the Analysis Section presented above, the message presented by these two almost jumps out. It is:

While on your pathway to your divine state of oneness with God, remember that you are doing it as a human. Act accordingly by honoring the fullness of your humanity.

JESUS CHRIST

Synopsis. Jesus Christ is thought to have been born in 0 CE, but his birth date was more likely in the period 4-7 BCE. He is believed to have lived for only about 33 years, the last three of which constitute his ministry. His followers believe that after he was: *crucified, dead and buried, he arose again on the third day. He ascended to heaven and sits on the right hand of God the Father Almighty, from thence he shall come to judge the quick and the dead.*

Although it is highly unlikely that he intended to found a new religion, the religion which bears his name has about 1.8 billion adherents worldwide, and is therefore the largest organized religion in the world. Jesus was a Jew. As such, he worshipped the God of Judaism. Consequently, there is a continuum between Judaism and Christianity which is often called the "Judeo-Christian heritage."

References. Since more books have been written about Jesus Christ than about any other human who has ever existed, he is so well known that nothing further need be said about references to him other than to describe the writing in *The Urantia Book. The Urantia Book* considers Melchizedek to be such an important world teacher that 78 pages are devoted to him. There are about 8 pages devoted to Moses, "the most important individual world teacher and leader

Messengers and Messages Sent from God

between the times of Machiventa Melchizedek and Jesus." There are about 5 pages devoted to Guatama Buddha, a "great teacher of truth in the Orient." However, *The Urantia Book* devotes 770 pages to the Life and Teachings of Jesus Christ! The message is self-evident.

Analysis. As a devoted Jew, Jesus supported the laws of Moses and the history which had developed them. As an example, he said: *Think not that I have come to abolish the law and the prophets; I have not come to abolish them, but to fulfil* [sic.] *them.* [Matt. 5:17]. However, many things had happened to the laws since Moses had received them, and the people who followed these laws did so to the letter, rather than the intent of the law. As a result, precisely defined laws were developed which covered almost every facet of daily life.

Jesus sought to change this. In a scene reported in the Bible, a lawyer came forward and asked him:

" *'Teacher, which is the great commandment in the law?' And he said to him, 'You shall love the Lord your God with all your heart, and with all your soul, and with all your mind. This is the great and first commandment. And a second is like it, You shall love your neighbor as yourself. On these two commandments depend all the law and the prophets.'"* [Matt. 22:36-40].

In this way, Jesus taught his lessons of love.

As an interesting part of this lesson of love, Jesus presented the thought that you should love yourself unconditionally, for you should "love your neighbor as yourself." Sometimes, we tend to think that we would love ourselves more if we were thinner, or prettier, or more intelligent; but Jesus does not teach that. In very simple words, he tells you to love yourself, and to love your neighbor as yourself. If you are to love your neighbor unconditionally, then you must do the same for yourself.

In this very important lesson, Jesus taught that *love* was the only commandment which really mattered, and that this love was to be given to all people, even to yourself and to your neighbor. Thus, while not abolishing the Law, Jesus did replace it with Unconditional Love, and therefore preached the intent rather than the letter of the Law. In order to understand what Jesus did, do the following exercise: take all of the Ten Commandments presented in Exodus, Chapter 20 and see if any of them would be necessary if everyone were to practice Unconditional Love. The answer is that none of these commandments would be required if everyone practiced Unconditional Love. In this way, it can readily be seen that Jesus did come to fulfill the Law. He fulfilled the Law by showing that the results of the Law and the results of Unconditional Love are identical.

The Message. Jesus Christ was a most important messenger from God, for by the time that he was sent to this planet, the people who felt they were remembering God had really forgotten what the Source wanted of them. Those created in His image had become so enamored with what they had accomplished, particularly as they developed the Laws which they believed that God wanted them to follow, that they completely forgot the major rule which God had given them. The forgotten message was that God wants us to <u>love</u> Him and to <u>love</u> ourselves and each other without any conditions beings attached. In other words, we had forgotten the rule of Unconditional Love, and Jesus came to remind us of it. That is possibly the most important message ever sent by God; for if all of us were to do nothing other than to love everyone and everything unconditionally, the Earth would become a heavenly place in which the divine could dwell. We would then be in oneness with God.

Christ's message is one of love for all which exists. It is arguably the most powerful message ever sent. In this way, Jesus taught us how to live, *if we would just do it!*

MUHAMMAD

Synopsis. Muhammad, whose full name is Abu Al-qasim Muhammad Ibn Abd Allah Ibn Abd Al-Muttalib Ibn Hashim, and whose name is interchangeably spelled either "Muhammad" or "Mohammed," was born in Mecca in present-day Saudi Arabia in about 570 CE. He is not only considered to be the founder of Islam, he is considered to be the founder of the Arab Empire. He is respected for having initiated religious, social and cultural developments which have had a tremendous impact on the history of humankind.

The Islamic message is none other than the acceptance of God as the One [*al-Ahad*] and submission to Him [*taslim*], which results in peace [*salam*]. Hence, the name of *Islam*, which means simply "to surrender to the One God," called *Allah* in Arabic. Today, there are over 1 billion Muslims, thus making Islam the second largest organized religion in the world.

References. Since Muhammad is recognized worldwide, few references are needed to present his credentials. However, it should be noted that he is not mentioned in *The Urantia Book*, which presents Jesus Christ as its last historical personage.

Analysis. In about 300 CE, a presbyter [i.e. a Christian lay leader] in Alexandria named Arius had a very difficult time accepting a major teaching which the early Christian Church was promulgating. That teaching presented the doctrine that Jesus Christ was divine, as fully divine as God, both in the quality and the quantity of that divinity. To Arius, this made it seem as if God had been divided. Consequently, Arius preached that there was only One God. The schism which this caused in the Church was the sole reason for the calling of the first Ecumenical Council in 325 CE, and was a major reason for the calling of the next five Ecumenical Councils. Arius was excommunicated from the Church because he could not, in good conscience, sign a document which declared that God and Christ were the same. He felt that to do this would diminish God, and Arius loved God too much to let that happen. He was willing to sign a compromise, but before he could do so, he died.

The major statement of Arius is as follows:

"We acknowledge one God, alone ingenerate, alone everlasting, alone without beginning, alone true, alone having immortality, alone good, alone sovereign; Judge, Governor, Provider of all, unalterable, unchangeable, just and good, God of the law and prophets and the New Testaments."

Much more information on the effects which Arius and Arianism had on the early Christian Church is presented in *The Christian Conspiracy*. The major effect was that many people were Arians during the following 300 years. Many wanted to follow Jesus Christ, but did not want to have him replace God at the center of their religious life. Consequently, they looked for a religion which centered on God rather than on his messenger.

Islam not only offered such an opportunity, it did so in the belief that it was returning not only to the religion of Abraham, but even of Adam. In this way, they felt that they were returning to the strongest of all monotheistic religions, one which was intended for all people, not merely those who were of a single tribe such as Judaism, or of a single event in history such as Christianity.

In essence, Islam believed in the same God presented by Judeo-Christianity, but with the belief that He was the God of All, and that there was nothing else to worship. The chapter on unity in the Koran says: *Say He is God, the One! God the eternally Besought of all! He begetteth not nor was He begotten. And there is none like unto Him.* Although the wording is different, this is the same message which Arius had presented 300 years earlier.

Muhammad is not worshipped as a God by Muslims in the way that Christians worship Jesus Christ. Instead, Muhammad is considered to be the "last and greatest messenger of God" in a line which started with Adam and included Abraham, Noah, Moses, and Jesus. The messengers were thought of as being holy men sent by God to specific peoples, but in no way were they considered to be divine. Muhammad was considered to be the greatest of these messengers not only because he was the final messenger sent by Allah to teach the "true faith," but also because he consolidated the messages sent by the others and made their messages into "true faith." He did this by removing the corruption which had been introduced into these earlier messages by those who became the leaders after the messenger from God had left. Muhammad hoped to prevent this corruption by writing all of his message before he died. Unfortunately, as we will see later, his writings did not prevent the subsequent corruption.

The Message. In the strongest of all possible terms, Muhammad stated that there is no God but God. He also said that God is the God of <u>all</u> people. The first message is, of course, in direct contrast to the Christians who had made Jesus Christ a God even though Jesus, himself, had said that he was <u>not</u> the equal of God [see Mark 10:17-8 and John 14:28 as well as the analysis presented in *The Christian Conspiracy*]. The second message is in direct contrast to the Jews who considered themselves to be the "Chosen People" through whom the rest of the world would have to come if they wished to be with the One God. Muhammad proposed the universality of a monotheistic God.

This is a powerful message. It is the same message presented by Melchizedek of Salem. We therefore have come a complete circle as we have examined the messages given by these eight messengers.

OTHER MESSENGERS

If the concept of messengers from God is a valid one, and if the messengers and their messages presented above have any merit, then it would seem that every 6-700 years or so, God has sent a messenger to remind us of the Source and of what the Source was like. If Melchizedek of Salem "lived" in about 2,000 BCE, then some 700 years later Moses came on the scene; followed about 700 years after that by Zoroaster, Buddha, Lao Tze and Confucius, all within a period of about 80 years; followed about 600 years later by Jesus Christ; and 600 years after that by Muhammad.

If you might like to speculate on other "messengers" who came at about the same time as one of these messengers, I would suggest that Quetzalcoatl came to Mesoamerica only shortly after the time that Muhammad came to the Near East. Many thousands of people fully believe that Quetzalcoatl brought the Christ Consciousness to the Americas. Many of the prophecies about Quetzalcoatl bear a striking resemblance to the prophecies about Jesus the Christ; and the teachings of Quetzalcoatl about the calendar, the arts and the sciences continue to be followed today.

If you have any curiosity about possible messengers who have come since the time of Muhammad/Quetzalcoatl and who support the 6-700 year cycle, I would suggest that you consider St. Francis of Assisi [about 1200 CE] who reminded us of the Unconditional Love taught by the Christ; or Meister Eckhart who lived about 1300 CE [died in 1327] and taught us that the soul of every creature has a "spark" which is the very likeness of God [see *The Christian Conspiracy*]. In our century, I would have three possible suggestions. The first would be Pierre Teilhard de Chardin, who not only taught that humankind *should* evolve mentally and spiritually toward a final spiritual unity with God, but that it is actually *doing* it! The second would be Pope John 23rd, the "Ecumenical Pope" who did more to open his people to the universality of God than all of his predecessors combined. His unfortunate, untimely death may have short-circuited that message, or it may not. Only God knows. The third, and possibly best candidate, would be Mohandas Gandhi, who taught that "all religions are true" and demonstrated that man could accomplish just ends without using violence.

SUMMARY

Returning to the eight messengers whom we have addressed in this chapter, the first said that there is only One God; the second that the One God has some thoughts about how He would wish us to live; the third that God created all things; the fourth that God wants us to listen to Him; the fifth that we are not isolated entities but instead belong in communion with nature; the sixth that our communion extends to all humankind; the seventh that all of God's "laws" can be replaced by Unconditional Love for Everything; and the eighth returned to that beautiful, prime message that there is only One God.

I fully appreciate that these six lessons do not represent the complete teachings of the eight messengers who have been described in this chapter. However, these messages do generate some useful understanding, both about the major messages and about how God can create order out of chaos.

Let those who have ears, *listen!*

CHAPTER 3
HOW THE MESSAGES SENT BY GOD HAVE BEEN ALTERED BY HUMANS

After each messenger sent by God left this Earthly plane, a normal human reaction set in among those who had become his followers. As their first official activity, the followers appointed someone to guide their efforts as they tried to follow the teachings presented by the messenger. Although the first generation of these leaders might adhere rather closely to the original thoughts, as each subsequent generation of leaders was selected, the stories about the messenger would get a little more exaggerated; until finally, the description of the messenger and his message would become one which had been almost totally composed by humans.

As one example of how this might happen, the first generation, the ones who had actually known the messenger, might say, "We follow the one who has told us about the Father." The next generation might say, "We follow the one who knew so much about the Father that he was almost like a son to Him." The next generation might say, "We follow the one who <u>was</u> a son to the Father." The next generation might say, "We follow the one who was <u>the Son</u> of the Father." The next generation might say, "We follow the one who was the Son of <u>God</u>." The next generation might say, "We follow the one who is the <u>Only</u> Son of God." The next generation might say, "We follow the one who is <u>God, the Son</u>"; and the next generation might say, "Since the one we follow is God, the Son, then he must *be* God, and not just the one who tells us about Him." Of course, the next generation would establish a religion centered around the messenger rather than centered around God. The succeeding generations would then spend their time defending and justifying their belief that the one they followed was identical to God in all ways.

By following this process, doctrines [i.e. that which is taught] have been converted into dogmas [i.e. that which must be believed]. This process would generally take a few hundred years and cannot be covered completely in this book. Instead, in this section will examine only a few specific ways in which the six messages sent from God have been altered by those who created the religion which followed the messenger. We will examine these six messages in the same order used in the preceding section. The six messages are: [1] there is only One god; [2] God has some thoughts about how we should live; [3] God created all things and they are good; [4] God wants us to listen to Him; [5] God wants us to be in communion with nature and with our fellow humans; and [6] all laws can be replaced by a compassionate Unconditional Love for Everything. The five major religious sects which will be examined to evaluate compliance with those messages are: Judaism, Buddhism, Confucianism/Taoism, Christianity and Islam.

MESSAGE 1: THERE IS ONLY ONE GOD

Judaism and **Islam** have been faithful to the message that there is only one God, and they have continued to hold their adherents to a belief in this message. Although that God is called by a different name, *YHWH* or *Yahweh* in the case of Judaism and *Allah* in the case of Islam, the latter religion considers their God to be the same as that of Father Abraham, i.e. the same as that of Judaism. It is interesting to note that in Aramaic, the language probably spoken by Jesus, the word for God is *Alaha*, a name which is generally translated as "the Invisible Source of Creation" and which is very similar to the name which Islam applies to their God. It is also interesting to note that when Judaism suffered, their prophets told them that they suffered because they had forgotten about the message that there is only one God. The Old Testament is filled with examples which specify the worship of one God.

One specific example is related to the hatred the Pharisees

felt toward the Samaritans. Although the reasons for this hatred are complex, they generally fall into one of two camps. The first is that when conquered by the Assyrians in the eighth century BCE, the Samaritans forsook the God of the Israelites and worshipped the God of the Assyrians. The second, and most recent explanation, is that although the Samaritans continued to worship the God of the Israelites, they did so in a temple of their own, several miles to the west of the Temple in Jerusalem. Since the Jews felt that their God had an earthly presence only in the Holy of the Holies, then those who worshipped in a different Temple must be worshipping a different God. Therefore, in either case, the hatred the Jews had for the Samaritans is explained by the belief that the Samaritans, although originally devoted to the worship of YHWH, had converted to the worship of a different God, thus disobeying the message originally given. Finally, it is interesting to note that the major reason that Islam was established was to proclaim that "there is no God but God." Consequently, Judaism and Islam were established as God-centered religions which worshipped the "one true God." They have remained faithful to that message.

Confucianism/Taoism and Buddhism were not established as God-centered religions, and they have not followed a belief system which requires that there be only one God. This is true despite the reference to the "Absolute God" in the early writings of Taoism. In fact, Taoism has been under recent criticism because of their practice of polytheism. Consequently, Confucianism/Taoism and Buddhism have never altered the message about one God, because they never subscribed to it in the first place.

It might be worthwhile to present a synopsis of God as visualized by Confucianism/Taoism and Buddhism; for their beliefs certainly differ from that expressed by Judaism, Christianity and Islam. In this way the response of Confucianism/Taoism and Buddhism to God-related issues can be covered in short paragraphs in subsequent sections of this book.

Confucianism is primarily based on the Chinese character *jen*, which is translated into English using various terms such as "virtue," or "magnanimity," or "humanheartedness" or "love," none of which is correct, but all of which combine to approach the correct meaning. When Confucius was asked to define *jen*, he replied, "Love men." The activities of *jen* lead to the *chun-tzu* or "superior man" who has neither anxiety nor fear, and who is always calm and at ease. In this religion, there simply is no Prime Cause such as that represented by God in the western religions. Consequently, the followers of Confucius would not alter the message that there is only one God, because they never subscribed to it in the first place.

A similar presentation could be made for **Taoism**, for the Tao [i.e. the Way] is considered to be a spontaneous rather than a caused thing.

Buddhism visualizes a plurality of universes, containing three planes: desire, materiality [or form], and immateriality [or formlessness]. The Buddha can be born only among humans, and can become the Buddha by achieving the state of the perfectly enlightened one. The goal of life is to pass from the temporal to the atemporal plane and thus overcome the cycle of rebirths into this material life. This is accomplished by a four-step process through meditation. The four steps are: [1] detachment from sensual desires; [2] denial of intellectualism to achieve inner serenity; [3] disappearance of all emotions including joy; and [4] abandonment of all attachment to any emotion whatsoever. After finishing this four-step process, the meditator enters into a state of supreme purity which is pure consciousness represented by indifference to everything. As can be seen, Buddhism also has no Primary Cause.

These paragraphs have given only a generalized picture about each of these religions and their thoughts about a God who is the Primary Cause. Not all adherents would agree that their religion has been fairly and completely represented. Nevertheless, dangerous as a little knowledge might be, there are times when a little knowledge is better than no knowledge at all. That has been the only intent of this condensed presentation.

Returning now to the message that there is only one God, in my opinion, **Christianity** has deviated furthest from this original message. Many of my Christian friends and former teachers will tell me that is not true and that I believe this only because I just do not understand the mysteries of the Trinity. However, Jesus never taught the Trinity, or that he was the same as God, or that *"Only* God and I are one." In fact, two times in the scriptures, Jesus states that he is <u>not</u> the same as God. In Mark 10:17-8 we read these words: *"Good Teacher, what must I do to inherit eternal life?" And Jesus said to him, "Why do you call me good? No one is good but God alone."* In John 14:28, Jesus says, *"...for that the Father is greater than I."* In at least these two cases, Jesus has said in no uncertain terms that he is *not* equal to God. And yet, the Christian Church not only proclaims that he *is* God, but that all who are to be called Christians must subscribe to the belief that he is God in *all ways*.

The Scriptures give a very incomplete picture of who Jesus was as interpreted during his time. The early church theologians also give a rather confusing picture. This subject is thoroughly discussed in *The Christian Conspiracy*, and therefore will only be touched on here. The important point to be made is that the Church felt that they had to define Jesus as God, even though the Scriptures did not. The Church needed to do this because the three central doctrines of [1] atonement, [2] incarnation, and [3] trinity had to come together as a complete package. To atone, Jesus had to be divine; but since he had been seen in the flesh, then he must be God incarnate; and since there is only one God or only one being, then there have to be at least two [later three with the Holy Spirit] persons in one being.

All of this is based on *one* simple belief which was accepted as a *truth* by the Church. That belief was that *only* God could generate atonement, with atonement meaning reconciliation [or "oneness"] with God. Since the Church believed it was an absolute truth that no man, no matter how talented or holy, could generate atonement, then if Jesus were to be the agent for reconciliation with God, he must be *divine*. Since there was *only* one God, and since the divinity of Jesus could not cause a multiplicity of Gods, then Jesus must therefore be *one with God in all ways and equalities*. This is the stand which the Christian Church took, and which it still takes.

If it ever could have been believed and accepted that God, who is all-powerful, was so powerful that he could have sent a message of redemption via a messenger whom He sent, and that with this message of redemption there would be reconciliation with God, then none of the debates and rationalizations about the definition of Jesus Christ would have been necessary at all. Jesus would have been a "one-of-a-kind anointed one," which is the correct translation of the Greek words *monogenes Kristos* rather than the mis-translation "only Son of God" which we read in our English-language Bibles. This "special anointed one" would lead those who follow him toward reconciliation with God; and possibly others sent by God could be another "one-of-a-kind anointed one" who would lead those who followed them toward reconciliation with God. Even within Christianity it is granted that God has sent more than one "one-of-a-kind [*monogenes*] messenger." In the original Greek, Isaac is called one in Heb. 11:17-8. In addition, John the Baptist is certainly called one in John 1:6 which says, *"There was a man sent from God, whose name was John."* It thus follows that Jesus simply could not have been the *only* one sent from God. God must have tried to reach His/Her children in *many* different ways.

However, because the Church insisted that the redeemer [i.e. one who sets others free] or savior [i.e. one who saves others] had to be *divine* in order to be the atoner [i.e. one who reconciles others to God], then he had to *be God* and not merely be a special messenger who brought God's powerful message for all to hear. Since there is only *one* God, then according to Christianity, Jesus had to be the *only* messenger who *was* God. In a nutshell, that is why humans had to define Jesus Christ as God in all ways, even though Jesus **did not**, and the Scriptures **do not**.

Does this not make Christianity an intolerant, Christ-centered religion rather than a tolerant, God-centered one? Remember the old hymn often sung in Christian Churches? It says: *Have thine own way, Lord! Have thine own way! Thou are the Potter; I am the clay...Fill with Thy Spirit 'til all shall see, Christ only always, Living in me!* It was God who made man out of clay, and it is God who needs to live in me in a God-centered religion, despite the fact that I follow Christ as a reflection of the God who calls to me. It seems that however Christians care to explain their beliefs and to justify the stands they have taken, they have abandoned the teaching that there is only one God.

I have often reflected on the thought that if there had been no Athanasius [a fourth century Christian Bishop of Alexandria who defended the divinity of Christ—see *The Christian Conspiracy*], there would have been no Islam; for it was the worship of Christ as God that got Islam established in a geographical area which was the original stronghold of Christianity. In the days immediately after the Resurrection, the strongest Christian establishments were in the Near East—not in Greece or in Rome. It was only after the early Church Fathers started to change the teachings of the Christ, and in so doing excommunicated sincere Eastern Christians such as Origen, Donatus, Nestorius, *et. al.*, that Islam was able to become established in this previously Christian area. They did this by reclaiming the prime principle that there is no God but God.

MESSAGE 2: GOD ADVISES US ON HOW TO LIVE

Every religion which accepts that there is a God, has also accepted that S/He gave us guidelines within which to live. However, every religion has altered those guidelines.

Judaism accepted the Ten Commandments from God, then augmented those with so many additional ordinances and laws that humanity was motivated by Law rather than by Divine Love. I especially enjoy the ordinance that stated that on the Sabbath, one could lift and carry a chair, but could not drag it because in the dragging, the chair would create a furrow and that would be plowing the earth. This is just one of many examples which could be cited to show how each generation of leaders in Judaism tried to improve on the lessons given to the original generation.

Christianity has developed many, many guidelines to add to the Ten Commandments. As just a few examples, at one time one could be thrown out of his or her branch of the church if one did not believe that Mary was a perpetual virgin; or did not accept that one had to kill a Jew before participating in the Holy Crusades; or did not declare himself subject to the Roman Pontiff; or tried to eat meat on Friday; or did not profess that Jesus is the only Son of God; or did not accept that homosexuals are despised by God; and on and on. The doctrines and dogmas established by the Christian Church have multiplied themselves far beyond the simple, yet profound, message that we are to lead a good life, based on universal, Unconditional Love. This is the message which was presented by the messenger from God.

In its origin, **Islam** developed six basic items of belief which are: *one God, angels, revealed books, prophets, Day of Judgment, and God's predetermination of good and evil*. In addition, there originally were five core religious practices, often called the "Five Pillars of Islam." They are: [1] the recitation of the *Shahadah* which makes a person a Muslim; [2] prayer five times per day; [3] fasting during the daylight hours of *Ramadan*; [4] giving alms to the poor; and [5] a pilgrimage to Mecca once during a lifetime. These five are still accepted as those which were given by their messenger.

Unfortunately, a significant number of Muslims believe that there is a sixth pillar which is *"Fight until allegiance is rendered to God alone."* Those who accept the sixth pillar have accepted a practice similar to that practiced by the Christians during the "Conversion by the Sword" times starting in the eleventh century. It means that if you do not accept my religion, I have the right to kill you in order to save you. Those who accept the sixth pillar believe that eventually there will be a Holy War, or even the "Mother of all wars." Although this belief in the sixth pillar may not be any more a part of mainstream Islam than some fundamental Christian practices are a part of mainstream Christianity, its acceptance by some Muslims is an alteration of the teaching presented by any of God's messengers.

Confucianism/Taoism and **Buddhism** have many guidelines for living, some presented by the messenger and others developed later. Some of the teachings of these religions about Earthly conduct and the relationship with their fellow man are among the greatest ever presented by any religion. The only question which might be addressed in this segment is whether these have been presented by God as a guideline for living. To those of these faiths, the question is a moot one; for if it works, why question the source?

MESSAGE 3: GOD CREATED ALL THINGS AND THEY ARE GOOD

One of the basic beliefs of Judaism is that God created all things and that when He looked at what He had created, He saw that it was good. This is emphasized in Genesis 1:31 which says, *"God saw everything that he had made, and behold, it was very good."*

Although **Judaism** later established ordinances, statutes, rules, regulations and laws about how one should live one's life, this did not change the basic principle that all which God created was good. Recently, some of the Christian Religious Right have been using the Judaistic rules for living to declare that certain sexual activities are against God's word. They specifically cite Leviticus 18:22 which says, *"You shall not lie with a male as with a woman; it is an abomination."* However, this is a Judaistic rule for living. It is not a statement about God's creations. As evidence, the 18th chapter of Leviticus starts with the words, *"And the Lord said to Moses...you shall not do as they do in the land of Egypt...and in the land of Canaan."* It then goes on to describe the things which are done in Egypt and Canaan which should not be done in the Holy land.

Jacob Milgrom is a Rabbi, a highly regarded Old Testament scholar and on the Editorial Advisory Board of *Bible Review* [*BR*]. In the December, 1993 issue of *BR*, Milgrom presents an article entitled "Does the Bible Prohibit Homosexuality?" Through a very reasoned argument, he comes to the conclusion that lesbians are not mentioned in the Bible, and neither are non-Jewish gay men unless they happen to live in the Holy Land. The point which this learned Rabbi is making is that the ordinances in Leviticus were developed about how life was to be lived in the Holy Land, and did not change, in any way, the basic belief of Judaism that God created everything and that all which God created was good. Although Rabbi Milgrom was criticized in many subsequent Letters to *BR*, he was strongly supported by biblical scholars, most of whom support his viewpoint that the Old Testament does not condemn such sexual acts except as a definition of the preferred way for Jews to live in the Holy Land.

As we will discuss more thoroughly in *Part Two*, compassion and understanding are required for all of life's activities. If we are to have Heaven on Earth, then there must be an understanding of the goodness in all which God created; there must be compassion for all who were created in God's image; and there must be Love given without any conditions being attached to that Love. In making this statement, I do not suggest, in any way, that I know what is God's will for another's life. I simply cannot do that and still follow the admonition in the scriptures which says: *Judge not, that you not be judged. For with the judgment, you pronounce you will be judged, and the measure you give will be the measure you get.* [Matt. 7:1-2].

However, I will say that as best I can determine, despite all the ordinances and statutes about how life should be lived, Judaism has not turned its back on the concept that God created everything and that everything which He created is good. Therefore, in my opinion, there has been no alteration of this message within Judaism.

Since **Confucianism/Taoism** and **Buddhism** have no God as the Primary Cause of all things, then an analysis of their following or altering this concept is not meaningful. However, it might be noted that in striving to become detached from all emotions via meditation, Buddhism implies that emotions are less than good; and in striving to become the "superior man," Confucianism makes a similar implication. If the Prime Cause [again, not recognized by Confucianism/Taoism and Buddhism] created things such as our emotions, then at least in some sense they must be good. If they aren't, then humanity has altered the message brought from God by the messenger.

The extremists of **Christianity** are arguably the world's most intolerant people, closely followed by the extremists of **Islam**. If God caused all things to be created in their beginning and is the Primary Cause for the religions developed by those created in His image, then even the religions of another person are good; and the denial of that "goodness" is an alteration of this message from God. In addition, the "Conversion by the Sword" practiced by each of these religions has killed beings which God created and which He stated were good—another alteration of this message. Finally, each religion has claimed God's support in their cause during a conflict with another state or government, thus implying that the other side, whether created by God or not, was not good—again an alteration of the message. It seems that these two religions, the two largest religions presently existing in the world, have decided for themselves that only that which *they* have created is good, even though in a primary causation analysis, God created it all. What have these religions done to themselves?

MESSAGE 4: GOD WANTS US TO LISTEN TO HIM

Some definitions may be necessary in order to understand the difference between prayer and meditation. The dictionary defines "prayer" as, *"The reverent petition made to a deity or other object of worship."* The word "petition" means, *"A request made to a superior authority."* The word "request" means, *"To ask for or express a desire for something."* Consequently, when we pray we reverently ask a higher authority for something.

The dictionary defines "meditation" as, *"A devotional exercise of contemplation."* The word "contemplation" means *"thoughtful observation."* Consequently, when we meditate, we devotedly observe what is happening.

Other definitions of these words, not found in any dictionary, are these: when we pray we *talk* to God; when we meditate, we *listen* to God. We are *loud* when we pray because we make our thoughts loud in supplication. We are *quiet* when we meditate, because we make our thoughts quiet in order to observe.

Meditation is the cornerstone of **Buddhism**, although there is some question as to whether there is a God involved in this quiet search or whether it is done solely to eliminate the illusions of this life. In a similar manner, the "superior man" sought by **Confucianism** is one who is developed not by asking God to become one, but by calming all outside influences until one *is* one. The pathway of **Tao** is also sought via quiet observation in the spirit of meditation. Consequently, in all three Eastern religions, meditation is a major source of support.

In **Judaism**, people pray. If you have ever visited the Wailing Wall in Jerusalem, especially during the week of Passover, you will see no quiet meditation or observation of the depths of life. Instead, you will see the bobbing men, clothed in their prayer shawls, loudly praising their God, giving testimony to the greatness of their God, thanking their God and submitting themselves to the wishes of their God. In orthodox Judaism, there seems to be a lot of prayer and little meditation. However, in the more mystic or esoteric sects of Judaism, especially those which involve the Cabala, meditation is a constant thing; and so is the belief that God may be reached by searching deep within one's own being.

In **Islam**, one of the "five pillars of Islam" is to pray five times each day. The call to prayer comes from the minaret, and all who hear its call immediately start their prayers of petition to Allah. As with orthodox Judaism, there seems to be little meditation, but a lot of prayer in orthodox Islam. However, as with Judaism, there is a mystic side to Islam, generically known as Sufism, in which deep meditation and deep searching are cornerstones.

On a personal note, a small chapel to the left of the Christian church I once attended had a sign which delighted me. It said, "Come in and Meditate." I mentioned this fact in my first book, *Christianity and the New Age Religion*. Shortly after that book was published, the sign was removed. I didn't know whether there was a connection or not, but I felt that something very dear to me had been lost; because prior to that, I had rarely heard of meditation being mentioned in mainstream **Christianity**. I do realize that the Quakers sit in meditative silence until their worship program is over; but unfortunately, they are not considered to be mainstream Christianity.

My experience in Christian worship has been that of noise. In the Baptist Church of my youth, the preacher shouted, not only during the sermon, but also during the time of prayer. It seems to me that every minute of weekly worship in a mainstream Christian Church is filled with noise. Everyone seems interested in telling God what they want Him to do, rather than listening to God indicate to us what He wills us to do. In the two years since I left the Christian Church, I have spent more time in meditation that I did in the previous 61 years of my life. I have sincerely and reverently tried to listen rather than to talk. As a result, I now feel closer to God, and even closer to the one known as Jesus, than I ever felt before. Try it sometime. You might be surprised at the results. Even Jesus said, *"He who has ears to hear, let him hear."* [Luke 8:8].

I believe there was a message sent by God to those created in His image via the messenger we presently call Buddha. It was the message to be calm and to listen. It is recorded in western scripture in Psalms 46:10 which states, "Be still, and know that I am God." However, this message seems to have been completely altered or even rejected by the orthodox religions of the West. It is a shame that this has happened; for there is an old axiom which states that you can never learn when you are talking—only when you are listening. Let those who have ears, **listen!**

MESSAGE 5: GOD WANTS US TO HAVE COMMUNION WITH NATURE/ HUMANS

The human element has been important to all religions. This importance will be described as each religion is discussed. However, having a human element within the religion is not the same as having the religion sponsor a communion with all fellow humans. In addition, for almost 4,000 years, very few religions of the world have felt the need to sponsor a communion with nature. Instead, most have felt the need to exploit nature for their own purposes, whatever those purposes might be. Recently, there has been some evidence that the world's major religions are realizing that communion with nature is a positive thing. If this trend continues, they will be recognizing that the earlier religions had some positive aspects to them [see pages 249-50].

The word "communion" has several meanings. One meaning is, *"A possession or sharing in common; participation."* Another is, *"A sharing of thoughts or feelings; intimate talk."* A third is, *"A religious or spiritual fellowship."* For the purposes of this book, a common thread running through all of these meanings is the thought of sharing, and then of using that sharing to develop an understanding or fellowship with nature and with all fellow humans.

Judaism believes in humanity and the human nature, else they would not have needed the Ten Commandments as guidelines through which the human nature could be expressed in a manner acceptable to their God. However, the thought of having communion with all humanity and nature has never been a part of Judaism; for the "Chosen People" were to stay apart in order to keep their religion pure and uncontaminated by others. An example is the hatred for the Samaritans previously described. In addition, one could not be of the faith without adhering to established rules, one of which was circumcision for the male. Those who did not adhere to these rules were not a part of the communion. And although Judaism worked with nature in order to generate the "land of milk and honey," this was more in the sense of exploitation rather than participation with nature or granting honor to nature as an equal partner.

Although the parts of **Islam** which I have experienced seem to contain the most tolerant people I have ever met, there are enough parts which accept the "sixth pillar" [see page 56] to raise the question as to whether Islam is in communion with all of humanity. I say this despite the tolerance and the commendable desire for a universal God practiced by the majority. In addition, in a manner similar to the practice of Judaism, Islam seems to exploit rather than to honor nature.

Christianity sponsored the colonization and exploitation of all the native lands which were "discovered" by the European society during the fifteenth through the twentieth centuries. This can hardly be called having communion with humanity. As one example, the "Gold, Glory and Gospel" philosophy of the Spanish Conquistadors during the sixteenth through the nineteenth centuries allowed them to conquer, enslave and exploit an advanced civilization of humanity which had existed in Central and South America. As another example, British colonization of the North American, African and Indian continents during the eighteenth through the twentieth centuries was promoted by exploitative economics as much as by evangelism. Neither activity supports the message of having communion [i.e. shared fellowship] with nature or with humanity. Today, when some of the extremists within Christianity hear of someone "communing with Nature" they will often accuse that person of practicing witchcraft or demonology.

Confucianism/Taoism and **Buddhism** have beliefs which differ from the Western religions in that they do not seem to feel the need to evangelize others to the same extent. Instead, they seem to inform others of their beliefs, rather than to force the acceptance of their beliefs onto others. In this sense, they seem to have some level of communion with humanity instead of having some sort of master-slave relationship. In addition, there are elements of nature respect, if not of actual nature worship, in all three religions as well as other Eastern religions such as Shintoism. Consequently, although communion with humanity or nature may not be practiced in the fullest sense of the word, these Eastern religions seem to have retained this message from God better than those of the West.

The **New Age** practices positive communion in their belief that when an individual has achieved higher energetics, he or she has raised the energy level of all of the rest of the world. This is true communion with humanity and nature.

MESSAGE 6: ALL LAWS CAN BE REPLACED BY UNCONDITIONAL LOVE

As a human being living a life on a planet filled with other human beings and with other creations of God, this is my favorite message. Since I follow the Christ, it would seem logical that this feeling of mine would have some basis in his teachings, and that is certainly true. Although this reference has already been mentioned, it is worthy of repetition. In Luke 10:25-28 we read the following: *And behold, a lawyer stood up and put him to the test, saying, "Teacher, what shall I do to inherit eternal life?" He said to him, "What is written in the law? How do you read?" and he answered, "You shall love the Lord your God with all your strength and with all your mind; and your neighbor as yourself." And he said to him, "You have answered right; do this and you will live."* And so, in this case as in many others, Jesus taught that Love is the only Law worth following; for if you follow the rules of Unconditional Love, no other guidance for life is needed.

Since it is believed that Jesus taught in the Aramaic language, possibly the essence of the original teachings can best be gained by a direct translation from the Aramaic to English rather than by taking the tortured translation trail from Aramaic to Greek to Latin to English as was done with the King James Version of the Bible. I am grateful to have been given the Aramaic version of the Greatest and the Second Commandments as translated by Dr. Michael Ryce.

"The Greatest and The Second Commandments expressed in Aramaic are: You shall *tidrakhim* [maintain the condition of pure love, encompassing judgment and behavior] for *Alaha* [the Invisible Source of Creation] in your entire mind and with your whole *naphshak* [true self], in all your actions and in all your thoughts. This is the greatest commandment and takes precedence over all. The second, which is like unto it, you shall *tidrakhim* [maintain the condition of pure love, encompassing judgment and behavior] for your *karebak* [neighbor—anyone near to you or anyone you think about] as your *naphshak* [true self]. Upon these two commandments hang the Law and its prophets."

I think that the shades of meaning generated by this version of the Great Commandments are truly refreshing. Returning now to the normal English-language Bible, in the scriptural passage presented above, the lawyer goes one step further in trying to test Jesus by asking, "And who is my neighbor?" And Jesus responds with the parable of the Good Samaritan [Luke 10:29-37]. This is a valuable parable to understand, for, again, the Samaritans were very much hated by the Jewish society in the time of Jesus. Therefore, Jesus was teaching his followers that they must love without conditions, even if doing so makes them love their enemies. Jesus said this again in the Sermon on the Mount when he said: *"You have heard it said, 'Love your neighbor and hate your enemy.' But I say to you, Love your enemies and pray for those who persecute you."* [Matt. 5:43-4].

Jesus brought us the message of Unconditional Love, and in doing so, he replaced the Law with Love. But those who followed him did not practice this lesson. **Christianity** has arguably put more conditions on their acceptance of an individual into their family than has any other religion. In doing so, it has become one of the world's most intolerant religions despite its being based on the teachings of the most tolerant human being ever to walk upon this Earth.

It is difficult to understand how this came about, and I will admit that I struggled with trying to understand it for many years. I am indebted to Father John Groff of the Mystic Journey Retreat Center in Guntersville, Alabama for generating some level of understanding when he told me that Jesus came into the Earth emphasizing Fourth Chakra characteristics; but the early Church Fathers were some of the most ardent Third Chakra people ever to appear on Earth. A description of the Chakra system and its meanings is presented later [see pages 114-16], but a short description of the type of love expressed by these two chakras will be presented here.

The Fourth [Heart] Chakra gives positive love in the sense that the love is compassionate, nurturing and understanding. This is a love which never tries to control another, but which instead generates compassionate understanding for the physical, emotional, mental and spiritual growth of the other. The Third [Navel or Solar

Plexus] Chakra, on the other hand, gives negative love of the strongly emotional and attached variety. This is a love which is so overpowering, that it can lead to complete control over the one being loved, often through the use of power.

Because of the Third Chakra love expressed by the early Church Fathers, the Christian Church became one which so loved its members that it would do anything to get them to accept Christ, even to the point of scaring them into submission; or, if necessary, of killing them to save their eternal souls. Jesus wanted those who followed him to do so from their own Free Will. To do this, he gave compassion and nurtured their belief system. The early Church Fathers, however, set the stage for the Church to generate a love which almost smothered individual initiative and proclaimed that since Jesus was the *only* Son of God and was divine, then humanity had no other choice but to follow him. As an example, the Third Chakra love of St. Augustine became so great that he even denied that humans have Free Will. In order to practice Third Chakra love, the Christian Church put so many conditions on being accepted into the Church that the Unconditional Love taught by Jesus was soon forgotten.

In a similar manner, **Judaism** and **Islam** have rejected Unconditional Love; for if you do not accept that Judaism is intended *only* for God's "Chosen People," or if you do not accept that Islam will fight you until you accept that there is *only* one God, then you are not completely loved by those who presently practice what they accept as the beliefs of those religions. To be loved by either requires conditions. Unconditional Love has been forgotten.

The association I have had with **Buddhists** makes me believe that they have heard the message of Unconditional Love; and I see **Confucianism** and **Taoism** asking for fewer conditions than the Western religions. However, a case can be made that these religions do not have a God to love. Thus, it would seem that none of the world's great religions gives Unconditional Love to both God and to their fellow humans.

SOME ESOTERIC THOUGHTS

The thoughts presented in the sections above were generated using conventional historical sources such as the Bible, *The New*

Encyclopaedia Britannica, The New Catholic Encyclopedia and the like. Although some might claim that *The Urantia Book, The Keys of Enoch* and *The Great Initiates* represent less-than-conventional resource material, much of what is presented in those sources uses, in turn, conventional resource material as background. Whether the material used so far is acceptable to the reader is up to him/her to decide; but to me, the material used so far is acceptable in a conventional sense and has presented little, if any, speculation.

This section is different. It will present material from what is considered by some to be "esoteric" sources. It could therefore be considered to be speculative material. However, esoteric material is not a source to be rejected out of hand, any more than mythology should be rejected as an inaccurate source [see pages 127-8]. Each taps the reservoir of human consciousness which is beyond the realm of our five senses; and each converts that resource into an understanding which can be accepted by our five senses.

The word "esoteric" is considered by some to be an evil word; but it is not. The major definition of the word "esoteric" is *"intended for or understood by a small group."* A secondary definition is *"Difficult to understand. Abstruse or confidential."*

When Jesus taught his followers in the parables, he was giving esoteric teaching. In Matt. 13:34, we read: *All this Jesus said to the crowds in parables; indeed he said nothing to them without a parable. This was to fulfil* [sic.] *what was spoken by the prophet: "I will open my mouth in parables, I will utter what has been hidden since the foundation of the world."* And in Matt. 13:10-11, we read: *Then the disciples came and said to him, "Why do you speak to them in parables?" And he answered them, "To you it has been given to know the secrets of the kingdom of heaven, but to them it has not been given."* The point is that although some who are Apologetics [i.e. those who prove Christian thought and defend their proof] decry the use of "esoteric material," in doing so, they are condemning some of the major teachings of the Christ.

This section will present two esoteric beliefs which have been developed outside the established religions. The first belief is the "Office of the Christ"; and the second is the lineage of the various messengers previously presented. Although some may consider this to be pure speculation, others will counter that it is as reliable as the recorded historical records. It is entirely up to the reader to decide which belief is more nearly correct for him/herself.

Some initial information about the Office of the Christ was presented in *Christianity and the New Age Religion*. In that material, the thought was presented that in this Office many work through an energy known as the Christ Consciousness to fulfill God's purpose; and that no one reaches the oneness of God without having processed through the essence of the Christ Consciousness. [For a personal experience which indicates this, see pages 266-7.] According to *The Keys of Enoch*, Ascended Masters work in this Office with Archangel Michael for the general liberation of this universe, and for the specific liberation of humans throughout all eons of time.

According to esoteric teachings, the Christ Consciousness is an energy which has been occupied at various times by the energy of various personalities, each working for the liberation of humankind. The personality known as "Jesus" was one such energy. According to the Brian Grattan book [see Bibliography], the energy known as Maitreya is the 35th Avatar of Christ Consciousness to embody that energy on Earth. Some believe that it was his energy which was incarnated as Jesus the Christ. Others believe that the personality known as Jesus was unique in that he was the only *human* ever to become the total vehicle for the Christ Consciousness, and therefore his name has come to us as Jesus the Christ. Although other personalities have been the total vehicle in the etheric form, they have not come to Earth in total humanity as did Jesus. Melchizedek could be considered as one such example, for his existence on Earth is reported to have been in an etheric body without organs. He, therefore, was not in total humanity. Others personalities who have come to Earth in total humanity, did not comprise the total vehicle of the Christ Consciousness, for they were not in the complete acceptance of their divinity at that time. Some of these personages will be mentioned in the following paragraphs.

The major point from this realm of esoteric teaching is that the energy of the Christ Consciousness has been available to the world in energies other than that of Jesus; and that the partial realizations of this Consciousness have been generated on Earth by humans other than Jesus. The uniqueness of Jesus the Christ was in bringing the total energy of the Christ Consciousness to this Earth in human form. In this way Jesus was a *unique* son of God; but not the *only* one. That message is clearly spelled out in the Greek version of the Gospels. The background on how the Greek word *monogenes* [meaning "unique" or "one-of-a-kind"] which is used in the Greek versions of the Gospels, got mis-translated into the English word *only* [as in "only son of God"] in the English versions of the Gospels, is presented in detail in both *Christianity and the New Age Religion* and in *The Christian Conspiracy*. The point of this particular discussion is that both by esoteric teaching and by the scriptures in their original language, Jesus the Christ is a *unique* son of God, but not the *only* one. In being a unique son, he represented the Office of the Christ on Earth. Through his teachings, we could learn to channel the energies of the Christ Consciousness as he did. Through him, but <u>not</u> *only* through him, we can experience the essence of the Christ Consciousness as we proceed on own personal pathway into oneness with God.

The next esoteric teaching has to do with the lineage of some of the messengers. Because of the need for reincarnation in God's universe [see Chapter 4], each of the messengers presented in this chapter represents energy or personality traits which have been on Earth before. In some of those incarnations, they were gaining experience in a way which has not been recorded by conventional history; but in others, their experiences were as a personality which is known to us. As just a few examples from this esoteric knowledge, it is believed that Jesus had visited Earth as a disciple of Zoroaster [according to Grattan], and as the biblical Joseph, Elisha and King David [according to Mark and Claire Prophet]. In the Alice Bailey book, Jesus is said to have been Joshua and Appollonius. In the Williamson book, Jesus is reported to have been Melchizedek, Guatama Buddha and Zoroaster. In the Edgar Cayce book, Jesus is reported to have been Enoch and Melchizedek.

According to Grattan, some of the well-known personalities in the lineage of Zoroaster are reported to be Akhenaton, Zoroaster, Peter, and Origen [third century Christian theologian]. The similar lineage of Mohammed would be Bartholomew, Mohammed and Patrick Henry. Because Melchizedek is reported to have lived for

92 years on Earth as an etheric body without organs, he therefore has no Earthly lineage. This is substantiated in the Bible where it says: *He is without father or mother or genealogy, and has neither beginning of days nor end of life, but resembling the Son of God he continues a priest forever.* Melchizedek is listed by Grattan as the one who has this universe as his body; whereas Sanat Kumara is listed as the one who has Earth as his body.

According to Williamson, Confucius previously had been Cato [great Egyptian artist], Cheops and Amenemopet [Pharaohs of Egypt]. Moses had been Ahmose I [Egyptian pharaoh] and Joseph who led the people of Israel into Egypt. Later incarnations of Moses were King David, Daniel, Joseph the father of Jesus, Barnabas [who worked with Paul], and Joseph Smith [who established the Mormon Church]. None of these references mention incarnations of Lao Tze.

As to whether or not any of this is historically true is up to the individual to accept or reject. In light of the "Third Viewpoint of Reincarnation" [see pages 89-93], it may not be completely correct to assign a lineage to anyone. To support the "third viewpoint," during a meditation in early 1995, the following was presented by an Ascended Master to my wife as a message for understanding:

"From our viewpoint, it appears that when there is a physical incarnation of great personage for a passage of energy which will effect all of mankind, more than one being will enter into the personage. Some may stay for a few years and another for the entire life. This would bring to fore several strength aspects which one alone would not have possessed. There is great cooperation in the higher realms which makes this possible."

And to that, I would reply that since God is omnipotent [all-powerful], then S/He could certainly make that happen.

COMMENTARY AND CONCLUSION

It is possible that someone who has read the comments presented in this chapter might feel that I have criticized all major religions, that I feel no good has come from any of them or their literature, and that I subscribe only to esoteric teachings. Nothing could be further from the truth. I do not condemn the religions of the world; nor do I accept everything that any author may put on paper, or that any spokesperson may say. Instead, I check in every way that

I can to see whether the message is from Spirit or from Ego; and I do this whether the message is orthodox or esoteric, and whether the message is presented in a book, from the pulpit, or from a channeler. I do this because it is my strong belief that God has tried in many ways to deliver messages to those whom he created in His/Her own image; but that the messages from Spirit have been often been altered by the Egos of humans. This alteration could happen to the humans of the orthodox religions, or to the humans of the New Age.

My basic belief is that participation in an organized religion is a positive activity during a major stage of spiritual development; but I further believe that at some stage of spiritual development, the restrictive teachings of orthodoxy have to be left behind. These points will be addressed further in Chapter 5 of *Part Two*.

Another reader may feel that this is an absolutely perfect world just as it is, and that all which is considered less-than-perfect by others, is really intended as a lesson for us. This belief system expresses the viewpoint that in gaining these lessons, we might need to learn how to reject fear in order to learn how to accept love, and how could we reject fear if it did not exist; or we may need to learn how to go to the Light, and how would we know to accept the Light if we had not experienced the Darkness? In many minds, this is a valid viewpoint. It is addressed further in the section on the Existence of Pain, Suffering and Evil [see pages 141-4].

As a meaningful conclusion for this chapter, I would ask each reader to imagine a world in which the organized religions accepted all of the messengers and kept their original messages without alteration. In that world, we would not need the lessons which we gain in this less-than-perfect world of ours. In that world, we would follow all of the messages presented in this chapter, particularly the last message presented in this chapter.

It is this last message, the message of Unconditional Love given to us by Jesus the Christ, that reflects the God who calls to me more than any of the other messages sent by God. That is why I remain a Christian, despite my objections to the altered teachings being presented by the Christian Church.

CHAPTER 4
SOME THOUGHTS ABOUT REINCARNATION

God is ineffable, which means that S/He cannot be described. Since God is beyond description, this means that S/He is beyond any full definition. However, this does not prohibit the human entity from trying to generate some partial definitions of God [see pages 17-24]. One of the partial definitions of God which can be made but which cannot be comprehended, is that God is infinite both in Time and Space. Many will say that this is not a proper definition, because in God's realm, neither time nor space exist. However, in human terms, there is time and there is space. Therefore, in human terms, God can be considered to be infinite in both time and space.

To be infinite in time means that God exists throughout all eternity. If this is true, then why would those who are created in His/Her image exist for only the microscopic term of one lifetime on this microscopic speck of cosmic dust called Earth?

In answer to this question, many believe that the human entity does not exist for merely one lifetime, but that the eternal and immortal soul of that entity will exist throughout eternity, even when united in oneness with God. Although the soul's journey to God may take less than an eternity, it is a journey which would be difficult to complete in merely one lifetime. Consequently, those who believe that the soul will exist for more than one lifetime believe that the eternal soul will occupy a form, possibly a physical form, many times and at many different places during the journey into oneness with

God. Such a belief means that the soul will "incarnate" [meaning enter into a body] many times. Such a belief is commonly called "reincarnation," or *"coming back into a body."*

This chapter on the concepts of reincarnation offers some understanding that might help one to define his/her individual pathway into oneness with God. Just as with all of the background information presented throughout *Part One*, it is up to the reader to accept or to reject the presented concepts. In order to generate a fairly complete understanding of reincarnation, this chapter will be presented in seven independent sections.

SECTION 1: TIME AND SPACE AS JUSTIFICATION FOR REINCARNATION

There is a series of questions which has been asked of me in respect to the expanded belief system I have developed as a Christian of the New Age. The first question is, "Why would a Christian study the New Age?" The next question is, "Do you really believe that the New Age brings you into a closer personal relationship with the Christ?" Then there is always the question, "Do you really believe in reincarnation?" The answer as to why I first started thinking in this new direction was presented in *The Christian Conspiracy*, but because its principle is so vital to understanding the need for reincarnation in God's universe, it will be repeated here.

Very simply, I started to become interested in the New Age and to accept the concept of reincarnation when I came to realize what the modern concepts of *Time* and *Space* implied for all of the established religions.

In respect to *Time*, if God were only just a little older than Judeo-Christianity, there would be no need for anyone to investigate the basics of the New Age religion; for all that S/He did would be represented by the study of Judeo-Christianity. But God is much older than that; for God was in existence even before there was a material universe. Otherwise, S/He could not have created it.

Although it is not certain, it is thought that the material universe was created at least 18 billion years ago. It is also thought that Earth is only about 4 billion years old, which means that some portions of the material universe have been in existence for almost *five times* as long as the Earth.

Judeo-Christianity is considered to start with Abraham, a man who is thought to have lived about 4,000 years ago. If the age of the <u>Earth</u> were to represent one year, then those "ancient days of Abraham" at the very beginning of Judeo-Christianity would constitute only the last 32 seconds of this Earth year.

If, on the other hand, we were to set the age of God's <u>Universe</u> so that it would be represented by one year, then those "ancient days of Abraham" would constitute merely the last 7 seconds of that Universal year; and Christ would have appeared in only its last 3-4 seconds. The point is that in relation to the time that God has been in existence and has been interested in those "created in His image," the time of Judeo-Christianity does not even make a ripple. It is but a minor part of the Time of God.

The question then becomes:

"What was God doing during all of that time which existed before Judeo-Christianity even began? Was He doing only that which has been reported by the Judeo-Christian heritage?"

A God who would do so little for all of that time is not the kind of God who calls to me. And since God seemed to want companionship by creating "man" [or "male and female"] in His own image [Genesis 1:26-27], then I have to believe that the living consciousness represented by the Biblical word "man" was also around for a long time before the Judeo-Christian period began.

Let us leave Time and think for a moment about *Space*. We tend to think that the moon is a great distance away from the Earth, but at about 230,000 miles, it is only about ¼ of 1% as far away as the Sun. We therefore tend to think that the Sun is a great distance away, and at 93 million miles, it is a big step. If we were to be able to cover the distance from the Earth to the Sun in one step, then it would take a mere ***657 million*** of those steps to walk across our Galaxy, the Milky Way. But our galaxy is not a very big galaxy as galaxies go, and it is only one of billions of such galaxies. In addition, there is more distance between the galaxies than there is within them. *God is present in all of this <u>Space</u>.*

The speck of cosmic dust upon which we live is similar to being only one grain of sand within the entire Sahara desert.

Although it is important to us and therefore to God, Earth certainly does not represent the "everything" that the Christian Church Fathers visualized when they established their doctrines and dogmas during the fourth through the sixth centuries CE.

This consideration of Time and Space then leads to a question posed by many people, including many Christians. It is:

Why does the Eternal God of the Universe allow those created in His/Her image only one existence of a mere 80 years on one small speck of dust, when S/He has all of this vastness of Eternal Time and almost eternal Space under His/Her control; and when S/He possibly could use the help of those created in His/Her image to bring other parts of His/Her creation along toward oneness with God? Why?

The consideration of Time and Space also leads to another logical question which is:

*With all of this time and space available to God, why does the recently developed religion of Christianity demand that it be so exclusive and be the **only** representative of God; and furthermore, why does Christianity as it has been developed by man believe that it is the final religion and that it is not possible for anything more representative of the ineffable God ever to come along?*

This analysis of Time and Space has been presented in respect to the Judeo-Christian world, but since all the Earth-based religions being examined in this book are more recent than the time of Abraham, then the conclusions apply to them as well. The *Time* of God, both in the past and in the future, and the *Space* of God, both within an expanding or a contracting universe, are simply too vast to believe that the final word on God has been delivered by any of the messengers who established these religions, especially since their followers have altered the messages which were delivered. In respect to *Time*, God simply cannot let those of His/Her image exist only for a period of 80 years or so; and in respect to *Space*, God simply cannot let those of His/Her image exist solely on this speck of dust, important though the Earth may be both to God and to us.

An analysis of *Time* and *Space* generates the belief that the eternal soul of each individual has been present in form more than one time on this planet, and present in form on more than just this one physical speck of cosmic dust within the vastness of God's space.

It is the belief of a large portion of the Earth's population of many different faiths, that the reincarnation process has gone on many, many times for each individual, eternal soul. An understanding of *Time* and *Space* supports that belief.

SECTION 2: BIBLICAL BACKGROUND ON REINCARNATION

The biblical and early Christian background on reincarnation has been presented in depth in each of the two previous books of this series. In *Christianity and the New Age Religion*, some five pages are devoted to a biblical background on reincarnation. This was increased to an eleven page section in *The Christian Conspiracy*.

This section will not repeat either of those previous messages in the same amount of depth. However, it will present enough of the story to indicate that reincarnation was a highly regarded concept during the time of Jesus.

That the concept of reincarnation was prevalent during that time is documented by Josephus, the Jew who became a Roman general and wrote *The History of the Jewish Wars* and *Jews in Antiquity*. These books present a good, non-Biblical, commentary on the mores and attitudes of the time. In fact, they are possibly the most reliable information we have on the thoughts and concepts of the Jews during the time of Jesus.

In respect to the Pharisees, Josephus stated:

"The Pharisees believe that souls have an immortal vigor in them and that the virtuous shall have power to revive and live again: on account of which doctrines they are greatly able to persuade the body of the people."

This is a powerful comment on belief in reincarnation by the Pharisees, the largest Judaic religious group at the time of Jesus.

In respect to the Essenes, Josephus says:

"They smiled in their very pains and laughed to scorn those who inflicted torments upon them, and resigned up their souls with great alacrity, as expecting to receive them again."

This again is a powerful statement on reincarnation, this time by the second largest religious group in Judea during the time of Jesus.

The Sadducees were also an influential religious group of the time. Although the Sadducees did not believe in reincarnation, this is understandable; for they did not believe in an afterlife of any kind, even the kind that an orthodox Christian of today would accept.

Leaving Josephus and looking at today's Bible, there are five pieces of scripture in the Gospels which are difficult to interpret in any way other than as substantial support for belief in reincarnation at the time of Jesus.

1. Mark 8:27 says:

And Jesus went on with his disciples, to the villages of Caesarea Phillippi; and on the way he asked his disciples, "Who do men say that I am?" And they told him, "John the Baptist; and others say Elijah; and others one of the prophets."

In this scripture, we have the disciples telling Jesus that the people believe that he is a prophet returned to them, an obvious description of reincarnation.

2. Matthew 17:9 comes right after the Transfiguration on the mountain, and says:

And as they were coming down the mountain, Jesus commanded them, "Tell no one the vision, until the Son of man is raised from the dead." And the disciples asked him, "Then why do the scribes say that first Elijah must come?" He replied, "Elijah does come, and he is to restore all things; but I tell you that Elijah has already come, and they did not know him, but did to him whatever they pleased."

In this scripture, Jesus is saying that Elijah has already come back into a physical form. In other words, he has reincarnated.

3. Matthew 11:13 is the next scriptural reference of note. It has Jesus saying:

"For all the prophets and the law prophesied until John; and if you are willing to accept it, he is Elijah who is to come. He who has ears to hear, let him hear."

In this scripture, we have Jesus stating that John the Baptist was the reincarnated Elijah, and that by this reincarnation, he had fulfilled prophecy.

4. The next interesting verse is Matt. 14:1, which says:

At that time Herod the tetrarch heard about the fame of Jesus; and he said to his servants, "This is John the Baptist, he has been raised from the dead; that is why these powers are at work in him."

In this scripture, we have Herod Antipas, one of the sons of Herod the Great and a man who ruled a major part of the Judean kingdom in the time of Jesus, stating that Jesus was John the Baptist, reincarnated.

5. The next verse of scripture is often used as a biblical reference on reincarnation. It is John 1:6 which says:

"There was a man sent from God whose name was John."

A comment on this powerful statement will be presented later.

In addition to these strong five verses of scripture, an author who has a Doctor of Divinity degree from an accredited theological seminary presents over 200 verses in the Bible which indicate some level of belief in reincarnation at the time of Jesus.

Furthermore, there is much evidence in the Bible which indicates that the preexistence of the soul was accepted at the time of Jesus. The preexistence of the soul is a basic requirement of the reincarnation concept. Three examples of this biblical evidence are:

1. The previously mentioned John 1:6 which makes absolutely no sense without there having been an existence of the soul of John the Baptist before he was born; for in what other way could the Bible have said: *There was a man sent from God, whose name was John.*;

2. John 9:2 also strongly suggests the preexistence of the soul. This is the verse in which the disciples see a man who had been blind at birth, and ask Jesus if the man had sinned and thus had become blind. One wonders how the disciples could have had the man sin before birth unless the soul was in existence before that birth; and

3. In Romans 9:10-13, it is strongly suggested by Paul that the Lord had loved Jacob but hated Esau before they were born. Therefore, Paul is strongly supporting the existence of the soul prior to birth, one of the primary requirements for reincarnation. In addition, since Paul teaches hate whereas Jesus taught only Unconditional Love, this is yet another example of how the teachings of the Christ were altered by those who followed him.

Finally there is a statement from Volume 13, page 471 of *The New Catholic Encyclopedia*. The pertinent quote is:

"The existence of the soul after death does not contradict the

belief that the soul did not exist before birth, since after death the soul retains previously acquired knowledge, a transcendental relation to matter, and even a certain exigency to be united with matter."

This description of the soul after death is fascinating; for a soul which *remembers* previously acquired knowledge and *desires* to be united with a body is the type of soul which those who believe in reincarnation talk about. But this definition is not from some New Age journal. It is from *The New Catholic Encyclopedia*, about as orthodox and doctrinaire Christian reference as one could find.

However, it is not the purpose of this review to state that reincarnation is taught in the Bible; only that it is not denied. Since the concept of reincarnation was prevalent at the time, it would have been denied if Jesus considered it to be wrong. John 9:2 in which a man was thought to have become blind because he sinned before he was born would have been a perfect time for Jesus to have refuted the concept of reincarnation, but he did not do that.

Jesus changed those things which he wanted to change. One need only look at how Jesus denied the prevalent concept of "an eye-for-an-eye" to understand this. To review that story, read the Sermon on the Mount in Matthew, Chapter 5, with emphasis on verses 38-48. In those teachings, Jesus completely refuted the current thoughts about revenge and substituted thoughts of love. He did this because he considered thoughts of revenge to be a false concept; and he wanted to change false concepts. But he did not refute the concept of reincarnation when he had a similar opportunity.

The fact that Jesus did not *deny* reincarnation is important and leads to the question of why Jesus did not *teach* reincarnation. Jesus did not teach reincarnation because he did not have to. He taught only those things which needed to be changed, and he taught them strongly. But he did not teach either reincarnation or the preexistence of the soul when he had the opportunity to do so because he did not feel that there was any need to change them. Consequently, in order to leave those concepts alone, he neither denied nor taught the concepts of reincarnation or of the preexistence of the soul.

In summary, there is a strong biblical background on reincarnation. In addition, there is a strong early Christian tradition about the concept of reincarnation, some of which will be presented in the next section. This subject was covered in depth in *The Christian Conspiracy* in which it is stated that I could find no documentation of any Church-wide condemnation of the concept of reincarnation. To confirm some of this thinking, on an Oprah Winfrey talk show in July, 1994, an ex-Roman Catholic priest stood up and stated that all the early Christian leaders taught the concept of reincarnation, but that the pope made it an anathema [i.e. placed a formal curse on it] in about 600 CE. However, at that time the pronouncements of the pope were not considered to be dogma unless they were verified by an Ecumenical Council of the Church. In my opinion, the Church has not done this. In other words, the Church has never officially *condemned* reincarnation, but has merely *ignored* it, possibly with the hope that it would go away. They have done this because if the congregation of the faithful were to believe that they might have another chance in another life, then the Church would have suddenly lost a great deal of control over its membership.

The Bible supports reincarnation, and so did the early Church Fathers. It is only as the Church continued to gain power and control over the thoughts of its membership, that belief in reincarnation started to disappear from its teachings; *for how do you control those who believe that they might be given another chance?*

SECTION 3: BACKGROUND ON REINCARNATION FROM THE GENERAL WORLD LITERATURE

In addition to the Bible, the concepts of reincarnation and the preexistence of the soul occupy a prominent place in the general world literature as well as in the early Christian literature. As reported in *The Christian Conspiracy*, the early Church Fathers made the following statements:

1. Within about a century of the death of Christ, Justin Martyr in his *Dialogue with Trypho* taught that human souls inhabit more than one body in the course of their earthly pilgrimage. He even suggested the possibility that those who live carnal lives may deprive themselves of the capacity to see God, and thus may be reincarnated as beasts. This, of course, represents reincarnation, transmigration and karma as taught by one of the earliest Church Fathers.

2. Toward the end of the second century CE, Clement of Alexandria in his *Exhortations to the Pagans* wrote that man was:

"...in being long before the foundation of the world...and God showed pity on us in our wanderings, He pitied us from the very beginning."

This is a stirring presentation of the preexistence of the soul by an outstanding Eastern theologian of the early Church.

3. About 30 years later, Origen, who was possibly the greatest theologian and teacher of the early Church, said:

"The soul at one time puts off one body, which was necessary before but which is no longer adequate in its changed state, and it exchanges it for another."

In later writing he said:

"Every soul comes into this world strengthened by the victories or weakened by the defeats of its previous life."

Origen thus teaches both reincarnation and karma.

4. In about 370 CE, Gregory of Nyssa, who with Athanasius was the early Church's greatest defender of the divinity of Jesus Christ, said:

"It is absolutely necessary that the soul should be healed and purified, and if this does not take place during its life on earth, it must be accomplished in future lives."

5. At about the same time, Arnobius, a Christian Elder, in his *Adversus Gentes* said: *We die many times, and often do we rise from the dead.* Some might suggest that Arnobius was merely referring to the small deaths and rebirths which occur often in life and which ultimately lead to the final physical death of the body. In response, the reincarnationist would state an acceptance of that belief, then continue to the larger picture in which there are many physical deaths and rebirths, all of which ultimately lead to the final exit of the physical life followed by a rebirth in spirit.

6. In the early fourth century, Lactantius, a Christian writer whom St. Jerome called, "the Christian Cicero," said that the soul was capable of immortality and of bodily survival only on the hypothesis that it existed before the body. He thus proposes the preexistence of the soul.

7. Augustine defined purgatory in the same manner as his teacher, Ambrose, who said that all departed souls await the end of the world in various "habitations" which vary according to their works on earth. This is quite a karmic statement. Augustine expanded on this in *De Civitate Dei* to say that the souls of men are judged immediately on death and then go at once to a place of purification. The reincarnationist who accepts the Monadic-influence concept of reincarnation [see pages 86-89] sees these "habitations" as the place where Soul and Spirit come together to evaluate the life just experienced, and to program the next set of experiences. This concept was explained in detail in *Christianity and the New Age Religion*.

8. In *The Confessions of St. Augustine*, Augustine writes:

" ...did my infancy succeed another age of mine that died before it?...and what before that life, O God, was I in any body? For this I have none to tell me, neither father nor mother, nor experience of others, nor mine own memory."

9. In the late fourth century, Synesius, Bishop of Ptolemais, in his *Treatise on Dreams* wrote:

"The soul which did not quickly return to the heavenly region from which it was sent down to Earth, had to go through many lives of wandering."

10. Among those whom the Church rejected, the Manicheans, the Priscillians, the Marcionists, the Paulicians, the Bogomils, the Cathars and many others openly taught the doctrine of reincarnation. The Cathars of the early twelfth century taught that our reason for being on Earth is that we all are fallen spirits forced to be incarcerated in bodies and to work out our liberation through transmigration from one body to another. However, they saw in Christ the instrument of divine redemption from the wheel of rebirth. By this time, the Church had decided to excommunicate those who did not completely accept its teachings. Consequently, the Cathars were excommunicated and presented with genocide by the Catholic Church for holding these beliefs, despite the fact that their beliefs on reincarnation were an echo of the thoughts presented by many of the earlier Church Fathers [see *The Christian Conspiracy* for details].

11. In the nineteenth century, John Henry Newman, after he left the Anglican Church and became a Catholic Cardinal, proposed that after death, the soul goes to an undesignated place where it has opportunities for further growth and development. This is very similar to the description which Augustine and Ambrose had previously presented and fits into the same interpretation by the reincarnationist.

In addition to the early Christian literature, reincarnation has been presented in the general literature of the world. The following Western authors or thinkers have been cited as reporting positively on the concept: *Dante, Michelangelo, Sir Francis Bacon, David Hume, Thomas Carlyle, Bertrand Russell, John Milton, Samuel Coleridge, Rudyard Kipling, Charles Dickens, Arthur Conan Doyle, Isaac D'Israeli, Lloyd George, Frederick the Great, Immanuel Kant, Goethe, Albert Schweitzer, Voltaire, Napoleon Bonaparte, Balzac, Victor Hugo, Tolstoy, Dostoevsky, Benjamin Franklin, Thomas Paine, Ralph Waldo Emerson, Henry David Thoreau, Henry Wadsworth Longfellow, Oliver Wendell Holmes, Walt Whitman, Mark Twain, J. D. Salinger, Henry Ford, William Randolf Hearst, Henry Houdini, Charles Lindbergh, Thomas Edison, William James, Carl Jung, Charles Darwin, Albert Einstein,* and many other Western authors. There also are many Eastern authors and thinkers who have expressed their belief in the concepts of reincarnation and the preexistence of the soul.

A few representative quotations from the world's general literature are as follows:

1. The Koran says: *God generates beings, and sends them back over and over again, till* [sic.] *they return to Him.* It then goes on to state: *And when his body falleth off altogether, as an old fish-shell, his soul doeth well by the releasing, and formeth a new one instead.* The Sufi sect of Islam is particularly strong on the concept of reincarnation.

2. Pythagoras often mentioned his previous lifetimes, and by indicating that he knew who he had been, he could remind others of their former existences in much the same way that a reader of the Akashic records will do today.

3. Julius Caesar wrote that the Celts believed that souls do not become extinct, but pass after death from one body to another; and by doing this the Celtic leaders would excite their ranks to valor and lead them to disregard the fear of death.

4. David Hume, the eighteenth century Scottish philosopher, stated that the soul, if immortal, existed before our birth. He went on to state that Metempsychosis [the scientific term for a form of reincarnation] is the only system which philosophy can harken to.

5. Thomas Carlyle said that death and birth are the vesper and matin bells that summon mankind to sleep and to rise refreshed *for new advancement.*

6. Robert Browning [in *One Word More*] says:

"I shall never in the years remaining, Paint you pictures, no, nor carve you statues. This of verse alone one life allows me; Other heights in other lives, God willing."

7. Rudyard Kipling [in *Naulahka*] says:

"They will come back, come back again, as long as the red Earth rolls. He never wasted a leaf or a tree. Do you think He would squander souls?"

8. David Lloyd George stated that the conventional heaven with its angels made him an atheist for ten years. He then went on to say: *My opinion is that we shall be reincarnated.*

9. Frederick the Great said that although he might not be a king in his future life, that was so much the better because he would nevertheless live an active life, and earn less ingratitude.

10. von Goethe wrote:

"The soul of man is like to water; From Heaven it cometh, To Heaven it riseth, and then returneth to Earth, For ever alternating."

11. Gustav Mahler stated:

"We all return; it is this certainty that gives meaning to life and it does not make the slightest difference whether or not in a later incarnation we remember the former life. What counts is not the individual and his comfort, but the great inspiration to the perfect and pure which goes on in each incarnation."

12. Albert Schweitzer, the great Christian theologian, said that the idea of reincarnation surmounts difficulties which baffle the thinkers of Europe.

13. Victor Hugo, in *Victor Hugo's Intellectual Autobiography*, wrote:

"I am a soul. I know well that what I shall render up to the grave is not myself. That which is myself will go elsewhere. Earth, thou art not my abyss...The whole creation is a perpetual ascension, from brute to man, from man to God. To divest ourselves more and more of matter, to be clothed

more and more with spirit, such is the law. Each time we die, we gain more of life. Souls pass from one sphere to another without loss of personality, become more and more bright.

With this magnificent quotation, we will close this sampling from the thousands of quotations on reincarnation which have been presented by the great authors, thinkers, and philosophers of the world. They accept the belief that the soul exists in a large number of bodies over a significant period of time. In the doctrines originally developed by the world's great religions, this same lesson was taught. In some religions, those doctrines were later changed by the humans of that religion.

SECTION 4: TWO VIEWPOINTS OF REINCARNATION

Although there are many viewpoints on reincarnation, two viewpoints dominate the scene. One presents the belief that reincarnation is a negative experience and that the purpose of life is to avoid experiences in order to achieve a life from which no more reincarnations need be developed. The other presents the belief that reincarnation is a positive experience which creates opportunities. It is therefore to be pursued, for if one is dying countless deaths in order to be born into *something else*, then one is growing more and more into immortality.

There is the tendency to call the first of these viewpoints the "Eastern Viewpoint" and the other the "Western Viewpoint," but such a distinction creates several problems. As one example, it divides the Earth into two contrasting spheres when we should be proceeding toward the unity of humankind. As another example, it tends to relate the first form of reincarnation to the Eastern religions such as Hinduism, when there are people of all faiths, including the Eastern religions, who are starting to accept the possibility of the other kind of reincarnation. As a further example, there are people of all religions, including the Western religions, who accept the belief that the purpose of their life is to run away from life's experiences, or to run toward experiences not found in a conventional life; and they have this belief whether they accept the concept of reincarnation or not. Many of these people have accepted the life which exists behind the cloistered walls of the monasteries or nunneries, whether in the East or in the West. But the biggest reason for rejecting the terms "Eastern" and "Western" for these differing viewpoints is the fact that the difference between the two thoughts is so great, that the words "Eastern" and "Western" simply do them a disservice.

In *The Christian Conspiracy*, a fairly detailed section presented the thought that the New Age divides itself into two groups, the "original belief system" and the "evolutionary belief system." In my opinion, the two viewpoints of reincarnation could be described in a similar manner as "origin reincarnation" and "evolution reincarnation."

The "origin reincarnation" viewpoint is very similar to the Hindu [or Upanishadic] viewpoint of reincarnation. In this version, the entity has an origin which is identical in all aspects with God. Through his misadventures, he falls from this ideal spot into the realm of matter. Because experiences in the realm of matter are considered to be a misadventure, they are to be avoided since they would merely dilute the original identity with God. Because of this belief, life and all experiences in the material world are to be avoided.

The "evolutionary reincarnation" viewpoint, on the other hand, believes that the entity starts with a small spark of God, and then separates in order to evolve through growth by having experiences in all realms of matter and non-matter. Through this involvement with experiences, the soul evolves to be where God once was; although because of the experiential evolution, God is no longer there because S/He also has grown and developed. Although God is always the ALL, and in this sense never mutates or changes, this viewpoint proposes that God does evolve as those who have been created in his image undergo their evolutionary development. In this way, the ALL which is God has evolved to something different than it once was.

The major difference in these two expressions of reincarnation is that in one, the purpose of life is to avoid experiences; for the more that experiences are avoided, the closer the entity becomes to breaking the chain of rebirth. By non-experiences in life, these reincarnations will lead the individual back to exactly where he/she originally was. The other expression of reincarnation believes that by experiencing life, these evolutionary reincarnations will lead the individual back to a point of being much closer to God than he/she originally was, because both the entity and God will have undergone evolutionary development. In essence, there is evolvement in one of the reincarnation viewpoints, but not in the other. Since a definitive experiment to determine which of these viewpoints is more nearly correct will be impossible to run as long as humans remain in their present three-dimensional existence, both beliefs will probably continue to remain within the belief systems of humankind.

But while each system remains, it should be understood that the difference between the "origin reincarnation" notion of personal immortality and the "evolutionary reincarnation" notion is enormous. In the origin view, the entity *is* an immortal soul temporarily clothed in a human body. In the other view, the entity has *become* a "soul" through millions of years of evolutionary development and struggle, and the "soul" it has become is capable of immortality. Throughout the earlier stages of its evolutionary development, the entity was entirely dependent on genetic factors for the inheritance of personal qualities; but at the point of becoming a human entity, it was granted the capacity to transcend biological processes by being able to move from one incarnation to another. The special change in becoming human is mentioned in the Bible which tells of God's having breathed into human in such a way that, by the divine *ruach* [i.e. the breath of God], human *became* a "living soul." This was a tremendous leap in evolution.

The acceptance, or non-acceptance, of any reincarnation belief system is entirely up to the individual. Whether any reincarnation belief system is accepted or not, there is a pathway into oneness with God which can be experienced, so long as it is acknowledged by the unique entity as being the one he/she should follow.

SECTION 5: THE MONADIC-INFLUENCE CONCEPT OF REINCARNATION

Although not all reincarnationists accept the concept of the monadic-influence, there are a growing number who do. As the remembrances of the time spent near to God continue to spread across the collective conscience of humankind, possibly more and more will join the ranks of those who accept that the Monad has a tremendous influence on the functioning of the reincarnation principles.

In Chapter 2, the *Monad* was described as being the first emanation from God. The Monad therefore became the agent for creation; and through the Monad, all created things were generated. Many of the established religions of the world, particularly Christianity, teach that God creates things out of nothing. In Christianity, the only exception to the belief that all things were created out of nothing was Jesus Christ who was not created, but was an emanation directly from God. As described in Chapter 2, one of the basic concepts presented in this book is the belief that there probably have been many messengers from God, some [or all] of whom *may* have been emanations and thus skipped the Monadic experience.

Other religions or philosophies have used other names as the agent of creation. As an example, the Old Testament in Hebrew names the *Elohim* as the creators in Genesis, a name which has often been changed to simply "God" in the English versions. Later, Judaism named *Wisdom* as the creating agent of God, a concept later picked up by the Christians when Paul named Jesus as Wisdom in the first Chapter of 1 Corinthians and expanded on this theme in the first Chapter of Colossians. Zoroastrianism believed that all matter was created by *Ohrmazd* [originally *Ahura Mazda*, the "Wise Lord"] who is the one supreme God and needed no intermediary in order to create material things. Philo, the Father of Hellenistic Judaism who lived about the same time as Jesus Christ, named *Logos* as the agent of God in the creation of the world. But most religions to which Greek philosophy has been applied have the Monad involved in some form as the first emanation, and as God's agent for creation.

By whatever name the creating emanation from God is known, the principle is the same. If, for example, the Monad is the agent of God's creation, then it is to the Monad that all created things will return as they proceed on their personal pathway into oneness with God. Reincarnationists who believe there is a Monadic influence on the reincarnation process believe that this influence happens every time a Soul has finished one incarnational experience and is being prepared for another incarnational experience.

To enter into the Monadic influence, the Soul will first sever itself from the bodies which it is leaving in order to join with Spirit.

Spirit is the messenger between God and the Monad. Spirit brings the message from God to the Monad and works within the Monad in conjunction with Soul to evaluate the experiential progress the entity made in the prior incarnation, and to plan for the experiential progress to be developed for the next incarnation. Whether the programmed evolution occurs is determined by the Free Will activities of the particular entity; but if God's will is followed at each step within the incarnational lifetime of that entity, then all programmed evolution will occur. If there are any missed evolutionary experiences, then these will merely be reprogrammed by Spirit into another incarnational experience for Soul.

Some knowledge about the severing of the soul from the body is needed to generate understanding about the way which the soul returns to the Monad for interaction with Spirit. Previously, there have been teachings presented which stated that the soul is connected to the physical body with a silver cord; and that after the death of the physical body, it takes the connection three days to separate. Consequently, it was believed that a body which is buried or cremated before those three days will have the soul still connected to it. Return to the Monad would, therefore, become difficult.

It is my firm belief that this is a teaching which has been misinterpreted. The teaching should refer to the attachment of the soul via the silver cord to the three *bodies*: the physical body, the mental body, and the emotional body. To enable Soul to attach itself to Spirit and therefore become a part of the spiritual body within the Monad, the cord must be detached from these three *bodies*, not take three *days*. In reality, the severance of the soul from the physical body can occur almost instantaneously; and therefore those who worry about such things as waiting three days to make certain the detachment is complete really have absolutely nothing to worry about. The detachment will be done in such a manner that even if the physical body were to be cremated, the soul would not be a part of the physical fire. As additional understanding, the reference to the silver cord is a reference to the energy or the light composition of the cord, and does not refer to any sort of metallic composition.

In summary, the Monadic-influence concept in reincarnation has to do with the bringing together of Spirit and Soul within the

Monad in a participative process to evaluate and program evolutionary experiences for the incarnations of Soul. It is a concept which is not accepted by everyone; but those who accept it feel strongly about it. They feel that it explains the roles of Soul and Spirit in the evolutionary progress of Soul through incarnational experiences. Those who accept this concept feel that it generates a powerful understanding of the entire reincarnational process.

SECTION 6: A THIRD VIEWPOINT ON REINCARNATION

This section is not for the fainthearted; and I would suggest that you skip this section if your belief in reincarnation is either of a recent nature, or if you have any doubts about reincarnation as a spiritual belief. I have lived for over twenty-five years with the firm belief that reincarnation not only *does* exist, but that it *must* exist in order for those who believe they were created in God's image to fulfill God's purpose for them. But even with this rather long background of full acceptance, it has been only recently that I have accepted this particular viewpoint of reincarnation. I think I needed all of the prior beliefs in order to accept this viewpoint without questioning the reality of reincarnation.

I had thought that I would not include this viewpoint in this book for fear that it would go too far, and consequently turn off those who had only recently become comfortable with their belief in reincarnation. However, because of a "coincidence," I have chosen to include this section. The spiritual meaning of "coincidence" and the particular coincidence which caused this section to be written are described more fully in Chapter 5 of *Part One*.

Since leaving the restrictive thinking present in today's Christian Church, I have had not only the time, but also the inclination to dig deeper into my thoughts in order to see what I truly believe. As a result, I have come to what I think is a more complete understanding of reincarnation. I do not mean to pat myself on the back in any way when I say that if the acceptance of either of the previously presented viewpoints on reincarnation is considered to be college-level spiritual material, then this viewpoint of reincarnation is graduate school stuff. For those of you who have specialized in a particular subject during graduate school, you may recall that some of the generalities which you had been taught as an undergraduate had to be "unlearned" so that you could delve deeper into your field of specialty. The original lessons had served a very valuable purpose, but it was now time to move on.

Although I will go further in Chapter 5 in describing the "coincidence" which directed me to write this section, I will say here that it came from one who has been a teacher and confidant to me for over twenty five years. Entirely independent of my development, he had come to the same conclusions; and said so in an audio tape which my wife and I received as I was writing this section of this book. As difficult as it was for me to accept this viewpoint, it must have been even more difficult for him; because he has spent a major portion of his life involved with the more generalized, less developed viewpoints of reincarnation presented in the earlier descriptions.

The reincarnation which I will describe will be called, for want of a better term, "trait-led" reincarnation. The examples I will use to describe it are based on the mathematical concept of permutations and combinations, with emphasis on the combinations part. As a simplified description of "permutations and combinations," they are ways in which small sets of groups can be combined from larger sets of groups. Combinations consist of small groups without regard to the order in which they are grouped; whereas permutations also consider the order. As an example, if you were to ask how many groups of two letters [e.g. AB] there are in four letters [e.g. ABCD], there would be 10 combinations [e.g. AB, BC, BD, etc.] and 20 permutations; because in the combinations, AB and BA would be the same, whereas in permutations, they would be different. In respect to reincarnation, we will consider only combinations, because the order in which they are used to create a personality is probably not relevant.

This small understanding of combinations will allow a description of trait-led reincarnation by using some examples of the concept. Let me say in advance that I have no idea of the actual numbers involved, and any number used in these examples is used merely to illustrate the concept.

As an example of trait-led reincarnation, let us suppose that to generate a "personality," it takes five "characteristics," or "personality traits," all of which we will describe by using the word "trait." In this use, the word "personality" means, *"a soul incarnated into a physical form or body."* Let us further suppose that the "oversoul" or "monad" or whatever term is used to describe that which is the emanation from God used to create all things, works with Soul to choose which traits will be incarnated in order to develop the experiences which Soul needs for evolutionary development. Let us also assume that Soul has available for its use, many more traits than the five which are needed to create a viable personality. The question then becomes this: *how many unique personalities, unlike any other personality which has ever existed, could Soul create while still having all of these personalities be of the same Soul?*

Before going into the examples, I feel the need to express a few words as to why I felt the need to explore the possibility of trait-led reincarnation. For many years "I" have known that I have been on this Earth plane before. It is much more than merely the sensing of past events such as might come from a group consciousness, important though that may be. Instead, it is a *knowing that I have been here before*. On the other hand, for many years I have known that I am unique, as are you; and that, in reality, neither of us has ever been here *in exactly our present personality*. Our present personalities may be *close* to that which has been here before, but the <u>exact</u> we which presently exists has never walked in these footsteps before. The question then becomes this: *how can we have been here before even though our present personality is unique?*

Going back to our assumption that 5 traits make a personality, then if the soul has 10 traits available to it, the soul could create 252 personalities without any two personalities having exactly the same five traits, even if the order in which the traits were placed into the personality made no difference. Since it is my belief that the soul has many more than 10 traits available to it, let us look at another example. Let us assume that the soul has 26 characteristics, just like the letters of the alphabet. How many groupings of five traits [e.g. ABCDE, or GOZQL, or BYPSV, etc.] could be made from an alphabet of 26 letters? The answer is about 67,000. In other words, if a soul had 26 traits available to it, and if it took 5 traits to create a unique personality, then that soul could create 67,000 personalities, all of the same soul and none of which would be exactly identical to any other personality. If, instead of 26 the soul had 60 traits available, then the soul could create almost 5.5 million personalities, each of which would be of the same soul, and no one of which would have the same five traits possessed by any other unique personality.

It is my belief that the soul has thousands of "traits" [whatever they are] out of which unique personalities could be developed. If a personality is composed of five traits, and if the soul had a mere one-thousand traits to work with, then many times the total of the world's present population could come from one soul, and yet no personality would have the same five traits as any other personality.

I have no idea how many "traits" are needed to create a personality; nor do I know how many traits each soul has to work with. Instead of needing five traits to create a personality, the soul may need 10,000. Instead of having 1,000 traits to work with, the soul may have a billion. The point I am trying to make is that anyone in present personality could have one [or possibly many] of the traits previously used by the soul to create a certain personality, but still be, in the whole, a personality who is unique and different than any who has ever been incarnated into physical form. In this way, one who can read the Akashic records to understand the past activities of this soul would "see" that the present personality would be, in some ways, exactly like a person of history, let us say Thomas Jefferson; and therefore this sincere and able reader would say that the person had "been" Thomas Jefferson. The fact is that if trait-led reincarnation has any validity, the present personality had not "been" Thomas Jefferson; although parts of the present personality certainly had been parts of him, else the reader would never have "seen" Thomas Jefferson in the history of the one being "read." In this way, although Thomas Jefferson has been reincarnated, or brought back into an incarnated form in this new personality, it is highly unlikely that his exact personality has returned *in toto*. Instead, there are parts of who he was, parts of who [say] Genghis Khan was, and parts of who Joe Brown and Jane Smith were, all brought together by Spirit [who is of God] working with Soul within the Monad in order to create the new and unique personality which is needed for Soul to continue in evolutionary development.

Another explanation of "trait-led" reincarnation has been previously presented [see page 69]. This explanation was presented to my wife during a meditation in early 1995. During another meditation a few weeks later, she was shown that an incarnate personality is somewhat like a soup which has been put together at a large soup bar. The major ingredient of the soup has been put into the individual's soup bowl from the large urn; but it has been augmented by a dash of several herbs from one part of the soup bar, by several essences from another part, and by the addition of certain cheeses or croutons from yet another part. The end result is then eaten by the individual. Any reader of the Akashic record would then see the added ingredients as a part of the individual who had eaten the soup. The Akashic reader might see an essence which gave the superb intelligence of Thomas Jefferson, a herb which gave the immense strength of Genghis Khan, and a cheese which gave the zest for life of Joe Brown or the pertness of Jane Smith. The individual would not "be" any of those prior persons; and yet he/she would have some of the qualities generated by that person of history. In this way the soul would have generated a unique personality which had "been" here before.

Some might say that none of these illustrations of "trait-led" reincarnation really represents a true reincarnation; but I would say that they do. I would say with all of my heart, that such a procedure is not only reincarnation in the sense of having that which has been here before returned in the form of a new body; it is the way that the return can be in the form of a new creation unlike any which has ever existed.

I have been here before; but I am unique. You have been here before; but you also are unique. Although each of us has been here many times in many different eras and many different places, we have never been put together in exactly the way we are now. This is the way that Soul and Spirit work together within the Monad in order not to lose what once was, but still to make evolutionary progress for the soul. Although the name of "trait-led reincarnation" may not be accepted by many, it is a name which could be applied to the third viewpoint of reincarnation—the form of reincarnation which creates unique personalities.

SECTION 7: THE NEED FOR PERSONAL REINCARNATION IN GOD'S UNIVERSE

There was an earlier section entitled "Two Viewpoints of Reincarnation." In that section, it was stated that one viewpoint believed that the entity had an origin which was identical with God, then through misadventure became trapped in the realm of matter. The other viewpoint believed that the entity was created with a spark of God, which would grow through experience into qualitative indenticality with God, even though the processing of such experiences might take an eternity to complete. In either case, the personal pathway into oneness with God is followed when the entity accepts God's will for its life with so much constancy that the two wills become identical. However, God has chosen not to order this to happen. Instead, S/He has allowed this to happen only when it is the Free Will choice of the individual. In addition, as suggested in Chapter 5 of *Part Two*, it is unlikely that this coincidence of wills can happen in the absence of Unconditional Love.

God is most likely not a local God as was frequently proposed in the historical times prior to the acceptance of monotheism [or "one supreme God"]. Instead, God is of the Universe with all of its vast Time and Space. In addition, God is most likely not an individual who has two legs, two eyes, one nose, and a blood-pumping circulatory system all contained within a piece of three-dimensional space. Instead, S/He probably has the ability to exist in all dimensions, even those which we cannot define or even understand by use of our five physical senses [see Chapter 5]. Finally, it is highly unlikely that God is a He, or a She, or even a S/He, although we often use those terms in order to communicate. Instead, God probably exists in all sexual states or in no sexual state, which possibly means exactly the same thing.

As a consequence of the preceding two paragraphs, for an entity to become one with God [i.e. to return to oneness with God], it is suggested that the entity would have to:

1. Be able to understand God enough to accept His/Her will in all instances and circumstances;

2. Be able to practice Unconditional Love with all who were created by God and to do this in all instances and circumstances;

3. Be able to experience, understand and accept all emotions of all sexes;

4. Be able to experience, understand, accept and survive all energies in all dimensionalities; and

5. On, and on, and on.

What is your thought? *Could all of this be accomplished in one incarnation, on one physical plane, in a single lifetime of, say, eighty years?* The true answer to that question is "absolutely YES," for it could happen in an instant and probably has happened many more times than most of us have realized. However, I still think that it is a rare occurrence, and possibly, although not necessarily, done only by those who have been created as an emanation of God rather than as a creation of the Monad. Consequently, I think that most of us had better plan on coming back again and again and again in many different forms and arrangements until finally, through incarnational experience, our soul has grown to such a level that the "we" represented by soul no longer needs reincarnation in form for experiential evolution. Instead, at that time "we" will be beyond form.

The Thiering book [*Jesus and the Riddle of the Dead Sea Scrolls*] is based on the premise that the gospels as we know them have a hidden meaning which can be interpreted by use of the "pesher," a technique adapted from Old Testament studies. This has been a highly controversial book within Christian communities. It is not my intent to judge the major premise of that book although it does seem to have great merit. Instead, I mention the book at this point to present one of its minor points. On page 76, the author says:

"By giving us the real history of Jesus, the gospels prepare the way for understanding that beyond the forms of religion is freedom from form. Jesus was human as we are human; he can take us only to our limit, and in taking us there, prepare us for God."

In other words, the author is saying that at some time we will be beyond form [i.e. a three-dimensional physical being], and when we get there, we will be closer to God. The major premise of this entire chapter is that it will take us more than one lifetime to go beyond form.

SUMMARY

In summary, because of all that must be experienced, accepted and understood by every entity as it defines and follows its unique and individualized personal pathway into oneness with God, there is a practical and fundamental need for the reincarnation of the soul into many diverse personalities. This is merely a way to experience all of God's Universe. Although the exact form of reincarnation which an entity will experience might differ from one belief system to another, the great majority of the world's population not only believes that reincarnation happens,

they believe that reincarnation is a necessity.

CHAPTER 5
ADDITIONAL BACKGROUND INFORMATION

Although much information needed to understand some of the elements on the personal pathway into oneness with God has been presented in the previous four chapters, there are other subjects which may prove to be of some help. In this chapter, six sections covering miscellaneous material will be presented as:
1. Dimensionality
2. God's Thermodynamic Universe
3. The Phenomenon of Coincidence
4. The Chakra System
5. Some Thoughts about Numbers
6. The Presence of God.

SECTION 1: DIMENSIONALITY
If there were any one subject which might help to explain what may be experienced or encountered on a personal pathway into oneness with God, that one subject would be dimensionality, or the understanding of dimensions. It is the one subject or belief which helps to explain the probability of many other beliefs. Although this subject was discussed in depth in *Christianity and the New Age Religion*, a significant portion of that discussion will be presented here in order to make this book more nearly complete.

In order to understand the concept of dimensions, there has to be some understanding of light. In reality, we don't know much about light. In the latter part of the 19th century, a furious debate was being conducted by physicists. Some thought that light was a wave; whereas others thought that light was a photon.

One of the most famous unsuccessful experiments of all time was conducted by Michelson and Morly in Cleveland in 1887. It was designed to prove once and for all whether light was a wave or a photon. The experiment proved that it was neither—or both. Even today we don't know much more; for we only know that under certain conditions, light responds as if it were a wave, and under other conditions, as if it were photonic. Even now, our best simple description of light is that it is energy—pure energy—which can be used in many diverse ways. In this description, light is not only the light which we can see, but includes all of the electromagnetic spectrum. In other words, light includes those parts of itself which do not respond to any of our physical senses, particularly to our physical sense of sight.

In general, light is dimensionless and has no mass. Of course, under the conditions in which light acts as a wave, the wavelengths of light are very specific and range all the way from the long wavelengths of the reds to the short wavelengths of the violets within the visible spectrum; and which extend into the longer infrareds or into the shorter ultraviolets as the wavelengths leave the visible region. However, in the sense that it is pure energy, light is dimensionless and without mass; and when the wavelengths of light are outside of the visible region, they still exist, even if we cannot see them.

Light has a place in the Bible. In the very first verses of Genesis, the Bible says that first there was God, who then created light, and who then created things. This could be paraphrased to say that first there was God who made energy and then used this energy to make things which have mass.

This interpretation fits very well into the "Big Bang" theory of modern physics which, when applied to the creation of physical things, states that first, there was just energy; and then the energy got together in such a way that every physical thing that has ever been created was created from that energy within a very short time period—within the microscopic part of a second. That was about 18 billion years ago. Since then, there have been questions as to whether or not there have been any new physical things created, or merely a rearrangement of the physical things created during the "Big Bang." The physical possibility of the Big Bang was first predicted by Einstein. In one application of his Theory of Relativity, it was predicted that mass could be converted into energy, and vice versa. Turning mass into energy creates an atomic bomb; whereas turning energy into mass creates the physical universe.

What is energy? In a classical sense, energy is defined either as the equivalent of work, or of having the capacity for doing work. It can be associated with a material body such as a coiled spring; or it can be independent of matter such as light in a vacuum. Energy leads to power which is defined as the rate of doing work and therefore the rate of energy flow. Since one partial definition of God is that S/He is omnipotent, which means "having all power," these descriptions of energy lead to a definition of God which says that S/He has control of all of the rates of energy flow. This, when combined with dimensions, generates a useable definition of God which might allow us to understand some of the pathway which could lead us into oneness with Him/Her.

To follow this reasoning, let us assume that for a creation of God, the energy flow will be the highest when that creation is in the spiritual form, and the lowest when that creation is in the physical form. In this concept, the highest spiritual form would be at such a high rate of energy flow that it would be dimensionless in terms of our three-dimensional physicality. It would not only be dimensionless because of the limitations inherent in our physicality, it would also be beyond the determination of our physical senses. In other words, our limited three-dimensional physical form is not capable of using our three-dimensional senses on creations which are other than three-dimensional.

As creations assume an energy flow which is higher than that of three-dimensionality, the creation exists in a higher dimension. As this continues, then the creation would ultimately approach the energy flow of the dimensionality of God, at least in the quality of those dimensions if not the quantity. At this point, the entity would start to become a Godlike spirit, for as Jesus said: *"God is spirit, and those who worship him must worship in spirit and truth."* [John 4:24].

As a spirit, God must be of the highest energy flow, which is energy itself—multidimensional energy from which all things can be made, and out of which all things may be said to exist. And yet, to those approaching similar multidimensional vibrations, the spirit would exist as an entity—as a God who was a person. This latter point is an important one, for there are more dimensions on the personal pathway into oneness with God than merely our present three-dimension form, or the infinite-dimensional form of God. The multi-dimensional ones other than these two levels represent all unseen things, or all things which occupy a different dimensional warp than that which exists in our restrictive, three-dimensional physical plane.

As the creation proceeds along the pathway, he/she soon comes to understand some parts of dimensionality. He/she knows that the present physical form into which his/her soul has incarnated is a three dimensional one which has length, width, and breadth and which, therefore, can be experienced by using the existing physical senses. The creation also recognizes that one-dimensional creations also exist; but since they have only one dimension, they cannot be determined by our physical senses, only by our mind or our mental senses. For although the geometrical representation of a one-dimensional object is a point, it is not a point like the period on a piece of paper. That point has three dimensions. However the one-dimensional object can be visualized in our mind, and because of this, we can do something with it.

In a similar sense, a two-dimensional object also could not be seen by our physical senses; because although it would have length and width, it would have no height and thus would not exist to our physical senses, but only in our mind. For although the geometrical representation of a two-dimensional object is a line, it is not a line such as the underlining of a word. That line has three dimensions. However, again a two-dimensional object could be visualized in our mind, and once visualized, we could describe it or do something else with it. Only when an object gets into the third dimension is it capable of being discerned by our limited physical senses. The geometrical representation of a three dimensional object is a plane, and it can readily be determined by the use of our physical senses. Of course, we can also visualize three dimensional objects in our mind.

We can therefore describe three-dimensional objects either from our physical or from our mental capabilities.

In some circles, the fourth dimension is defined as being time, for if you wish to locate a moving object, you need more than just three dimensions in order to establish its location. You also need to know when it will be there in order to see it. There is no use knowing that an airplane will be 25,000 feet over a certain latitude and longitude unless you also know when it will be there. Otherwise, if you know only the three dimensions and not the fourth, the airplane would be invisible to you unless you were lucky enough to guess the fourth dimension and be looking not only at the correct three dimensional coordinates, but also doing it at the right fourth dimensional coordinate—at the right time. In a similar manner, the normally three-dimensional blades of a spinning fan will disappear because the physical eye cannot time them properly. Of course, if you know what kind of an airplane it is, or can remember how the fan blades looked when stationary, then you could mentally visualize these fourth dimensional objects at any time.

It would seem fairly simple for a human caught in this three dimensional world to see how anything in a one- or two-dimensional world would be invisible to his physical senses, but might be captured by his mental senses. It also seems fairly simple for such a human to understand how he/she could physically experience things in a fourth dimensional world, but only if all four dimensions were known so that he/she could be at the right spot at the right time. However, he/she could mentally experience a fourth dimensional thing without knowing anything about any of its dimensions.

At the present time, physics has not defined the fifth or higher dimensions, but it should be fairly simple for a human caught in this three dimensional world to accept that a creation operating in the fifth [or higher] dimension would not be discernible as a physical object to the human's physical senses. That creation might be available as a mental object to its mental senses, or it might even conceivably be available as an emotional object to its emotional senses, or as a spiritual object to its spiritual senses; but it would never be physically seen, heard, tasted, smelled or felt unless the "one who sees" and the "one who is seen" are of the same dimensionality. In other words, as long as we stay three-dimensional, then other-dimensional creations will not respond to our limited, human physical senses. That lack of response, however, does not mean that those creations do not exist.

That is one of the points which the contemplation of dimensionality will generate. It is the point that although you cannot determine something with your physical senses, you might be able to determine it with your mental, emotional or spiritual senses. During prayer or meditation, have you ever heard God speak to you? Many believe that they have; and yet, it was not a physical voice which was heard, nor was it imagination. It was something which touched the Soul with a definite message, possibly of an emotional or a spiritual nature. Have you ever felt love? With what physical sense did you feel love? Could it have been of such a nature that its dimensions were beyond those of the three-dimensional physical world? Yet, wasn't it real, even though it was something which had to be determined by the emotional or the spiritual senses rather than the physical ones?

To be on a personal pathway into oneness with God, it is useful to understand that God is a higher dimensional being than the three or four dimensions which fit into our three dimensional world. In fact, it helps to accept that God is of such a high level of energy flow, and is at such a high frequency of energy, that S/He is beyond dimensions, meaning that God is capable of assuming any dimension including the fourth dimension of time. This allows Him/Her to fit the second and third definitions of God—those of being omniscient [or "all knowing"] and omnipresent [or "in all places"].

In addition, the individual on the pathway will accept that there are other beings who are in dimensions both higher and lower than the three dimensions in which we exist as we incarnate in our low-frequency physical state. Some of those beings are locked into their dimensions just as our present physical forms are locked into our three dimensions; whereas others are able to go into or out of those dimensions at will because they are multidimensional. As one minor example of the usefulness of multidimensionality, this would be the only way that extraterrestrial travel could be possible—by going into a frequency dimension which is higher than the slowly vibrating three dimensional physical world into which all of our matter belongs. Staying three-dimensional is just too slow for meaningful space travel!

If a three-dimensional being can mentally or emotionally visualize dimensions to which his physical presence cannot take him, then many puzzling things become explainable. Why, for example, are extraterrestrial activities or beings sometimes seen and sometimes not seen? Do they or their vehicles merely slip into dimensions unavailable to our physical senses? How could Jesus ascend when his followers seemingly could not? Did he merely follow his available capabilities by going multidimensional? Why can some people seemingly see Mother Mary, while others cannot? Is she merely bringing parts of them up into a dimension which is not available to all? When the paranormal happens and has been accepted not to be involved in some sort of chicanery, has the experience been dimensionally related?

Finally, wasn't Billy Graham talking about dimensionality in his book entitled *Angels* when he said:

"*Angels speak. They appear and reappear. They feel apt sense of emotion. While angels may become visible by choice, our eyes are not constructed to see them ordinarily any more than we can see the dimensions of a nuclear field, the structure of atoms, or the electricity that flows through copper wiring. Our ability to sense reality is limited.*"

An understanding of dimensionality, and an acceptance of its existence, can answer many questions which otherwise would make a personal pathway into oneness with God a very difficult concept to accept or to understand, and an even more difficult one to experience.

SECTION 2: GOD'S THERMODYNAMIC UNIVERSE

In human terms, time and space are very important, for we live in three-dimensional space which is encompassed in barriers of time. It is because of this importance to the human endeavor that we presented so much detail about time and space in Chapter 4.

However, since God is eternal in respect to both time and space, then these subjects are meaningless in God's Universe. Instead of being concerned with the time and space which occupy human thought, it is my belief that God's Universe is concerned with transformational events, or those events which change the form of energetic beings or material within the universe. These transformational events are caused by changes in energetic formation. On Earth, such changes are examined in a branch of physics entitled "thermodynamics"; whereas the time which such changes take is examined in a branch of physics entitled "kinetics."

Thermodynamics is defined as "the physics of the relationships between heat and other forms of energy." There are three Laws of Thermodynamics, none of which will be discussed here; for the sole reason for addressing thermodynamics in this book is to present the rule that certain transformational events will occur if there is a change in a thermodynamic function known as the Gibbs Free Energy. In other words, certain kinds of energy, at certain energy levels, can cause a transformational event to occur, such as the transformation of two chemicals into a third chemical unlike either of the starting two.

All physicists will accept that the Gibbs Free Energy is a known, physical energy which can cause transformations to occur. It is my belief that other kinds of energy, at other energetic levels or other levels of dimensionality, can cause other kinds of transformational events to occur. In both the transformational events acknowledged by our physical scientists and those presently not acknowledged, calculations of the energy changes will generate no knowledge about the time necessary to make those events occur.

The concept that God's Universe is concerned with events and not with the timing of those events may be difficult for humans to accept, because we are so concerned with time as a measurement of all of our activities. We do this because our world is concerned with temporal things or those things which are limited by time. We want to know when something did happen, or when it will happen. We even study history by learning the "when and where" rather than the "why and how," because we are more interested in the time capsule of historical events rather than trying to understand the long-range impact of those same historical events. As the ultimate in concern about time, most humans would like to know the time of their death so that they would know how much "time" is left to them.

Additional Background Information

Most humans are more concerned with temporal matters such as these, than with the eternal matters of God.

Because we live in a world so oriented toward time, we would like God to tell us *when* things will occur. Since God is omniscient [i.e. has all knowledge], then it is easy to believe that God knows when things will happen; but a God who was concerned with time would be a God created in our image instead of the other way around. God is concerned with eternal things; we are the ones concerned with temporal things. God's Universe concerns itself with the transformational events and their impact on the eternal universe rather than the time at which such transformational events occur. God is the Primary Cause in a thermodynamic universe based on transformational events—not a kinetic universe based on the timing of those events, especially when timing is related to this small speck of cosmic dust called Earth.

As a consequence of all of this, whenever a sincere channeler presents a message from Spirit and not from Ego, that message will be event-oriented. It will rarely, if ever, have time as a part of the message. When a sincere channeler tries to tell the when, it is often in an attempt to help the humans who are listening; and it often proves to be incorrect.

This is because the channeler who is led by Spirit rather than by Ego has been allowed to see an event, but since that event has come from the eternal Oneness, it has no time frame associated with it. The sincere channeler may try to associate related events in order to get some perspective on the time factor just as the prophets in the Bible did; but each reporting of a time factor is done in an attempt to help relate humans to the event, and not to give the message as presented by God. The only incident during which a Spirit-led channeler would be presented with a time frame is when the events being described require human participation and therefore need to be done within a particular, human time frame. When that happens, the message has been converted into our language for our benefit. It is for our benefit because God's Universe simply does not run on our concept of time.

There is a reason for this being true. As most physicists would state, it is impossible to change thermodynamic events directly into kinetic information. Instead, a lot of additional measurements must be taken in an isolated thermodynamic system.

In the same way, it would be virtually impossible to place universal transformational events into a time capsule which has meaning in this temporal world of ours, because we would have to isolate ourselves from the rest of the universe in order to get an accurate measurement of the time associated with that time capsule. When we do that isolation, then we have isolated ourselves from God, and all God-related events would have been changed. In other words, we would know the <u>when</u> of transformational events on this Earth only if we were to isolate this Earth from the rest of the universe. If God is to be involved in those transformational events as the Primary Cause, then such an isolation is not possible. Try as we might, we simply cannot know the timing of any transformational event if God's causative efforts are to be involved in that event.

Understanding that God's universe functions as a thermodynamic universe rather than a kinetic one has tremendous impact on an individual's pathway to God, for it means that the pathway is concerned with events and not with time. In Chapter 5 of *Part Two*, we will describe a pathway which has seven transformational events or milestones at certain points along the pathway. Let us assume that because of the Free Will of a particular individual, it has taken many hundreds [or even thousands] of reincarnations in order to pass the transformational event described by the first milestone. To a human, this might cause concern, because the time associated with those many reincarnations would imply that similar times might be necessary at each subsequent milestone. That is thinking in human's terms, and not in the terms which describe the functioning of God's Universe.

Although it is possible that God would be surprised that anyone created in His/Her image might take so many attempts to understand God's will and thus create an event which would be a transforming one for them, it is the transforming event rather than the time associated with it which is observed by God. God sees this event because it is a transforming event through which an individual has been able to satisfy God's will for him/herself.

As a consequence of God's Universe being a thermodynamic rather than a kinetic one, each stage on the pathway into oneness with God is associated with a transformational event, and not with the time which we humans would associate with reaching that event. It is possible that although a single milestone on the pathway to God may have taken a significant amount of time in human terms, many other milestones on that pathway may be covered in what would be a short period of time in human terms. Again, it is the transformational event and not the time associated with that event which is meaningful to God.

The experience of creating a transformational event must be a fascinating thing for God to observe as S/He evolves with us [or as we evolve with Him/Her]. As an example, it is my personal belief that God has never experienced the separation into the duality or polarity of sex, but instead has gained an understanding of this fascinating process by experiencing our growth as we learn to handle this difficult opportunity. Consequently, each transformational event which shows that another of God's children has learned how to handle duality and polarity must be one which is met with great joy at the doors of heaven!

As a summary of this thermodynamic-kinetic discussion, humans should concern themselves either with time, or with God, but not with both; for time and God are two separate subjects. It is the thermodynamics of the event, and not the kinetics which is of importance within an eternal universe.

SECTION 3: THE PHENOMENON OF COINCIDENCE

Possibly one of the most misunderstood words in the English language is the word "coincidence." The primary meaning of the word is *"the state or fact of coinciding"*; whereas the word "coincide" means *"to occupy the same position simultaneously, to have identical dimensions, or to happen at the same time."* I have no quarrel with any of these definitions. In fact, I think that they are correct in describing the fact of coincidence in which, for example, two things happen at essentially the same time, especially those *"having identical dimensions."* However, a secondary definition of the word, "coincidence" does bother me, for it presents a connotation which I believe is not correct. That secondary definitions is, *"An accidental sequence of events that appears to have a casual relationship."*

If there is a God, and if S/He is the Primary Cause of all things, then how can any sequence of events be an accidental one? It would seem that all things are either a part of God's will, or a part of our own Free Will as we ignore the messages which define God's will for us. Consequently, to toss off those things which "happen at the same time" from two or more non-identical sources as being "an accidental sequence of events" seems to be ignoring a powerful message which could have been sent specifically to us from God.

If it is not ignoring a message sent to us from an outside source, and if the accident of coincidence is merely an accident, then what we are denying is that God has a causal relationship with the world; and that this phenomenon of two [or more] identical things coming at us from more than one non-connected source at the same time, has no source which is the One. In other words, if coincidences are accidental, then there is no God who is the Primary Cause of all things and who, therefore, has a causal relationship with us.

I believe that there is such a God, and I therefore believe that the concept of coincidence being an accidental happenstance is an attempt to soft-pedal, or even to avoid an issue of utmost importance in our relationship with God. I believe that the phenomenon of coincidence is one of the most powerful messages that God does exist, and that S/He cares about what we do with ourselves. Others also believe this. Some have been so strong in this belief that they have defined coincidence as "God's way of remaining anonymous!"

To generate some sense about the phenomenon of coincidence, I will relate four incidences. The first two are personal ones; the third is a publishing phenomenon of 1994; and the fourth is a message from one of the more interesting intellectuals and teachers of the New Age [or better, of the New Pilgrimage].

On the Monday before Thanksgiving, 1994, I was reviewing some reference work which related to the scriptures as they had been before being translated into English. I came across the remark that since Aramaic was a major spoken language in Palestine from 300 BCE until about 650 CE, then it is highly likely that Jesus and the Apostles spoke Aramaic, a fact which I already knew and which had been mentioned in the previous books of this series. This triggered a desire to see some translations of scripture directly from Aramaic in order to see if there were subtle differences from the Bible we have in English, a Bible which was written in Greek, and subsequently was translated into Latin from which it was translated into English [see *The Christian Conspiracy* for details]. To me, this desire was a somewhat difficult one to achieve, since it has been reported that most of the scriptures written in Aramaic were destroyed by the Catholic Church and the Islamic conquests during the seventh century. The Church had done this because they wanted only Latin scripture to be the accepted version; and the Islamic conquests had done this in an attempt to establish Arabic, rather than Aramaic, as the language of the region. Consequently, my desire, although fervently expressed, seemed to be a difficult one to fulfill.

The next afternoon, I was playing a game of golf with a friend who was leaving Atlanta to work with a spiritual man near St. Louis. After our game, he told me that he was going into training to teach the activities which Dr. Michael Ryce had developed, many of which were based on his translations of the scripture directly from Aramaic. It turned out that my friend had several examples in the trunk of his car, one of which was used in Chapter 3.

Although this could be considered somewhat unusual, it does not necessarily meet one of the "coincidence requirements" such as "happening at the same time." The second step happened on the Friday after Thanksgiving. On that day, I received a thick letter from a friend in Albuquerque. The handwritten note merely said, "Dave, thought you might look this information over since it deals with Christianity." The enclosed material consisted of several flyers from the Noohra Foundation which was founded to "universalize the Aramaic understanding of the Bible." Almost all of the reference material in the flyers concerned interpretations of Scripture which had been directly translated into English from Aramaic. The material had been posted to me by a friend in Albuquerque at almost exactly the same time that my friend and I had finished our golf game in Atlanta. Neither friend knew the other.

At this point, I had one of two choices to make. I could either consider the coincidence as "an accidental sequence of events that appear to have a casual relationship," or I could assume that someone who can control such activities was trying to send me a message.

Because I believe in a God who has a causal relationship with those who are created in His/Her image, I accepted that this was a message for me, possibly in response to my prayers or my desires.

The second of these personal examples of coincidence caused me to include the section entitled, "A Third Viewpoint on Reincarnation" in Chapter 4. As described in that section, I have long suffered from a dichotomy. I had a strong belief in reincarnation in the sense that *I have been here before*; but I had an equally strong sense that I was unique and as such, *I had never existed in exactly this form before*. I felt that I had worked this dichotomy out in my mind, and I also had a fair level of confirmation during meditation that the concept which had been presented to me was as close to the factual working of reincarnation as the human mind could comprehend. However, I had decided not to include that explanation in this book for fear that it would turn off some who had not become confident in the reality of reincarnation.

On Friday, January 13, 1995, I had just finished the first rewrite on Chapter 4, the chapter on reincarnation. The section on the third viewpoint had not been included. As a result, I had the nagging feeling, and possibly even the message, that the chapter was not complete. My wife and I discussed this, but we decided to leave the decision on whether or not to include the additional section for another time.

The next day, an audio tape arrived in the mail. It was from an old and dear friend, one who had been a guide and counsel to my wife and me for over twenty-five years. His spiritual name is Elias DeMohan. We had previously known him as William David, founder of the Esoteric Philosophy Center in Houston, Texas and the Foundation of Sound, Color and Vibration in Phoenix, Arizona. He is the author of *The Harmonics of Sound Color and Vibration*, is one of the world's premier readers of the Akashic records, and is a reader whose life readings for clients are presented in a complete sense of service and with a complete lack of ego. Elias is also an accomplished artist. One of his paintings was on the cover of *The Christian Conspiracy*.

In life readings given by Elias to my wife and to me many years ago, we had learned that we had "been" certain well-known persons in history. I had always been able to gain much insight into myself from those associations, but I never really felt that I had "been" that particular individual. I never shared those thoughts with Elias; but in the audio tape we received from him, Elias discussed for several minutes some new insight which he had received. It was related to how the soul will use various characteristics from historic personages who have had an impact on humanity, in order to continue those positive impacts on humanity through the activities of a personality who recently incarnated.

As Elias was telling us this, which incidentally was quite an expansion on his life's work, my wife and I got wide eyed as we looked at each other, then we each got a big grin, and then we nodded to each other in agreement and kept nodding in agreement until he was done with his explanation. I then went to the computer and did a first draft on the section presented in Chapter 4—the section entitled, "A Third Viewpoint on Reincarnation."

Was it an accident that a friend in Albuquerque had the same thoughts about Aramaic translations that I and another friend were having in Atlanta, or is this coincidence an act of the Primary Cause of all things? Was it an accident that a friend in Phoenix was generating the same thoughts about reincarnation that I was having in Atlanta, even though those thoughts were a change-of-direction for him, or is this coincidence also an act of the Primary Cause of all things? Is it an accident that two people will invent the same thing in widely disparate parts of the world at almost exactly the same time, or is this coincidence also an act of the Primary Cause of all things, possibly by introducing a wavelength of new energy which is tapped by more than one person? Are any coincidences accidental? I strongly believe that they are _not_ accidental. I have been helped to accept this belief by the following two examples of "coincidence" about which I had prior knowledge.

The first of these examples concerns an unusual publishing event which occurred in 1994. It is a publishing miracle which has rarely, if ever, been duplicated. A man named James Redfield wrote a book entitled *The Celestine Prophecy*. That is not unusual, for people write books all the time. However, since this book was not accepted by any publisher, Redfield published it himself. Again, this is not unusual, for that also happens all the time. Soon, by word-of-mouth, the first, small printing of the book was sold out. That is unusual. Then a major publisher bought the book, at a price which was very unusual. Finally, the book spent a major part of the year on the *New York Times* best-seller list. At year's end, it was still highly rated on that distinguished list. That is indeed unusual. It is obviously a book which meets a public need.

The Celestine Prophecy is an adventure story which presents nine insights into the spiritual journey of humankind. The first insight is presented early in the book. As stated in the book: ...*the First Insight occurs when we become conscious of the coincidences in our lives.* This part of the book goes on to say that although we might not understand these mysterious coincidences, they are real; and they generate a sense that there is another side of life and some other sort of process operating behind the scenes.

Are coincidences real? They certainly are, for they can be documented. Are coincidences accidental? Again, I think not, but you must decide that for yourself. Are coincidences an insight into the spiritual journey of humankind? Since I have started to pay attention to them, I have come to the conclusion that they are. Others must think likewise; for if a lot of other people do not accept the reality of coincidences, then how did *The Celestine Prophecy* become such a runaway best-seller?

Which brings us to the second non-personal example of the phenomenon of coincidence. Drunvalo Melchizedek is thought by many to be one of the more interesting teachers of the New Age. In a video tape entitled *The Story of England, Part Two*, he spends several minutes describing the three steps necessary to make contact with the Higher Self. During this discussion, in the second step he tells that two angels appeared to him, and that following their appearance, all sorts of "coincidences" started to happen to him. These coincidences ranged from the smallest thinkable coincidence to those which were virtually miraculous. In further discussion, he states that rejection of these coincidences by thinking them accidental rather than causal would have meant that he rejected the angels, and that consequently he would have made no contact with the Higher Self. Following this discussion, in the third step, he relates how all of the sudden, everything about which he had a thought, actually happened;

and he asks, "Were these activities merely coincidences?"

If you believe that there is a God, and that S/He has a causal relationship with us, then these "coincidences" are not accidents. The final "coincidence" of thinking something and then having it actually happen, is the same phenomenon which occurs when God's will and your Free Will coincide by coming into synchronicity.

In the part of the definition of "coincidence" which I liked so much, the word can mean *"to have identical dimensions."* When your dimensions and God's are the same, then you are One with God. In that instance, your will and His/Her will become the same and remain that way throughout eternity. This is the oneness with God which some of His/Her messengers have described. As a few examples of these descriptions, in Zoroastrianism, it is said that everyone faithful to the wise *Ahura* can commune with him, meaning that intimate thoughts can be exchanged; in Buddhism it is thought that all can become enlightened, and in this enlightenment become a "fully awakened one" [*sammasambuddha*] and therefore realize the "immortal" [*amata*]; and in the Christian Bible, in John 10:30 Jesus said, "I and the Father are one."; and later in John 14:3 he said, "...where I am you may be also."

There is a "phenomenon of coincidence." It can either be considered to be an accident as is popularly accepted, or it can be considered to be a spiritual message, as is accepted by those who read *The Celestine Prophecy*; or who hear the messages given by New Age teachers such as Drunvalo Melchizedek; or who believe that God expresses Unconditional Love for those created in His/Her image and wants to give them a message. It is up to you to decide how you might want to look at the phenomenon of coincidence; but it seems to me that if coincidences are only accidents, then a lot of other things will also have to be considered as accidents. Some of these might be the person of the Christ, or the answer to prayers, or even the existence of life itself. I know where I stand on those subjects. It is my sincere belief that they were <u>not</u> accidents. It is my sincere belief that coincidences are not accidents either!

SECTION 4: THE CHAKRA SYSTEM

Chakra is the English version of a Sanskrit word meaning "wheel." To many people, the word "chakra" has come to represent the center of an energy vortex in our bodies. Possibly the most important chakras are located in our etheric bodies; but the ones which most people know about, are those which are associated with our physical bodies.

It is not the intent of this book to become a definitive reference on the Chakra System, for there are many books which are totally devoted to the subject. Many books present the Chakra System in deep esoteric detail and with all of its nuances; whereas others merely give an adequate introduction. For those who want an understanding of the Chakra System beyond that which is offered here, but do not want to take a graduate course in chakraism, I would recommend *Kundalini and the Chakras* by Genevieve Lewis Paulson [see Bibliography]. This outstanding book presents a number of diagrams of the Chakra System as well as a good level of understanding *via* the written word; and it does all of this in a totally non-threatening manner. The "entry-level understanding" presented here uses that book as its reference.

One of the major reasons for mentioning the Chakra System in this book is that the personal pathway into oneness with God which is described in Chapter 5 of *Part Two* contains seven stages, most of which could have some level of correlation with the seven chakra points normally associated with the human body. Those who spend a lot of energy understanding the Chakra System know that there are more than seven chakras associated with the bodies of an entity. Those who spend a lot of energy trying to perceive the complete personal pathway into oneness with God know that there are more than seven stages which mark progression along the Way. For the vast majority of people, a tremendous amount of understanding can be generated by accepting and working with only the "basic seven," whether that basic seven relates to the Chakra System, or to the Pathway, or to a correlation of each.

Another possibility for correlation which I considered using in this book is the system of colors and vibration known as the Seven Rays, or the forthcoming Twelve Rays. Although I decided not to use

Additional Background Information 115

them, the Seven Rays correlate with the Pathway at least as well as the Seven Chakras do.

The remainder of this section will merely present some basic background information for understanding the Chakra System of the physical body. This background information will be useful in understanding the seven stages on the pathway as described in Chapter 5 of *Part Two*.

The first chakra is called the "root" chakra in English. In Sanskrit, it is known as the *Mudlahara*. In the physical body, it is located near the coccyx [base of the spinal column]. It affects the adrenal gland. The root chakra can give positive messages of good self image and security to the personality; or it can give negative aspects of insecurity which the personality may try to overcome by a variety of techniques.

The second chakra is called the "middle sex" chakra in English. In Sanskrit, it is known as the *Svadhighthana*. In the physical body it is located between the coccyx and the navel. It affects the sex glands [ovaries or testicles]. The sex chakra can give positive messages of vitality or sexuality; or it can give negative messages of lust or other base emotions such as greed, the desire for power, etc. These negative messages are often associated with aspects of insecurity. These aspects of power and insecurity, as well as the insecurity of the first chakra, tie in with "The Worship of Material Things" in Chapter 5 of *Part Two*.

The third chakra is called the "navel" or the "solar plexus" chakra in English. In Sanskrit, it is known as the *Manipura*. In the physical body, it is located near the navel. It affects the leyden [or leydig] gland. The navel chakra can give positive messages of peace and emotional rest; or it can give negative messages of strong, emotional, attached love. This attached love can become so overpowering that it can lead to the desire to use power in order to gain complete control over the loved ones. This issue of control through love is one of the major messages presented in the section on "The Worship of Gods as Defined by Humans" in Chapter 5 of *Part Two*.

The fourth chakra is called the "heart" chakra in English. In Sanskrit, it is known as the *Anahata*. In the physical body, it is located near the center of the chest. It affects the thymus gland. The heart chakra can give positive messages of compassion and understanding intuition; or it can give negative messages of being hardhearted or closed to others, which will often lead to despair. The lesson of compassion and service to humanity is one of the major messages presented in Chapter 5 of *Part Two*.

The fifth chakra is called the "throat" chakra in English. In Sanskrit, it is known as the *Visudha*. In the physical body, it is located near the center of the throat. It affects the thyroid and the parathyroid glands. This chakra can give positive messages of reason and logic; or it can give negative messages of being so prejudiced that the personality will accept only its own viewpoint, thus leading to a rejection of Unconditional Love. The lesson of Unconditional Love is one of the major messages presented Chapter 5 of *Part Two*.

The sixth chakra is called the "third eye" chakra in English. In Sanskrit, it is known as the *Ajna*. In the physical body, it is located behind a spot between the eyebrows. It affects the pituitary gland. The third eye chakra can give positive messages of brotherhood and creative thinking; or it can give negative messages of egotism. Again, the lesson of giving up Ego in order to grant Unconditional Love to all and thereby give service to divinity is one of the major messages presented Chapter 5 of *Part Two*.

The seventh chakra is called the "crown" chakra in English. In Sanskrit, it is known as the *Sahasrara*. In the physical body, it is located near the top of the head. It affects the pineal gland. The crown chakra can give positive messages of oneness with all and of cosmic understanding; or it can give negative messages of being put-down or alienated from life. The lesson of cosmic understanding is one of the major messages presented Chapter 5 of *Part Two*.

This brief description of the Chakra System is not intended to enlighten those who have spent energy understanding the chakras and their effect on the personality. Instead, it is merely intended to enlighten those who know essentially nothing about the chakras. It is intended solely as background understanding. Its major purpose is to explain the milestones along the personal pathway into oneness with God which are presented in Chapter 5 of *Part Two*.

SECTION 5: SOME THOUGHTS ABOUT NUMBERS

In our modern society, we have an almost reverent feeling about the precision of numbers which leads us to accept them as truth. In other words, if someone were to say "forty" to us, we would automatically think of it as the absolute number which comes after the number thirty-nine, but before the number forty-one.

Other societies often have had a different feeling about numbers. In many of those societies, a number would represent a philosophical concept as well as a numerical one. Our society has a tendency to translate the symbol which represents a number into its numerical concept whenever we can. However, in those other societies, translation into the philosophical concept is equally as likely.

The purpose of this section is to indicate that there are other ways that the symbol which represents a number could have been meant to be used; and that we should not automatically assume that the translation into a number was either the correct translation, or that the resultant number represents the precision which such a number would have for us.

A case for the philosophical meaning of numerical symbols could be made for many societies; and we could also cite the Pythagorean doctrine that "all things are numbers," which means that the essences and structures of all things can be determined by finding the numerical relations contained in them. However, such a presentation would go beyond the scope of this book. Instead, this section will merely use biblical material to present the point that when a Jewish writer used the symbol for a number, he may have been meaning something quite different from what we might presently think.

Have you ever wondered why the number 40 or "forty" appears 99 times in the Bible whereas the numbers 39 or 41 are never used? The answer is that the number 40 is represented by the character in the Hebrew alphabet we call "Mem," but *Mem* also represents the simple, philosophical thought of "a sufficient amount." Thus, in the story about Noah [Genesis, Chapter 8] when it rained for forty days and forty nights, and when the flood continued on Earth for forty days, and when Noah waited for forty days before sending out a raven, the Jewish author is not saying that all of these things happened on the day after the thirty-ninth day for each episode. Instead, the author is probably saying that it rained for a sufficient amount of time to fulfill God's purpose, and that the flood also lasted for a sufficient amount of time, and that Noah waited for a sufficient amount of time before releasing the raven.

Likewise, when the people of Israel escaped from Egypt and wandered in the wilderness for forty years before finding habitable land [Exodus 16:35], again the author is probably stating that they wandered in the wilderness for a sufficient amount of time before they found the promised land. Because of the difficulty that the Jews had in telling time and defining years [see page 119], there is simply no way that the term "forty years" would have the same precision to them as it would to us. As a final example, when Jesus "fasted for forty days and forty nights, and afterward he was hungry" [Matt. 4:2], again the author is presenting the thought that Jesus had been in the wilderness for a sufficient amount of time to fulfill God's purpose, and not necessarily for a period of time which was one day longer than thirty-nine days, or one day less than forty-one days.

In a similar manner, the number 7 is used 410 times in the Bible, and the number 70 is used 77 times; whereas 6 is rarely used and 69 or 71 never appears. The character in the Hebrew alphabet used for 7 is *Zain*, and for 70 is *Oin*. The symbolic meaning of each is "an excess amount." Thus when Jacob worked for Leban for seven years in order to wed Leah, and then for another seven years to wed Rachel [Genesis, Chapter 29], the Jewish author was probably indicating that each was an excess amount of time, and not that each contract was for 84 months.

The Creation Story in the first Chapter of Genesis is possibly the most famous use of the number seven in the Bible; for many have accepted as literal truth that God created all which has ever been created in one of our weeks, or 168 of our hours. There are several problems with such a belief. In the first place, since the Earth's spin has recently been slowing down at the rate of about one second every ten thousand years, and may have had a higher rate of spin slowdown in the early years, then at the time of the creation, a day would have been much shorter than the length of a present day. In addition, it somewhat boggles the mind to think that God would use the spin of

Additional Background Information

one small speck of cosmic dust to determine the length of His/Her working time before getting some rest. Finally, as described in Section 2 of this chapter, time is a meaningless term to an eternal God.

Instead of meaning one of our weeks, the Jewish writer is probably indicating that his God is so great and powerful that seven days would be an excess amount of time for Him to create all that has ever existed. If the "Big Bang" theory of modern physics has any validity, that certainly is correct; for this theory states that all matter was created in the microscopic part of a second, actually 10 to the minus 43 power—an extremely short period of time. As Job indicated in the Bible, the God of the Jewish people was indeed a very powerful God!

As far as the ability of the Jewish society of biblical times to tell time and generate a year in the same sense that we presently do, again that is something which we should consider in their terms rather than ours. In the Sanders book, it is stated that at the time of Jesus, the Jewish month was defined as a lunar month and the year as a solar year. In addition, the new moon which established that each new month had arrived had to be *observed*, not calculated. If the night were cloudy such that the new moon could not be seen, then the old month was continued until the new moon was actually *seen*. Because of this, although months were supposed to be either 29 or 30 days long, sometimes there were 35 days in one month, with the subsequent month being only 25 days.

In addition, because 12 months of 29-30 days each [on the average] made a "year" of only 354 days, then every third year or so, the year would have to consist of thirteen months in order to make the solar year correct. Because of this rather haphazard system of months and years, any reference in the old Jewish texts which presents a definite number of months or years, simply cannot be judged by our present standards of precision. That is why it is probable that the author was using the symbol to express its philosophical meaning rather than its numerical meaning.

Another use of numerology in the times of Jesus had to do with the translation of names. Many times, names were translated from one language to another by their numerical equivalent rather than their literal equivalent. As a striking example, that is probably the way that Jesus got the name which we presently use.

The name "Jesus" is the Latin equivalent of the Greek name "IESOUS." In Aramaic, the name of the person whom we call Jesus is believed to have been *Yeshua [or Yashua] ben Yoseph*. Consequently, his name in Greek should have been Joshua if it were a literal translation. However, in both the Greek and the Aramaic alphabets, the letters correspond to numbers. According to the Fideler book, in the Aramaic alphabet, the letters used in the name which we would call "Joshua" total to the number 888. In the Greek alphabet, the letters used in the name "IESOUS" also total 888. As a consequence, it is highly probable that the name was translated from Aramaic into Greek by using the numerical route, rather than by using the literal translation route; for if a literal translation had been used, today we would be calling him Joshua rather than Jesus.

As with the other sections of this chapter, in this section we are merely trying to generate some understanding which might help in the development of an individualized pathway into oneness with God. It is possible that by generating some knowledge about the probable meaning of certain symbols in the Bible which we have assumed were meant to be numbers, we can lift some of the restrictive thinking which we have put upon ourselves.

SECTION 6: THE PRESENCE OF GOD

If there is a God, and if that God created All that is and is therefore the ALL, and if it were important for us to discover where that God might be, then it seems to me that there are two highly likely locations into which we could look. Such a God would be either outside of all which S/He created with nothing placed within the creation to tie itself back to the Primary Source; or such a God would have put some parts of Him/Her within all which was created in an attempt to leave therein some residual memory of the Source. I will grant that there might be intermediate possibilities which would have the "spark of God" within only a few selected things which were created [e.g. the human soul]; but for sake of this discussion, let us consider only the possibilities of God being totally "without" or totally "within."

The God mentioned first would be considered *transcendent* in the sense of being above and independent of the material universe. The other God would be considered to be *immanent* in the sense of being within. In neither case would the God have to be considered to be less than transcendent in the sense of being preeminent.

There are those who believe that the Creator is greater than the Created and therefore simply cannot be a part of that which was created. I understand their point; but I would suggest that my parents left a part of themselves within me, even though at one point in time they were much greater than I; and that my wife and I have left a part of ourselves in each of our children; and that in each house which we have made into a home, a part of us remains behind in that which we created there, etc. etc. I would submit that there are many other arguments which could be made in which a part of the creator would have been left behind within that which was created.

Since I fully understand the Creator-Created argument which the learned theologians have proposed, I can fully accept that the God in whom I believe would not create another who would be equally supreme, because in doing that, S/He would have destroyed the definition of the One. In fact, it is just such a problem which led the early Church Fathers to declare that Jesus the Christ was an emanation from God and not a creation. But I agree with the teachings of Meister Eckhart, a fourteenth century Dominican whose spirituality was described in *The Christian Conspiracy*, when he taught that the God who created those in His/Her own image left a "spark" or "ground" of Him/Herself within the eternal soul of that which was created; and that this was done without compromising any of the Creator-Created arguments.

Remember the story of the Catholic priest in India who approached a group of children? He asked those children where God was. Each Catholic child responded by pointing to the sky; whereas each Hindu child responded by pointing to his/her heart. To those who believe in the absence of God, the answer given by the Catholic children is probably acceptable. To those who believe in the Presence of God, the answer given by the Hindu children is probably preferable.

Determination of the absolute position of an effable God is

beyond the capability of the human mind. In this way, His/Her position is like an electron which follows the Heisenberg Uncertainty Principle. This law of physics was used to introduce a section on The Definition of God in *Christianity and the New Age Religion*.

In essence, the Heisenberg Uncertainty Principle states that the closer one tries to measure the position or the velocity of a subatomic particle, the more uncertain at least one of those measurements will become. As previously mentioned [see page 22], such a principle also applies to the position or the definition of God. The closer we try to determine the location or the definition of God, the more uncertain at least one of those determinations will become; and we simply cannot determine both of them at the same time.

Despite this, each individual who wants to generate his/her personal understanding should address the issue of whether God is outside, or a part of Him/Her is within. I personally spent over 50 years of my life within the confines of the mainstream Christian Church with its lessons about how since I had fallen from God, then God was outside of me. Despite the absence of the God within me, the Church did say that if I would just accept Jesus, I could have salvation and be redeemed with God. I can now freely say that in the years since I left those confines, I have searched and found the God within; and in so doing have become closer to the Unconditional Love of the one known as Jesus the Christ than I ever was able to when I was within the confining restrictions of the Church. I can also say that although the decision to leave the Church was a terribly difficult one for me to make, it was the correct one for me. It was time to move on.

When I was in the Church I enjoyed teaching adult Sunday School. I especially enjoyed teaching the parables of Jesus, because they can be taught on so many different levels; for there are many lessons in each parable, not just the most obvious one which is often taught. One of my favorite parables was the Prodigal Son as presented in the fifteenth Chapter of Luke. This is often taught as a lesson in forgiveness, but it goes much deeper than that. It is the only parable which is the third part of a triad of parables; for Jesus presents three in a row with no explanation given between any of them. This is the only time he does that. Consequently, he must have been teaching a lesson which requires all three in order to make true sense. The truth from within the Parable of the Prodigal Son describes the reason that it was time for me to move on from the restrictive teachings of the Church.

The first parable of this triad is the Lost Sheep. In this teaching, a shepherd who has a hundred sheep loses one of them. He leaves the rest of his sheep in order to find the one which is lost. This parable is often taught to show that God cares about every single one of us. That is a good lesson, but it has deeper meanings. The second parable is the Lost Coin. It is similar to the first in that a woman who has ten silver coins loses one of them. She searches diligently until she finds it. Again, this parable is often taught to show that each of us is important to God. Again, there is a deeper meaning; for without pause, Jesus tells the story of the man who had two sons, one of whom decided to ask for his inheritance so that he could leave the father and go out on his own. Later, after his wherewithal was gone, he decided to go home to his father and to ask forgiveness. The father forgave him and welcomed the lost son home. This parable is often taught as a demonstration of forgiveness.

Even though the lesson from each parable is important, the three parables taken together present a much deeper lesson. It is a lesson in Free Will. The sheep which was lost has no Free Will, and so the shepherd had to go out to find it. The coin which was lost also has no Free Will, and so the woman diligently searched for it. The son who got lost has a Free Will; and so the father does not go out and search for him. Instead, the father waits patiently until the son, of his own Free Will and in his own way, decides to return to the father.

The Prodigal Son has to be looked at as a part of three parables in a series in order to understand its deeper message. It is a repeat of the Eden Story from the Old Testament. In each story, humanity, which has a Free Will, decided to leave the Father; and because of Free Will, God cannot go out to find those who are lost. Instead, S/He must wait patiently until humanity, of its own Free Will and in its own way, decides to return. Note that humanity will not do this at the exhortation of one in the church, or in the temple, or in the mosque. It can happen only by humanity choosing to do so by use of its own

Free Will and in its own way; for only by the choice of truly exercising Free Will can the Presence of God become real.

It is my present belief that the Presence of God *is* a real thing which can be experienced by those who choose to open themselves to such a possibility. But this is just my belief. I would ask you to decide for yourselves, and not to let words found in any book, or heard in any church, synagogue, mosque or other sanctuary, make that decision for you.

SUMMARY

This chapter has presented background information on several different subjects. In the section on Dimensionality, it was proposed that those who have come closer to oneness with God, have done so in the spirit realms of higher energy flow. In these realms, they have existed in dimensions which are beyond the ability of our five physical senses to detect. However, although not presented as evidence in this section, there have been instances of multidimensional ones making themselves known to our senses. This has possibly occurred most often with our hearing them; but some have seen them, and many have used their sense of smell to receive the comforting confirmation of the delightful angelic smell of heaven for just a brief instance. It is not imagination; it is real!

The section on God's Thermodynamic Universe was presented to indicate that those who try to interject God into our time frames are trying to create a God who acts like us rather than trying to think about how we could act like God; for time and God are two separate subjects. In addition, if God's universe is a thermodynamic one rather than a kinetic one, then it is one which uses transformational events rather than the passage of time in order to generate experiential evolution.

In the section on Coincidence, a rather controversial subject was introduced; for in spite of all the background information which could possibly be developed, many will continue to believe that coincidences are accidental rather than being a message from the Primary Cause of the Universe. It is my belief that the more you become aware of the coincidences in your life, the more you will open yourself to understanding God's will for you.

Additional Background Information

A brief section on the Chakra System was presented to establish some background for a further understanding of the milestones along the personal pathway into oneness with God which will be presented in Chapter 5, *Part Two*.

The section on Numbers was presented to show how some topics which seem so obvious to us may not really be obvious at all when looked at from the viewpoint of a different society. This lesson is an important one to accept, for it relates to much more than the mere expression of numbers.

The final section of this chapter presented some thoughts about the Presence of God. I believe that God is present; for only by His/Her presence can God make His/Her will evident to those who are here. However, in this subject as well as all the other subjects, the decision as to whether or not to accept these thoughts as having any meaning for you is yours alone to make. Again, no one should allow someone else to make that decision for them, whether that someone else is a minister, a rabbi, a priest of any faith, or the author of any book.

SUMMARY OF PART ONE

The purpose of *Part One* was to present some Background Information as an aid in understanding some aspects of one's personal pathway into oneness with God.

The material covered a wide range of subjects including:

1. Some definitions of God with the conclusion that God needs to be experienced rather than to be defined;

2. A description of eight messengers sent from God and a description of the messages they presented;

3. A presentation of how the established religions of the world have altered these messages with the conclusion that if this had not happened, the world would be different than it presently is;

4. A presentation of many thoughts about reincarnation with the conclusion that a majority of the world's population not only accepts reincarnation, they also believe it to be a necessity; and

5. A number of miscellaneous subjects which might help each unique individual to experience his or her personal pathway into oneness with God.

It is not required that any unique individual accept all, or even any, of this Background Information in order to experience his or her personal pathway, or even to have a fuller understanding of the lessons to be found in *Part Two*. Instead, the material has been presented in the hopes that some of it may be found to be interesting, or useful, or possibly even helpful.

PART TWO
COSMIC CONCEPTS
AND
PERSONAL PATHWAYS

CHAPTER 1
THE FIRST COSMIC CONCEPT:
THE CREATION

BACKGROUND INFORMATION

The first Cosmic Concept states that there is one God who created *all things*, and all of the things which S/He created are *good*.

There are, of course, a number of legends and myths from throughout the world which support this Cosmic Concept. The myths which are a part of the seven great religions of the world are presented in this chapter. Additional myths from other cultures are presented in Appendix B which also suggests how these myths might fit with the first Cosmic Concept. Before evaluating any of these myths, it is probably useful to gain some understanding about what myths really are.

One of the major definitions of the word "myth" is: *Any real or fictional story, recurring theme or character type that appeals to the consciousness of a people by embodying its cultural ideals or by giving expression to deep, commonly felt emotions.* In other words, a myth is not necessarily fiction or a made-up story. It can be real.

On pages 243-4 of his magnificent book *Introducing the Old Testament*, John Drane says:

Many books on the Old Testament refer to the early stories in Genesis as "myths." But this is not a particularly helpful term to use. Most people think of a myth as something that is untrue. Scholars do not normally use it in this sense, but ...[use it] to describe a story which expresses a truth about human life which cannot adequately be described in terms of science or history. In this sense, myth is as valid and respectable a way of thinking about life's deepest meaning as science, art or philosophy.

Joseph Campbell has done a magnificent job in putting the understanding of myths in front of the American public via his famous TV interviews with Bill Moyers. In regard to myths, he has said: *Myth is the secret opening through which the inexhaustible energies of the cosmos pour into human consciousness manifestation.* The point to be made here is that no one has any reason to be ashamed of myths. They often are able to touch our deepest soul with truths which are every bit as valid as today's newspaper—and possibly even more so.

The creation myths of the seven great religions of the world will be presented in the probable order that their written records appeared. We will start with the "Western Four" led by Zoroastrianism; and follow that with the "Eastern Four," led by Hinduism.

Zoroastrianism

Although most forms of Persian religion prior to Zoroastrianism had seen the world in terms of a constant conflict between good and evil forces, each of which came from the same divine source, Zarathustra [known in the West by his Greek name, Zoroaster] rejected the notion that this duality was from the same source. Instead, he proclaimed one supreme God, *Ahura Mazda* ["Wise Lord"], who is entirely good and is the source of all which is right in the world.

In the remainder of this section, Ahura Mazda will be called "Ahura" for easier reading. Under Ahura are lesser gods, and opposed to Ahura is a <u>lesser</u> spirit, *Angra Mainyu* ["Destroying Spirit"], who is opposed to goodness. This spirit will subsequently be called "Mainyu," again for ease in reading. Zoroaster believed that evil was not a matter of nature, but of choice; and further believed that humans use their Free Will to choose to be loyal to Ahura.

In the creation myth of Zoroastrianism, Ahura first produced certain spiritual beings who remained for three thousand years in a perfectly spiritual state: motionless, without thought and without tangible bodies. At the end of this time, Mainyu perceived Ahura as being powerless. Thus, when Ahura approached Mainyu with an offer of peace, Mainyu believed it was from a point of weakness. However, unknown to Mainyu was the fact that Ahura was omniscient and omnipotent, and therefore knew things unknown to Mainyu.

Because of his great insight, Ahura proposed a period of nine thousand years of intermingling conflict, for He knew that his will would prevail for three thousand years, there would be intermingling of the two wills for three thousand years, and during the last three thousand years, after the birth of Zoroaster, the will of the evil one would be broken. Together with the three thousand years of the stationary state already behind them, this would comprise all twelve thousand years of creation's existence before the return of the messiah, *Saoshyant*. Mainyu thought this was a good deal, because he did not know what Ahura knew. Consequently, he accepted and Ahura began to create.

As the first step, Ahura created Good Mind and Sky. Good Mind, in turn, created the Light of the World, the Good Religion, Righteous Order, Perfect Sovereignty, Divine Piety, Excellence, and Immortality. As the second step, Ahura created the stars with four captains in the corners of the starry constellations; and then created the moon and the sun. Following this, he created water, earth, plants, animals and man. All of this was created by the goodness and rightness of Ahura, the Wise Lord. Consequently, all which was created was good.

In the meantime, Mainyu slept for the first three thousand years of creation. When he awakened, he was angry at all the good which he saw. Consequently, he created a whole slew of troubles for humankind.

But the point to be made is that in the beginning, *Ahura Mazda*, the Wise Lord of Zoroastrianism, created all that was created; and all which He created was good. Consequently, the creation myths of Zoroastrianism support the first Cosmic Concept.

Judaism/Christianity

Since the creation stories of Judaism and of Christianity are identical, these two religions will be presented together. In the Judeo-Christian creation myths, there is much support for the first Cosmic Concept.

The major creation myth which supports the first Cosmic Concept is found in the first chapter of Genesis which states:

In the beginning, God created the heavens and the earth...and light...and firmament...and dry land...and seas...and vegetation...and the sun, moon and stars...and living creatures...and man and woman...and God saw everything that he had made, and behold, it was very good.

This concept was supported by Isaiah [Is. 44:24] when he reports:

Thus says the Lord, your Redeemer, who formed you from the womb: "I am the Lord, who made all things, who stretched out the heavens alone, who spread out the earth—Who was with me?"

Consequently, if those of the Judaic and the Christian faiths accept the words of their Holy Scripture, and if they accept that there is only one creator God, a belief which is a major part of each faith, then those of the Judeo-Christian heritage must accept the first Cosmic Concept as being a part of the truth which has been given them. However, as described later in this chapter, there is much evidence that neither faith has practiced this Concept.

Islam

As mentioned previously, Islam was born with the cry, *La ilaha illa 'llah*, or "There is no god but God." This cry, obviously a slap at Christianity which had made the Son as divine as the Father at the First Ecumenical Council at Nicaea in 325 CE, was followed by many who wanted to return to a Yahweh unencumbered by the doctrines of the followers of Jesus Christ. This is understandable, for

First Concept: The Creation

the name Yahweh, the name used by Judaism for their God, is of Arabic and not of Hebrew origin. Therefore, Mohammed's claim that his people were the original followers of the God proclaimed in the Bible probably has merit, even though neither the startled Jews nor the astounded Christians have ever accepted it [see page 430 of Joseph Campbell's book on Occidental Mythology].

Because of this belief, the creation myths of Islam are essentially identical to those of Judeo-Christianity. As a few examples, the Koran says:

Allah is the Wonderful Originator of the heavens and earth, and when He decrees an affair, He only says to it Be, so there it is; ...certainly We created man, and We know what his mind suggests to him, and We are nearer to him than his jugular vein; Allah is He who made the earth a resting-place for you and He formed you, then made goodly your forms, and He provided you with goodly things; that is Allah, your Lord; blessed then is Allah, the Lord of the worlds.

Such statements certainly support the belief that God created all and that all which He created is good, especially when it is realized that the Koran is accepted by Islam as an addition to the words of the Old Testament of the Bible. As an example, the Fall of Man in the Koran uses the same people [e.g. Adam] and presents the same end result as the Bible. In addition, the entire story of the patriarchs, the Exodus, the Golden Calf, water from the rock, the revelation on Mount Sinai, Father Abraham and a lot more which Judeo-Christians hold as their own, are repeatedly reflected in the Koran as well as in the part of the Bible accepted by Islam. In fact, Father Abraham is probably more revered by Islam than he is by Judeo-Christianity.

But the main point being made here is that Islam supports the first Cosmic Concept in the same manner as it was supported by Zoroastrianism, Judaism and Christianity; for almost every syllable of the Koran continues the Zoroastrian-Jewish-Christian heritage. The only difference is that Islam claims to restore all of these stories to their proper sense and to use them to carry the heritage to its final formulation. In other words, Islam claims to be closer to the original God of the Bible than either Judaism or Christianity. In relation to God, the major differences between Islam and Judeo-Christianity relate to the method of worship, and not with the God being worshipped or with the good things which that God created.

Hinduism

In Hinduism, there is a very strong relationship between the Brahman and the world. Brahman has various translations such as the "Absolute," the "Creator," or the "Holy Power." The word comes from the root *brh* meaning *"to grow, to increase, to roar."* Although this may make it seem that the relationship which the individual Hindu has with the Brahman is similar to that between a Christian and his God, the concepts are really quite different. The Brahman of Hinduism refers not to a transcendent, personal God such as that believed in by the Western religions, but instead refers to an immanent being <u>within</u> all things which the individual may call forth by the use of roaring sounds or a *mantra*. Thus, it is the "God within" which is important to the Hindu; and the Brahman does not create the world as something "outside" the Absolute Being, but as the extension or manifestation of himself as the Absolute Being. As a result, the Brahman is considered to be the "inner self" of all things.

The relationship between the creator and the created in Hinduism can be illustrated by a creation story, dated ca. 700 BCE. The story says that in the beginning, the universe was nothing but the Self in the form of a man. He was alone, so his shout would be, "It is I"; and when he was afraid, he would say, "There is nothing here but I, so why am I afraid?" and the fear would disappear.

However, since he was alone, he lacked delight; and since he was exactly the size of a man and a woman embracing, then Self divided into two parts and with that, there was a master and a mistress. The male embraced the female, and from that the human race arose. Later, she became a cow, and he became a bull; and from this, cattle arose. Then she became a mare and he a stallion; and still later, she became an ass and he a donkey; and from these, all the solid-footed animals arose. Still later, she became a goat and he a buck; she a ewe and he a ram; and from these, all the goats and sheep arose. In this manner, all paring things arose, down to the ants. Then Self realized, "I am creation, for I have poured forth all of this." Thus arose the Creation, which comes from the Sanskrit word *systih*, meaning *"what is poured forth."*

As can be seen from this story, God and man were both involved in Creation as visualized by the Hindu.

A later Hindu creation story [from the *Mundaka Upanishad*] states that the Heavenly Person is without body. He is both without and within, not produced, without breath and without mind, pure higher than the high Imperishable. When He decided to create, then from Him came breath, mind and all organs of sense. In addition, from Him came ether, air, light, water, the earth, and the support of all. He is indeed the inner self of all things.

From this story, it can be seen that God created, but became a part of the creation as the inner part of all things.

It may be difficult for these types of creation stories to be fit into a support system for the first Cosmic Concept, especially since the Hindu wants to reject most things of this world. However, the Hindu believes that the true nature of Self [*Atman*] is that of union with the divine; and that true Self is eternal and immortal and in some way is one with the Ultimate Reality [*Brahman*]. This union of Atman and Brahman is prevented by things which were created by man rather than by God. These things created by man are things such as believing that the personal self is the ultimate reality, and that the worldly existence is desirable. Consequently, the Hindu will believe that all things created by God are good. The only lack of support for the first Cosmic Concept could be the belief that man has created undesirable things, and thus all things were not created by God.

But as said in the final verse on Creation from the *Rig-Veda*:

He, the first origin of this creation, whether he formed it all or did not form it, Whose eye controls this world in highest heaven, he verily knows it, or perhaps he knows not.

In other words, the Hindu might say, "Who knows whether God created all things, or whether he didn't?"

Buddhism

Buddhism has an even greater problem identifying with the first Cosmic Concept than Hinduism, for although Buddhism takes for granted the Hindu gods, demons and other spirits, the Buddhist feels that they are irrelevant to the attainment of *Nirvana*, and totally unnecessary for following the "eightfold path." A Buddhist might feel that all has been created by God, but that this feeling is of no real substance, just as the self of the human being is of no real substance. Because of this, the belief that "God created all and that all which He created is good," has no relevance to a devoted Buddhist.

Nevertheless, the understanding of how the Buddhist fits into this pattern is important, for it directly impacts on the steps presented in Chapter 5 of *Part Two*. At this point, it is important to reiterate the fourth Cosmic Concept which is that "each individual is unique and therefore has a unique personal pathway into oneness with God." Those who have chosen during this lifetime to accept the pathway proposed by the Buddha have used their Free Will to decide to eliminate a number of experiences. No one knows whether the path chosen by the devoted Buddhist is a shortcut, or a detour; and no one can make that judgment until after the experiences of this particular lifetime have been completed, and we can all look back.

On the other hand, possibly it is a correct thought that although God exists, this fact is completely irrelevant during the life we live. This is not a conclusion which I accept for myself, for I feel God's presence often and use that presence as a guide for life. However, many men whom I admire have believed that God is not active in the daily affairs of humankind. In this manner, they would be supporting the irrelevance of God in our daily life, just as the devoted Buddhist does.

The men who feel this way are called Deists. Their movement, Deism, occupied the thoughts of many intelligent men during the period from the latter part of the seventeenth century through the early part of the nineteenth century. Basically, they believed that God created the Earth and all that is in it, but then He left us alone to run matters without His presence or counsel. The Founding Fathers of the United States of America were mostly Deists. This group included George Washington, Benjamin Franklin, John Adams and Thomas Jefferson among others. Being a Deist did not exclude a belief that the Christ had been in existence since the beginning of creation; and thus these men could be called Christians. However, their belief that God had no say in the affairs of men is a belief which is similar to the "no relevance" attitude of the devoted Buddhist about God. Deism, as an alternative to the presence of God, is discussed in greater depth in *Christianity and the New Age Religion.*

In essence, Buddhism could support the belief that God created all that is; but would have a difficult time accepting that all which He created is good, primarily because they accept that many of His creations are simply irrelevant.

Confucianism/Taoism

Many have stated that because of its emphasis on moral conduct and its de-emphasis of theology, Confucianism is more of a code of ethical behavior than it is a religion. Even Confucius himself, when asked about God said, "I prefer not speaking"; and throughout his life, the efforts of Confucius were directed at turning men's minds away from the contemplation of the eternal imponderables and toward the ever-present, the practical, and the more easily understood problems of human behavior. In the Scriptures of Confucianism [the *Li Ki*], it is said that man is the product of the attributes of heaven and earth. He is created by the interaction of the dual forces of nature, the union of animal and intelligent souls, and the gathering together of the finest matter of the five elements.

Because of its emphasis on the present rather than the eternal, Confucianism has very little to say about the creation of the universe and all the things contained therein. Consequently, although we will find little support for the first Cosmic Concept in Confucianism, we will also find little, if any, denial.

Taoism, like Hinduism, describes the ruling principle of the universe as a single intangible, indescribable force [*Brahman* in Hinduism and *Tao* in Taoism]. As an example, Chinese translations of the first verse of the Gospel of John say, *"In the beginning was the Tao, and the Tao was with God, and the Tao was God."* In this way, they have replaced "the Word" of Christian theology with "the Universal Pathway" of Chinese Taoism.

In the *Tao-Te King*, the basic scripture for Taoism, it is stated that Tao is "not capable of being expressed"; is the "infinite profundity"; is "the eternal"; was "in existence before heaven and earth"; is "supreme"; and is the "origin of all things." In its poetry, the *Tao-Te King* states: *Infinite profundity is the gate whence comes the beginning of all parts of the universe.* These definitions and statements sound very familiar, for they are the same type of definitions or statements which the Western world uses to try to define its God. Consequently, the theology of Taoism fits well into the first part of the first Cosmic Concept, in that their expression for God created all things.

Later in the *Tao-Te King*, it is stated that: *Tao is the source of all things, the treasure of good men and the sustainer of bad men.* And still later, it is stated: *Between yea and nay, how much difference is there? Between good and evil, how much difference is there?* This particular poem then goes on to imply that the difference is not relevant. Consequently, although it may be a stretch, it could be concluded that Taoism would not only agree that God made all things, but that all things are good. Taoism would therefore, be in support of the first Cosmic Concept.

Other Creation Stories

Appendix B presents several creation stories from all over the world. Many of these stories are from peoples such as the Native Americans, the Native Australians, or the Native Africans. Many of these stories lend support to the first Cosmic Concept.

ANALYSIS

Based on the background information presented above, it would seem that at the time they were established, the world's seven great religions endorsed the first Cosmic Concept. There is no question that the four Western religions have the first Cosmic Concept as a vital part of their initial teachings, myths and legends. Among the Eastern religions, although Buddhism and Confucianism might feel that God was irrelevant in their lives, they do give some credit to a source which created; and Hinduism and Taoism would seem to give an even stronger association, albeit not as strong as that expressed by the Western religions. On the balance, it would seem as if the first Cosmic Concept has been accepted by the great religions of the world.

The major question then becomes this: have these religions practiced the principles of the first Cosmic Concept throughout history, and do they do so today? In other words, do these religions practice the principle that God created *all*, and that all which God created is *good*?

Zoroastrianism

Zoroastrianism is not a major world religion today. Although there are small Zoroasterian congregations throughout the world, the principle practitioners are the Parsees, a minority group in Iran and India. In addition, the documented history of Zoroastrianism has not received general acceptance. Consequently, to evaluate Zoroastrianism in its practice of the first Concept would not be worthwhile. Instead, let us look at the religions which descended from Zoroastrianism and evaluate their performance against this principle.

Judaism

In the beginning of Judaism, this religion represented only a very small tribe in a very small corner of the world. Only after exposure to Zoroastrianism during the Babylonian exile did the religious leaders of this small tribe record their holy works and start to talk about the universal sovereignty of their God, Yahweh.

Despite their belief in the universal sovereignty of their God, the Jews believed that they were the "Chosen People" and that other people were not as accepted in the eyes of God as they were. Consequently, they implied that some of the "good" created by God was not as good as some of the other "good" which He created. In addition, during the time of the Kings when the nation was being formed under Saul, David and Solomon, these people of God waged war on others of God's creation, thus not only violating the principle that the others were good [i.e. the first Concept], but also violating the second Cosmic Concept, that of Unconditional Love.

Finally, among other violations which could be cited, Judaism rejected other religions which accepted their God—first Christianity and then Islam. Now if their God created all things, and if all that he created was good, then why reject others who accept that same God? It seems that all could be accepted as brothers, each trying to find his or her unique pathway into oneness with God [i.e. the fourth Cosmic Concept]. Why fight those who are trying to do the same as you, albeit in a slightly different manner? Does God care *how* S/He is approached—or merely *that* S/He *is* approached? It is a question worth thinking about, isn't it?

Christianity

Christianity, of course, has one of the world's worst records in practicing what they preach. Much of this was documented in *The Christian Conspiracy*. Consequently, only a little will be presented here.

As one example, Arius [see page 45] was a Christian presbyter who loved God so strongly that he defended His uniqueness against what he felt was a desire to divide Him into another God—Jesus Christ. If all that God created was good, then why wasn't Arius, created by God, good enough to be accepted by orthodox Christians as merely one who is taking a uniquely different path. Why kick him out of the Church?

As other examples, if the Jews were created by God and therefore were good, why did the Medieval Church require each Crusader to kill a European Jew in order to prove his worth before he could go on the Crusades? And why did John Calvin feel the need to burn Michael Serventus at the stake merely because Serventus had questioned the existence of the Trinity, a concept *not* presented in the Bible? And why do Catholics and Protestants still fight each other in Northern Ireland, a fight which has been going on for much too long?

Further, why are women prohibited from the ministry in some Christian denominations? Were they not created by God and are they not good? Why does the Religious Right have such a hatred of men and women whose sexual preferences are different than the majority? Were they not created by God and are they not good? On and on this could go.

The Bible, which is accepted by most Christians as being at least directionally correct if not His absolute Word, says that God created *everything*, and that God believed that everything which He created was *good*. Why has that principle not been accepted by those who follow Him as they follow Jesus Christ? Do those who decide such matters feel that they can state what is not good, even though God saw that everything He created was good?

Possibly, the Christian feels that there have been things which were not created by God? If so, then they are saying that there is another creator. Doesn't this deny the concept of one God? We will return to this issue of one God later in this chapter.

Islam

Let us now examine the follower of Islam, a word which means "submission" or "surrender." As previously mentioned, Islam was founded on the principle that, "There is no god but God," an obvious slap at the Christians who had made Christ identical to God in all ways. Again, the God which the Muslims [meaning "those who have surrendered to God"] worshipped, at least in the beginning, was the same God worshipped by Judaism and Christianity. Within the Christian camp, Marcion, a second century Christian leader, had tried to say that the Father taught by Jesus Christ differed from the Yahweh worshipped by Judaism. As a result of this attempt, he was excommunicated from the Church, a Church which demanded that the God for Christianity and the God for Judaism were identical.

Islam not only accepted this God, they gave a fair amount of credence to the belief that they had been worshipping Him for much longer than the Jews. Consequently, a Muslim believes in the God who created all, and who saw that all which He created was good. However, the Muslim did not practice this belief when he decided to kill the Christians who accepted Jesus Christ. Wasn't Christ created by God and wasn't he good? Now I recognize that the Christian Church teaches that the Christ was not created, but existed from the beginning. However, that begs the question. Wasn't he part of the goodness of God? As such, why was he the reason for one good creation of God to decide to kill another good creation of God in the name of the "right" religion?

Why do some [though not all] Muslims believe that there are six "Pillars" to Islam rather than the five proposed by Mohammed, with the sixth Pillar being the *jihad* or "Holy War," a war which is to be fought against all until "allegiance is rendered to God alone." Isn't this holy war a fight against others who were created in God's image and thus are good? Yet, it is a war which is believed to be demanded by the God who creates only that which is good. There is no question that even in their doctrinal beliefs, Islam rejects the practice of the first Cosmic Concept.

Buddhism, Confucianism, Hinduism and Taoism

Because of their soft support for the first Cosmic Concept, Buddhism and Confucianism, will not be analyzed as to their practice of this Concept. However, Hinduism and Taoism will.

Hinduism believes that God created all the good things that were created, but not necessarily all things. They see many things as having been created by man, and they see these things as not being good. The devoted Hindu will accept God's creations, but reject the creations of man. As a consequence, the Hindu will not fully accept the first Cosmic Concept as a belief. It is, therefore, difficult to evaluate his practice of this Concept.

As previously described, Taoism, in its original form, more nearly accepted the first Cosmic Concept than any other major Eastern religion. About two centuries after the establishment of Taoism by Lao Tze, Chung Tze greatly furthered its spread through his teachings which were much more understandable to the masses than were the teachings originally presented in *Tao-Te King*. These new teachings are reported to contain some of the most beautiful and profound stories to be found in religious literature.

However, since then Taoism has been reported as having gone into serious deterioration from its original high ideals. This is a scenario which has been repeated by almost every religion as it became organized and as it established its doctrinal practices. This deterioration from the original in Christianity has been extensively documented in *The Christian Conspiracy*. According to *The Portable World Bible*, similar deterioration happened in Taoism as it became demeaned by polytheism, witchcraft, demonolatry and a degenerate papacy far removed from the purity of Lao Tze's conception.

I have no personal knowledge of the decline of Taoist ideals such as I have personally seen in the Christian Church; but the record presented in *The World Bible* is confirmed in other books which say that Taoism has developed an elaborate cult of supernatural beings, and has become preoccupied with magic and alchemy, particularly as these relate to the search for physical immortality. All of these seem to be far removed from the lofty ideals originally proposed for Taoism; and possibly could be considered to be a far cry from the support which Taoism originally gave to the first Cosmic Concept.

EXISTENCE OF PAIN, SUFFERING AND EVIL

This chapter could not be complete without expressing some thoughts about the existence of pain, suffering and evil in the world; for if God did create everything, and everything S/He created was good, then why do pain, suffering and evil exist? Why is the world not an idealistic place in which we would live with nothing more on our minds than the worship of God's goodness?

First, let us make a premise about the relationship between God and the existence of things on this Earth such as pain, suffering and evil. We will then attack that premise to find the weakness.

The premise is as follows:

If there is only one God, and if that God created all things, and if all the things which God created are good, and if all the things which God created exist only on this planet Earth, then it stands to reason that there is no pain, suffering and evil on this planet Earth.

Since there is pain, suffering and evil on this planet Earth, then something in this premise is not correct. Is the incorrect part the clause which states that there is only one God? Is there more than one Primary Creator, more than one Ultimate Reason, more than one Prime Mover of the Universe, more than one One; and does the other "God" create pain, suffering and evil while the God we recognize creates only good?

This is a question which has been addressed throughout the ages. Some have called the creator of pain, suffering and evil the Devil, or Satan, or some other such name; and these people have fought against that "God" with all their might, including that of killing those who supposedly followed Him. If you doubt that statement, then I suggest you read the "Conversion by the Sword" section of *The Christian Conspiracy* or other reference books of that type which document such behavior on the part of "right thinking" people. But you do not have to return to the Middle Ages to find such an activity. Today's pursuit of homosexuals by the Religious Right is as much of a "Witch Hunt" as that which the "right thinkers" of 1692 addressed in Salem, Massachusetts; for the Religious Right considers homosexuality to be another creation of the Devil.

Personally, I do not believe that there is more than one Primary Creator. Consequently, I do not think that this is the incorrect part of the premise presented above.

For my own part, I believe that there is only one God who created, and that all the things which S/He created are good. However, I do not believe that S/He created things *only* for planet Earth; and I believe that is the incorrect part of the premise presented above. Instead of being a creator only for planet Earth, I believe that God created all things in the entire universe; and that His/Her creations are made for the good of the entire cosmos. In this sense, that which God created could have a good *cosmic purpose*, even though in a particular part of that cosmos, the creation might produce pain and suffering or might be considered to be evil.

As an example, let us suppose that someplace within the cosmos, God is trying to build a perfect society which can be entered into only by the free-will choice of each applicant. God might want to make certain that the applicant would not commit murder, or generate mental or physical abuse on another when that applicant entered into the perfect society. How could S/He be assured that the applicant would not do such a thing if he or she had never been exposed to these things and, by free-will choice, had rejected them?

Is it possible that Earth is one of the training grounds from which free-will choices can be made to allow those who have experienced pain, suffering and evil to decide never again to participate in generating such an activity? If rape did not exist on planet Earth, and if you had never experienced, either directly or indirectly, the pain of rape, then how could you know to make the free-will choice never to participate in such an activity? Could you? And the same analysis could be presented for murder, abuse, infidelity, domination, wars, hatred, superiority, etc., etc., etc.

Pain, suffering, and evil <u>do</u> exist on planet Earth. The God I believe in could eliminate all of this if S/He chose to do so, because God is omnipotent [i.e. has all power]. If that evil had been created by another God of whatever nature, then the omnipotent God I accept could eliminate such competition with the batting of His/Her eye. However, I do not believe that such beings exist, unless they do so to serve a purpose as a part of God's ineffable plan and thus are "good" in a <u>cosmic</u> sense.

In addition, if the God I believe in wanted to have His/Her children generate no pain, suffering or evil, then S/He could do this in an instance merely by passing a Law which would forbid such activities. However, to do so would violate the free-will option which His/Her children have. I believe that God is too omniscient [all-knowing] to let that happen.

The point is that pain, suffering and evil are part of the lessons which individual personalities have been given in order to have knowledge of them through experience. This experience, either direct or indirect, would not be available if these lessons did not exist. The opportunity to be in oneness with God via free-will choice would not be available if an alternate choice did not exist. Such a possibility would reject the third Cosmic Concept presented in this book.

I firmly believe that there is a part of God's vast universe in which pain, suffering and evil do <u>not</u> exist, and where Unconditional Love is the sole reality. I fully believe that those who reside there could, and would, introduce activities such as pain, suffering and evil if they had not been exposed to these activities and had personally learned to reject them during their experiences in places where these activities <u>do</u> exist. I believe that in this free-will rejection, these entities have cleared themselves from any further participation in activities such as pain, suffering and evil. I believe that planet Earth is one such place for exposure to these activities, and that those who are here have chosen to experience such an exposure, possibly for many thousands of years during many Earth-bound lifetimes. By this choice, the causes of pain, suffering and evil can be experienced, practiced and rejected in order to move on.

If this reasoning has any validity, then pain, suffering and evil are a created *cosmic* good, even though they may not seem to be a created good from our present, parochial viewpoint. I believe that if anyone thoroughly thinks this through as a sequence of logic, they will accept this reasoning as being beyond a reasonable doubt; for to think otherwise would be to think either that God was not powerful enough to control evil, or was not loving enough to let us experience it. It must be painful for Him/Her to see us experience pain in order to learn to reject it; but if God loves us unconditionally, then S/He simply has to be loving enough to let us experience all of these shortcomings in order to overcome them.

CONCLUSION

The first Cosmic Concept states that there is one God who created *all things*, and all of the things which S/He created are *good*. A preponderance of the world's great religions have teachings which support this Concept; but few of the established religions practice this Concept. Instead, most seem to want to state for themselves that there are created things which are not good; which means either that they believe there is more than one creator, or that the one creator which they believe in has created that which is not good.

Because of the information which has been presented in this chapter, I conclude that the first Cosmic Concept exists. As a test of that conclusion, I would ask each reader to try to visualize what our world would be like if the first Cosmic Concept were to be accepted by all. The results of that test would undoubtedly generate a world which would be quite different.

As one difference, the judgment of others would immediately cease, and we would be following the Scripture which states: *Judge not, that you not be judged. For with the judgment you pronounce you will be judged, and the measure you give will be the measure you get.* [Matt. 7:1-2]. In such a world, all would be looked at for the good which is in it; and all would soon reject that which was imperfect, for the imperfection would have been used to teach the *folly* of its very existence.

Think of what the world would be like if the first Cosmic Concept were to be accepted by all.

Could an acceptance of the first Cosmic Concept be a part of your evolution?

CHAPTER 2
THE SECOND COSMIC CONCEPT: UNCONDITIONAL LOVE

The second Cosmic Concept states that the one God practices *Unconditional Love* for all which S/He created, and requests that all of His/Her creatures and other creations also practice Unconditional Love.

This Cosmic Concept will probably be the hardest of any of the four concepts to fully accept for two reasons. The first reason is that love, itself, is so difficult to understand; and the second is that since humankind has been practicing conditional love for so long, accepting the practice of Unconditional Love will be a giant step for our emotional bodies, possibly one which will be virtually impossible in this restricted, three-dimensional existence.

The Background section of this chapter will present some thoughts about love as proposed by the philosophers; followed by a description of love as proposed by the seven world religions using their scriptures as the primary source of this description. This will be followed by a description of the practices of Unconditional Love on the part of those established religions which teach it. The seven religions will be presented in the same order used in Chapter 1.

The Background section will be followed by a section on the Issues Concerning Unconditional Love; followed, in turn, by a section on the Guiding Principles of Unconditional Love.

BACKGROUND ON UNCONDITIONAL LOVE
Philosophy

It is difficult to describe physical feelings to another person. There have been times in my life when I have been involved in very deep muscle spasms in my lower back. I have found it impossible to describe to another just how frightening that pain is, and just how helpless that pain makes one feel with each movement. The pain soon generates a fear in making a movement of any kind. Even more than that, after the spasm had been relieved, the memory of that intense pain still makes one afraid to move. That feeling of residual fear after the fact is also impossible to describe to another. Although I have never had what is called a migraine headache, others have tried to describe that feeling to me. I guess it would rank with the physical pain of my lower back in its intensity.

I have never given birth to a child; but from what I have heard, the pain which is involved must be truly unforgettable, for the memory seems to linger even 40-50 years after the fact. Such an unforgettable physical feeling seems almost indescribable to one who has not gone through it. The point to be made is that it is very difficult to describe physical feelings to another person. I feel certain that many people have experienced the frustration of trying to communicate such a difficult subject.

But as difficult as the communication of physical feelings is, that difficulty pales in comparison with the difficulty of communicating emotional feelings. I once tried to describe the difficulty of communicating emotions by composing a poem which said:

I can't hear you.
The sound of
My own pain
Is too great!

Whether or not that poem "resonates" with you, the thought that emotions are virtually impossible to communicate is one which many people have shared with me. Of all the emotions, hatred or rejection is one of the easiest to communicate; whereas love or acceptance is one of the most difficult. For this reason, both philosophy and religion have tried to define love. Their attempts have not been very successful. Nevertheless, a few of those attempts will be reported here.

One of the earliest of the Greek philosophers who tried to define love, was Epedocles who lived in ca. 490-430 BCE. He believed that all matter was composed of four basic elements or essential ingredients: fire, air, water and earth. He further taught that nothing is ever brought into being or destroyed, but is merely transformed by varying the ratio of the four essential ingredients. He believed that two forces caused this transformation as they brought together or separated the four elements. Those forces were Strife and Love; with Strife causing the elements to pull apart, and Love making them mingle together. Parts of this philosophy have been picked up by every religion which says that we can all come together under the love of God.

Later, Plato [ca. 427-347 BCE] expanded the concept of love to include two forms; the physical which he called *Eros*, and the spiritual, which the Christians later called *Agape*. Platonism believed that Eros was the soul reaching out for a hoped-for good. In this sense, the love of a beautiful person would be an attempt to gain immortality by having an offspring with that person. The more spiritual form of love would generate a desire to be with a kindred soul in an attempt to gain immortality by giving birth to improved rules for life; with the highest of all spiritual love being a generation of improved rules for life via dialogue.

These two kinds of love were so prevalent in Greek thought, that they were still in existence 800 years later, when Augustine declared that man's destiny is determined by choosing spiritual love, and by completely rejecting physical love. In this example, and in other presentations by the early Church Fathers, the Greek thoughts of love were changed considerably. Although most of the changes in these definitions will be reserved for the section on Christianity, it should by noted here that the early Greek philosophers accepted both Eros and Agape as noble activities, for each was a Love in which the soul reached out to another. However, Christianity decided to define Eros as a Love which was ignoble because it devoted itself solely to the fulfillment of self; whereas only Agape is a noble Love because it devotes itself to the fulfillment of others.

Teachings of Love Based on Scripture

Zoroastrianism presents a marvelous story of love. As previously mentioned [see pages 128-30], a major theological premise of Zoroastrianism is that there are two powers: good and evil. The good is represented by *Ahura Mazdra* ["The Wise Lord"] who is entirely good and is the source of all that is right in the world. The evil is represented by the lesser spirit, *Angra Mainyu* ["The Destroying Spirit"].

Ahura Mazdra loves humanity and reveals himself for its good; whereas Angra Mainyu hates humanity and wants to destroy it by "the Lie." The basic belief of Zoroastrianism is that love and good will triumph in the end; and that those who follow Ahura Mazdra will attain heaven, whereas those who oppose Ahura Mazdra will be punished in hell along with the evil spirit.

The central scriptures of Zoroastrianism are called the *Avesta* which means "The Law." This scripture presents many similarities with the scriptures of Judaism. As one example, when Ahura Mazdra is asked his name in a manner similar to that which Moses asked of God in Exodus 3:13 [see page 18], he replies with twenty names, followed shortly thereafter with six other names. Then much later in a long monologue he says, in essence: *He that recites these names...[will be kept safe]...for it will be as if there were a thousand men watching over one man.* This is somewhat similar to the reward system established by Judaism.

Later in the scriptures, Ahura Mazdra [or actually his agent *Ohrmazd*] describes how in the end, all men shall be returned to him. In the belief system of Zoroastrianism, all humans had been judged independently at death. In the resurrection, all humans will pass through molten metal as Ohrmazd melts the world. Those who had called on the names of Ahura Mazdra and who "did good" during their lifetime were considered to be just. They would pass through the molten metal as if it were a pleasant bath; whereas those who were considered unjust would go through a terrible torment. Through their torment, the unjust would be purified and made just. In this way, all would return to Ahura Mazdra.

Zoroastrianism is considered to be a religion based on "doing good" rather than on love. However, their God must love His people, for he permits them to love Him by calling upon His name, and then to show that love for Him by doing good deeds. As a result of these good activities, He permits them to pass through molten metal without torment.

This act of kindness is love, whatever term is used to describe it. However, it seems to me that the love expressed by the God of Zoroastrianism is a conditional love rather than Unconditional Love; for although His is an Unconditional Love in the sense that all can return to Him, it is a conditional love in the sense that some must go through a terrible torment in order to do that. Consequently, Zoroastrianism seems to give love on the condition that their followers "do good" or be "purified through torment."

Based on their scriptures, Zoroastrianism is a religion which seems to teach conditional love, or at least love in which judgments are made. Unconditional Love is non-judgmental love.

Judaism established a base for the Judeo-Christian heritage of love. However, there is a great difference between the love described by Judaism and that described by Christianity.

As an example, in the King James Version of the Bible in English, the word "love" is used 356 times. In the much larger Old Testament [Judaism] the word is used only 105 times or about 30% of the total. This means that 70% of the time that the word "love" is used in the Bible, it is used in the New Testament [Christian] portion of the Bible. Of the 105 times in the Old Testament, 30 of those times are from the Song of Solomon, one of the shorter books of the Old Testament. The Song of Solomon is generally considered to by biblical scholars to be the most erotic book in the Bible. In essence, it is a book which expresses love by describing the joy to be found in the natural order of human relationships.

Statistical data can be very misleading; and they generally are boring anyway. However, these data do make a point. That point is that based on scriptural data, the God of Judaism is not presented as being a God of Love to the extent that He is in Christianity. That description of the presentation is true. Despite the fact that the God for both religions is the same God, and despite the fact that Christianity put forth a lot of effort to make certain that all of her followers accepted the fact that the God of these two religions is one and the same God, the presentation of that God on the part of Christianity differs from the presentation on the part of Judaism.

The basis for the love of God in Judaism is the covenant-fidelity relationship which God established for His "Chosen People." In this relationship, God creates a covenant with His people, and loves them if they are faithful to the terms of that covenant.

The first covenant for Judaism is the one which God made with Abraham. That covenant is presented in Genesis 12:1-3. In this covenant, God gives Abram [before his name was changed to Abraham] an order [or commandment] and the promise of a reward if Abram's people are faithful to that commandment. The commandment is to *"Go... to a land that I will show you."* If they are faithful, the reward is, *"And I will make of you a great nation..."* None of this agreement between God and Abraham uses the word "love." Instead, it is a familiar reward-punishment system which states, "Do what I ask of you and you will be rewarded. Deny it, and you will be punished."

The next major stage in the development of Judaism started when the Hebrew people were in Egypt. They were not free there, but were held in bondage and slavery. Then the daughter of the Pharaoh found a young baby floating in a basket on the Nile. She named him Moses, and raised him in the house of the Pharaoh where he remained until he questioned the treatment of the Hebrew people. This led Moses to feel that he might be killed. Consequently, he fled from the house of Pharaoh, married a Hebrew woman and settled among the Hebrew people as a shepherd for his father-in-law, Jethro.

At this point in time, God made contact with Moses. As a result, Moses led the people of Israel out of Egypt, with a lot of help from God. This led to the next major covenant which God had with the people of Israel. It was given at Mount Sinai when God gave to Moses the Ten Commandments under which the people of Israel would become the "Chosen People" of God. Those Ten Commandments are presented in Exodus 20:1-17. In the second commandment, the word "love" is used for the only time when God says:

"...for I the Lord your God am a jealous God, visiting the iniquity of the fathers upon the children to the third and the fourth generation of

Second Concept: Unconditional Love 151

those who hate me, but showing steadfast love to thousands of those who love me and keep my commandments."

Other than that love which is conditional on His people being faithful to God's commandments, the closest thing to "love" in the Ten Commandments is "hallowed" as in *"...the Lord blessed the sabbath day and hallowed it.";* and "honor" as in *"honor your father and your mother...."* Even the single use of "love" is based on reciprocity in that God will love you if you love Him; but will punish you if you hate Him.

Later, in Deuteronomy 6:4-5, we read:

"Hear, O Israel: The Lord our God is one Lord [or the Lord is one]; and you shall love the Lord your God with all your heart, and with all your soul, and with all your might."

In this case, the reward comes some five verses later, when God tells how he will give them a fully developed land which they did nothing to earn other than to love God. There are many other commandments to love God in Deuteronomy; and in the Psalms, there are references to God's loving you. An example is in Psalms 145 where it says, *"The Lord preserves all who love him; but all the wicked he will destroy."* This, again, is a reward-punishment system similar to that previously described.

The scriptures of Judaism tend to present the same message throughout. That message is that you should show your love for God by being faithful to the covenant He has made with you; for if you do not, then He will punish you. It says that God will love you *only* on the condition that you are faithful to the His covenant or commandments. It is love; and it is love which has been a positive force in this world. However, it is a love based on conditions. It is not the Unconditional Love proposed by the second Cosmic Concept.

Christianity changed the Judaic concepts of love; for when the Christian scriptures started to circulate throughout the Mediterranean world, an entirely new concept of love was presented. This concept of love used the Greek philosophical concepts as their basis, but then expanded those thoughts both backward to the Source [i.e. God] and forward to humanity. It is proper that Christianity should take their lead from Greek thinking; for although Christianity had

Judaism as its birthplace, it had Greek philosophy as its tutor. This "learning from the Greeks" was presented in detail in *The Christian Conspiracy*.

Possibly the best way to describe how the Christian concept of love expanded the Greek philosophy on which it was based, is to repeat a paragraph presented on page 1040, Volume 8 of the *New Catholic Encyclopedia*. This quotation represents what the Christian Church interprets Christian love to be. As will be demonstrated in the following paragraphs, this definition of love is not only changed from that of the Greeks, it is considerably changed from the teachings about love given to us by the Christ. The Church's definition of love reads as follows:

"Christianity brought a basic shift in man's thoughts about Love. Instead of Plato's Love based on man's spiritual poverty, or Aristotle's Love which was based on the needs of nature, Christian thought sees Love's source in the infinite perfection and creativity of the Divine Being. God, Himself, is Love as presented in 1 John 4:8. His very substance is a loving community of three Divine Persons. He creates the world out of Love. Out of Love, He sends His Son to redeem man. The Word made flesh is Love incarnate who calls man, made in His image, to share in His life. Man's basic vocation is now one of generous Love."

There are many pieces of New Testament scripture which speak of the type of Christian love which existed before the Church developed their doctrinaire definitions such as the one just presented. Out of these many, three have been selected to demonstrate the power that love had in the newly established religion of early Christianity. Those three are 1 John 4:7-8; Matt. 5:43-48; and Matt. 22:35-40 or the corresponding Luke 10:25-28.

In the first reference, 1 John 4:7-8, we read:

Beloved, let us love one another; for love is of God, and he who loves is born of God and knows God. He who does not love does not know God; for God is love.

This is indeed powerful scripture. It is the supreme message of the Christ as presented in the scriptures. It says that <u>God is love</u>. I can find no previous references to a God who is defined in exactly this manner. It is a simple but powerful definition. It is the basis of all that I believe in. God is love! What else need be known?

The earliest message that you should love your enemies is given in our second message of love. In Matt. 5:43-48, when Jesus is speaking as a part of the Sermon on the Mount, he says:

"You have heard that it was said, 'You shall love your neighbor and hate your enemy.' But I say to you, Love your enemies and pray for those who persecute you, so that you may be sons of your Father who is in heaven; for he makes his sun rise on the evil and on the good, and sends rain on the just and on the unjust. For if you love those who love you, what reward have you? Do not even the tax collectors do the same? And if you salute only your brethren, what more are you doing than others? Do not even the Gentiles do the same? You, therefore, must be perfect, as your heavenly Father is perfect."

This powerful message is quite a change from its Judaistic precursor with its railings against those who do not obey Jehovah and those who are the enemies of the Chosen People. This message is also powerful in that when Jesus states that the Father makes the sun and the rain available to all, he again is implying a global, if not a universal, love.

Our third message of love is given in Matt. 22:35-40. Although this message has previously been used, this scripture is so powerful that it must be repeated here. In these verses we read:

"And one of them [i.e. a Pharisee], *a lawyer, asked him* [i.e. Jesus] *a question to test him. 'Teacher, what is the great commandment in the law?' And he said to him, 'You shall love the Lord your God with all your heart, and with all your soul, and with all your mind. This is the great and first commandment. And a second is like it, You shall love your neighbor as yourself. On these two commandments depend all the law and the prophets.' "*

Jesus is saying that all of the rules and regulations which the Pharisees had been defining for over 1,000 years were meaningless unless the basic rule was first established; and that basic rule was to love God and to love your neighbor. In the corresponding reference in Luke, when Jesus was asked just what he meant by the term "neighbor," he answered in a way that completely astonished the Pharisees who were listening; for it is at this point that Jesus tells the Parable of the Good Samaritan. As was previously mentioned [see pages 50-1], the Samaritans were very much hated by the Jewish society of Jesus' time; and when a Pharisee asked Jesus who was his neighbor, Jesus replied that their enemies, the hated Samaritans, were. This must have left his audience perplexed, but it should not had done so; for earlier, in the Sermon on the Mount [see above], he had told all who would listen that they should love their enemies.

In this, and in many other examples which could be cited, Jesus states that his concept of love is one in which all humans are to be included. It is a global, if not a universal, love. This is the third time I have used this scriptural reference to speak of the love which was taught by Christ. In the first instance [see pages 42-3], the reference was used to demonstrate that one should love him/herself, and then love his/her neighbor in a like manner. In the second instance [see page 63], the reference was used to demonstrate how Jesus was replacing the Law with Love. In this instance, we have added the teaching that one should also love his/her enemy.

In all I read, I see Jesus as teaching a Love which is to be given to *all* things, without any conditions being attached. Jesus is teaching the practice of Unconditional Love; and he is saying that his Father in heaven [Note: God was always masculine in the Jewish society of Jesus' time] also teaches the practice of Unconditional Love, else why would He give everyone the sun and the rain? God is omnipotent, meaning that He has all power. If His love were to be conditional, then why would He not use His power in such a way that He would give sunshine or rain only to those who had met his "conditions"—only to those who "deserved" it?

Christianity was established as a religion which taught Unconditional Love. However, as we will describe in the next section, Christianity is not a religion which practiced Unconditional Love for a very long period after the Christ left.

Islam is primarily based on the worship of Allah; and as you read through the pages of the Koran, there is absolutely no question that the Muslims *do worship* Allah. In the early part of Chapter 5, I will state that although it is possible to love something without worshipping it, it is virtually impossible to worship something without loving it. In this sense, the Muslims must love Allah; and, in fact, they do call him the Beloved.

However, in their scriptures their references to their love of

God are rare. This sort of reminds me of the husband who never told his wife that he loved her because he assumed that she knew it. Then suddenly, she left him because she felt he didn't love her. It seems to me that one of the requirements of loving something as important as God, is to tell Him/Her that you truly do feel that love, and to make that expression of love often.

As you try to understand orthodox Islam, you come to the feeling that it is very much like Judaism in that God is supreme, but that He is to be obeyed, both in the hope that obedience will generate a reward, and in the fear that disobedience will generate punishment. It is back to the old reward-punishment idea with the admonition to "do it or else."

This obedience is implicit in the name of the religion; for Islam means "submission" or "surrender." Thus, a Muslim is expected to submit to the will and the guidance of Allah; and when he does so, he is rewarded with divine favor in the world to come. As a part of the will of Allah, each Muslim is expected to submit to the doctrine of social service by which he will alleviate the pains of those who suffer and will give help to those who are in need. But as you read about these duties, you get the feeling that the devotion given to Allah, and the help given those in need, is done without a major feeling of love for either one of them.

The fact that Islam considers Allah to be the God of everyone, rather than merely the God of the Chosen People, would indicate that if love were to be a part of Islam, it could be a global or universal love. However, the "sixth pillar of Islam" means that any love coming out of Islam would have to be a conditional love; for those of Islam who accept the sixth pillar are determined to fight to death anyone who does not accept that there is only one God.

If there is love in the scriptures of orthodox Islam which translates into a doctrine of love, it seems to be love of a conditional nature rather than being Unconditional Love. However, the mystic part of Islam is different. In a manner similar to the difference between the orthodox and the mystic parts of Islam in regard to meditation [see pages 59-60], there seems to be a difference in attitude about love; for many will state that Sufism is love, and its poetry describes that love with great feeling.

Hinduism covers all life in that it consists of religious, economic, social, literary and artistic aspects. It is also broken into literally hundreds of different sects, each of which tends to have its own scriptures and religious beliefs. This makes an all-encompassing definition of Hinduism rather difficult.

Nevertheless, there are three religious principles of Hinduism which are common to all sects. Those are *samsara*, *karman* and *moksha*. *Samsara* refers to the transmigration of each individual soul; *karman* refers to the applications of acts presently done to a good or a bad future; and *moksha* refers to the liberation of the soul from the consistently recurring cycle of life, death and rebirth. There are three paths or means to *moksha*. They are: the path of ritual or disinterested action; the way of true knowledge; and the method of intense devotion to God.

In no way does this short description present a full picture of Hinduism. Nevertheless, it does allow us to address the present issue which is whether or not the doctrines of any established religion present the concept of Unconditional Love as its principal teaching.

The intense devotion to God which is mentioned as one of the pathways to *moksha* would allow the Hindu to apply the concept of Unconditional Love to the deity. However, there is little, if anything, in the basic doctrines of Hinduism which suggests an Unconditional Love of fellow humans. This conclusion is emphasized when one considers the caste system which is so prevalent in Hinduism. In this concept, which some have identified as <u>the</u> central unifying institution of Hinduism both as a religion and as a way of life, individuals are placed into certain social and religious strata based on the relative purity of their soul at the time of birth; and they have virtually no chance to change the caste into which they have been born. Even secular laws have had little effect on the practice of the caste system.

Although I do not mean to judge such an activity, I do have a hard time seeing how this system could possibly fit into the concept of Unconditional Love for a fellow human being in any way. Instead, it seems to me that there are conditions for love and acceptance throughout the entire structure of Hinduism; and that the caste system is a strong deterrent to the practice of Unconditional Love.

Another example of the absence of Unconditional Love in the practice of Hinduism [as well as Islam], is the Hindu-Muslim communal riots in the late 1940s. They were accompanied with a religious persecution of non-rioting civilians which can be ranked with the Holocaust as an atrocity. This broke Mohandas Gandhi's heart.

As with Islam, if there is love for humans in the doctrines of Hinduism, it seems to be of a conditional or judgmental nature, rather than being Unconditional Love.

Buddhism believes in a plurality of universes. Therefore, they believe in a plurality of people. To one who is not a Buddhist, a Buddhist might say, "Be calm; be happy; be peaceful." He then might go on to say that if you are relaxed, happy and peaceful, then you will never create a war; and if everyone would stop creating wars, then there would never be another war.

To me, one who says these things is giving a lot of love, and is giving it without conditions being attached; for this message is given to anyone who will listen. In addition, as previously mentioned [see page 38], universal love is one of the ten great virtues of Buddhism. Finally, the great mantra of Buddhism and Hinduism, *Om Mani Padme Hum*, was accepted as the personal mantra of Lord Chenresik, the Tibetan name for Avalokitesvar Bodhisattva, the Buddha of Compassion. Lord Chenresik has vowed to save *all beings* without exception. To have a Lord devoted to a saving compassion for <u>all</u> is a close approach to having Unconditional Love for all.

As a result of all of this, I feel that there is a lot of love in the teachings of Buddhism; and possibly more love in the practice of Buddhism than in any other established religion in the world. This thought is developed further in the next section of this chapter.

However, the giving and receiving of Unconditional Love is not the guiding principle of Buddhism. Instead, the guiding principle of Buddhism is "live in the now," with other major principles being "do no harm," and "take no action." Finally, a practicing Buddhist will attempt to reject all things and to detach him/herself from all earthly desires. In the *Path of Dhamma* which is found in Buddhist scriptures, the following statement is made:

"Some people are born again; evil doers go to hell; righteous people go to heaven; those who are free from all worldly desires attain Nirvana."

In *The Buddha* which also is in the scriptures of Buddhism, the following statement is made:

"He who takes refuge with Buddha, the Dharma and the Sangha; he who, with clear understanding, sees the four holy truths: viz. pain, the origin of pain, the destruction of pain, and the eightfold holy way that leads to the quieting of pain; that is the safe refuge, that is the best refuge; having gone to that refuge, one is delivered from pain."

The place where suffering and pain no longer exist is *Nirvana*. The attainment of Nirvana by overcoming all worldly desires is the principle goal of the practicing Buddhist for him/herself; whereas the principle goal of a practicing Buddhist for another is not necessarily to love that other person, but to do him/her no harm.

I think that love could <u>seem</u> to exist by the practice of not harming or hating another; for the absence of hate can make it <u>seem</u> as if love is present. But I would submit that the absence of hate, or the detachment from all worldly emotions does not necessarily give the presence of love, especially if love is considered to be one of the worldly emotions from which detachment is desired in order to attain *Nirvana*. In other words, detachment to achieve a feeling of nothingness is not necessarily the same as an attachment to the presence of love, even if in that nothingness there is bliss.

In the next section I will indicate that I appreciate the <u>practice</u> of Buddhism even more than I appreciate the practice of the Christianity in which I was raised. However, I will also state that the doctrine of Unconditional Love exists more in the teachings of the Christ than in those of the Buddha. This is one of the reasons I still follow the Christ, even though the present practice of Christianity continues to bother me.

Although others may disagree, I do not see the concept of Unconditional Love as a guiding principle in the teachings of Buddhism.

Confucianism does not teach the concept of Unconditional Love, although the love which they do teach is arguably closer to Unconditional Love than that of any other established religion. Confucianism teaches that love should reach to all, but that this love should be expressed in varying degrees, starting with the most to oneself, then to one's family, followed by lesser amounts to the community, the country and the world in that order. The teachings go on to say that these various amounts of love are not to occur by a natural sequence of feelings, but are to be deliberately lessened as the distance from self proceeds.

Although this love for society is admirable, it is not the teaching of Unconditional Love; for the amounts of love are based on the conditions of family relationship. This overlooks the concept that *all* are one with God; but then Confucianism overlooks God anyway.

However, although Confucianism does not seem to teach Unconditional Love, a break-off sect once did. A philosopher named Mo Tse [or Mo-tzu] was born 72 years after Confucius, in 479 BCE. He originally was a follower of Confucius, but broke away to found his own school. He did this because he felt that Confucianism laid too much emphasis on rituals and too little on religious teaching.

Mohism became the major rival to Confucianism for several hundred years. There were several minor differences between these two schools. As a few examples, whereas Confucianism taught "humaneness" as the key virtue, Mohism taught "righteousness"; whereas Confucianism centered on human values, Mohism centered on religion and actually taught that there was a heaven; whereas Confucianism promoted ritual and art, Mohism promoted the well-being of the people.

But the major difference between Confucianism and Mohism had to do with their thoughts about love. Mo Tse insisted on Universal Love for all without distinction for their family or national relationship. These thoughts are presented in their scriptures. In one section, after defining what things are injurious to the nation and stating that they are caused by a lack of mutual love, the writings of Mohism say:

"Here is a ruler who only knows to love his own state, and does not love his neighbor's; he therefore does not shrink from raising all the

power of his state to attack his neighbor's. Here is the head of a family who only knows to love it, and does not love his neighbor's; he therefore does not shrink from raising all his powers to seize on that other family. Here is a person who knows only to love his own self, and does not love his neighbor's; he therefore does not shrink from using all his resources to rob his neighbor."

The writings go on to give many other similar examples, then say: *They may change it all by the law of universal mutual love and by the interchange of mutual benefits.* Later, the writings say that although the rulers might say that Universal Love is too difficult, it is because they simply do not understand the advantages of such a law to everyone. The writings give several examples of this advantage, then say:

"*As to mutual love, it is an advantageous thing and easily practiced—beyond all calculation. The only reason it is not practiced, in my opinion, is because the superiors do not take pleasure in it. If superiors were to take pleasure in it...stimulating people to it by rewards and praise...nothing would be able to stop them.*"

Universal, mutual love is the basic cornerstone of Mohism. It is the major teaching. It is very close to the concept of Unconditional Love. Mohism disappeared in about the second century BCE. Most scholars blame the disappearance on the belief that although Mohism should be desired for its high moral tone, its teachings were over-demanding and contrary to human nature. With this demise, China went back to Confucianism with its teaching of "love by degree."

Taoism, or the mastery of the Way, is not a religion of Unconditional Love. The following is one example from its scripture: *It is only the virtuous person who can love or who can hate others.* Another part says: *There are four things which the Master taught: letters, ethics, devotion of soul, and truthfulness...four things from which the Master was entirely free: forgone conclusions, arbitrary predeterminations, obstinacy and egoism.* Although there is no hint of Unconditional or Universal Love in these, in another part it is recorded: *do not to others what you would not wish done to yourself.* The "Golden Rule" is wonderful philosophy, albeit not Unconditional Love.

It would seem that for a short period of time, the traditions of Confucianism/Taoism spawned a religion of Universal, Unconditional Love which was discarded because it asked too much of humans. Too bad it was not tried for a longer period of time!

The Religious Practice of Unconditional Love

Of all the religions mentioned above, only two use their scriptures to present Unconditional Love as the basis for their teaching. One has not survived. That is **Mohism** with its teaching of universal, mutual love. As we will later show, the other has not followed its original teachings. That is **Christianity** which had the teachings of Unconditional Love as originally presented by the Christ, but which has failed in the practice of those teachings, at least within the Church which bears his name.

Buddhism tends to practice some, if not all, of the principles of Unconditional Love without having this concept as one of its basic teachings. Buddhism teaches good works which some equate with love. Buddhism also teaches the practice of calmness which tends to establish an atmosphere in which hate does not exist. If one can consider that love is demonstrated by the practice of good works and by the absence of hate, then Buddhism can be considered to practice Unconditional Love; for they are unconditional in their desire to do good works and to abolish hate.

However, good works can be driven by a number of emotions other than love. Some may wish to do good works because they fear what might happen to them otherwise; others in an attempt to gain an earthly reputation; still others in hopes of receiving a reward in return. In my opinion, the existence of good works does not necessarily demonstrate the presence of Unconditional Love; and neither does the absence of hate.

If these opinions are correct, then Buddhists do not practice Unconditional Love, merely the unconditional acceptance of good works, the unconditional condemnation of hate, and the desire to become so detached as to become one with the nothingness. Despite this soft criticism of Buddhism, there is true merit in practicing the absence of hate, for it would seem that the absence of hate can lead to the absence of intolerance. Buddhism is a religion which is very tolerant of the beliefs of others.

One interesting analysis of rating a religion's practice of Unconditional Love and its consequent practice of intolerance would be to evaluate the harshness of their Seven Deadly Sins; in this case by comparing those of **Judaism, Christianity** and **Hinduism**.

One would think that the Seven Deadly Sins of **Christianity** would be based on the Seven Deadly Sins of **Judaism** as presented in Proverbs 6:16 which says:

There are six things which the Lord hates, seven which are an abomination to him: haughty eyes, a lying tongue, and hands that shed innocent blood, a heart that devises wicked plans, feet that make haste to run to evil, a false witness who breathes out lies, and a man who sows discord among brothers.

These are all things which are to be avoided and they are in what Christianity considers to be Holy Scripture.

However, by the sixth century CE, Pope Gregory I, known as Gregory the Great, made the Sins seem much more harsh. He also made the punishment for committing them much more harsh; for his Seven Deadly Sins would prevent a person from receiving God's Grace. Denying God's Grace to anyone hardly represents the practice of Unconditional Love. Gregory's Seven Sins for **Christianity** were: *pride, lust, envy, anger, covetousness, gluttony and sloth.*

In the twentieth century, Mohandas Gandhi presented a softer picture. Gandhi was a practicing Hindu who had studied all religions during his lifetime. He had been fascinated by Tolstoy's writings on Christianity, and had read the Koran thoroughly. He also delved deeply into Hindu scriptures and philosophy. His study of comparative religion and his discussions with the scholars of each, led him to the conclusion that "all religions are true."

This quotation is often used by those who are working for ecumenical accord within the established religions of the world. However, the Gandhi quotation is longer than that; for he goes on to say that although all religions are true, they all are imperfect because they were "interpreted with poor intellects, sometimes with poor hearts, and more often misinterpreted." If you were to carry these thoughts further, it would lead you to the thought that when one religion expresses intolerance by feeling superior to another religion, it is because it is seeing the imperfections or misinterpretations rather than the basic truths of that other religion. I would also like to extend the thoughts of Mohandas Gandhi by suggesting that there are no differences between religions—only by the way in which their cultures view the world. Gandhi's softer Seven Deadly Sins for the universality of religion were:

wealth without work; pleasure without conscience; knowledge without character; commerce without morality; science without humanity; worship without sacrifice; and politics without principle.

I like these; and I would suggest that they represent teachings based on love to a much greater extent then do the Christian ones of Pope Gregory.

Returning to an analysis of Unconditional Love, it is my present opinion that no presently established religion follows the practice of Unconditional Love, or holds out to their members the desire for them to practice Unconditional Love.

If **Christianity** is the only major, existing religion which has Unconditional Love as a part of its original teaching, then I can tell you that in the fifty years I spent within the walls of that Church, I saw a lot of wonderful love; but I never saw or heard the advocacy of Unconditional Love as a policy of the Church. I have heard the Presbyterian Church, which was my religious home until recently, argue endlessly against the ordination of homosexual ministers and against allowing any time or space to those who believe that femininity has a place in the worship process. Neither represents a policy of Unconditional Love.

Other Christian sects deny the ordination of females in their ministry. I recently had a very pleasant discussion with an ordained Presbyterian minister who complemented the Episcopal Church on its recent decision to permit the ordination of women, and on the expanded thinking presented by two of its Bishops: Bishop Pike and Bishop Spong. I agreed, but then countered that any Church is composed of people; and that there is the Episcopal Bishop in Texas who has publicly stated that despite what the Church teaches, he refuses to ordain women. He went on to say that as soon as he retires from his Episcopal bishopric, he will become a Roman Catholic where they still know that only men are to be priests. Is this Unconditional Love?

This is not the only example of the established religions giving love only to the men of the church. The following two paragraphs present examples which were cited in Susan Haskins great book, *Mary Magdalen: Myth and Metaphor.*

In respect to **Judaism**, she writes:

"Whilst women were known to have supported rabbis with money, possessions and food, their participation in the practice of Judaism was negligible. Although they were allowed to read the Torah at congregational services, they were forbidden to recite lessons in public in order to "safeguard the honor of the congregation." In the first century CE, one Rabbi Eliezer was quoted as saying, "Rather should the words of the Torah be burned than entrusted to a woman!" It was for this same reason that the women were seated separately from the men in the synagogue itself....They were forbidden to carry out any liturgical functions."

In respect to **Christianity**, she writes:

"In Acts and from the Letters of Paul, women such as Phoebe and Junia were able to have important functions as bishops and deacons. This, however, occurred only in the fledgling Church where their work generated the admiration of Paul, himself. However, this state of equality lasted for only a few generations after Christ's death. Toward the end of the second century, Tertullian wrote, "It is not permitted for a woman to speak in the church, nor is it permitted for her to teach, nor to baptize, nor to offer the Eucharist, nor to claim for herself a share in any masculine function, not to mention any priestly office."

In addition to these two references, there is a traditional prayer of **Judaism** which says:

"Lord God of our Fathers; God of Abraham, Isaac and Jacob: All praise and glory to you for that I have not been born a woman."

It would hardly seem as if any of these references present an example of Unconditional Love for the female within Judeo-Christianity.

Islam also denies women leadership roles within the religion. Like most Americans, I had heard of the intolerance with which women are treated by Muslim adherents. Consequently, I was surprised to learn that all Muslims venerate Mary, the Mother of Jesus, and believe that she gave virgin birth to Jesus. It is probable that Mary has been chosen for this veneration because the mother of Muhammad died when he was a young boy, and Muhammad was raised first by his paternal grandfather and later by a paternal uncle. Consequently, his mother had little influence in his life.

However, despite this adoration of Mary which I learned about during a trip to Turkey in the spring of 1995, I cannot accept that Islam practices Unconditional Love for their females.

Returning to the religion which had Unconditional Love as its originating teaching, there are three examples which lend support to the belief that **Christianity** does not practice Unconditional Love. The first example is an incident which I found to be very strange. On September 7, 1994, during a telecast in Atlanta, Billy Graham said, *"The only sin which God will not forgive is the sin of refusing Jesus Christ."* This was strange to me, for it not only showed that Christian spokesmen require acceptance of Jesus Christ before they will love you enough to grant forgiveness, it was strange in showing how far the teachings of the present-day Church have drifted from scripture; for the scriptures do not say that. Instead, they say something entirely different. In Mark 3:28-30, Jesus is reported to say:

"Truly I say to you, all sins will be forgiven the sons of men, and whatever blasphemies they utter; but whoever blasphemes against the Holy Spirit never has forgiveness, but is guilty of an eternal sin"—for they had said, "He has an unclean spirit."

Now how is it possible that the men of today's Church could change scripture by substituting Jesus Christ for the Holy Spirit? As described in *The Christian Conspiracy*, this is the result of the efforts made by the early Church Fathers as they defined Jesus during their debates on Christology during the fourth through the seventh centuries, CE. The scriptures do not say what Billy Graham said, and neither did Jesus. It is one example of how the Church has not only changed the teaching of Unconditional Love, it has lost its practice.

A second example is the Christian belief that "you can hate the sin but love the sinner." Within the concept of Unconditional Love, this is not possible. You cannot hate one characteristic of a person without making the love you feel for that person become a conditional love. The reasons for this are presented in detail in the next section.

The third and final example is related to *"imprecatory psalms."* This term was first used by the Scottish theologian and Semitic scholar, W. Robertson Smith, in 1881. The word "imprecatory" comes from the Latin *imprecatus* which means *"to invoke or pray."* The word has come to mean *"to call down evil or curses on a person."* Smith used the term to describe certain Psalms which, in the whole or in part, invoke Divine vengeance. Examples of the Psalms which he cited are: Psalm 58; Psalm 68:21-3; Psalm 69:23-9; Psalm 109:5-19; and Psalm 137:7-9. These Psalms indeed are prayers that God will curse the enemies of the one doing the praying. As an example, Psalm 109 says:

> Appoint a wicked man against him;
> > let an accuser bring him to trial.
> When he is tried, let him come forth guilty;
> > let his prayer be counted as sin.
> May his days be few; may another seize his goods!
> May his children be fatherless, and his wife a widow!
> May his children wander about and beg;
> > may they be driven out of the ruins they inhabit!
> May the creditor seize all that he has;
> > may the strangers plunder the fruits of his toil!
> Let there be none to extend kindness to him,
> > nor any to pity his fatherless children!
> May his prosperity be cut off;
> > may his name be blotted out in the second generation!
> May the iniquity of his fathers be remembered before the Lord,
> > and let not the sin of his mother be blotted out.

There is no question that the God of Judaism was a Lord of vengeance. Since the teachings of the Christ changed that God into a God of Love, I suppose some might wonder why such a cursing Psalm would be used as an example of how Christianity has failed in its practice of Unconditional Love. The reason is simple. Some who profess to be loving Christians continue to recommend the use of "imprecatory psalms."

In the November 4, 1994 edition of the *Atlanta Constitution*, an issue which was printed during the week before the elections, there is an article on the use of imprecatory psalms in order to defeat Democratic foes. A group called the Capital Hill Prayer Alert urged all their members to use imprecatory psalms as "supernatural weapons of prayer" to defeat Democratic officeholders in Tuesday's elections. A letter which this group circulated says, "Don't hesitate to pray imprecatory psalms over them. These people have ruined our country and must be prayed out!" Just as in the days of old, these imprecatory psalms are the equivalent of a curse, asking that evil come upon the subject. As a few examples of these imprecatory psalms, the letter suggested that one might say, "Let his days be few, and let another take his office. Let his children be fatherless, and his wife a widow." Or possibly, "Let death seize upon them, and let them go down quick into hell."

The prayer list to which the Capital Hill Prayer Alert group wished to send such dire threats included two Democratic governors, seven Democratic senators, and 16 Democratic House members. It would seem that this is ample evidence that at least some who believe themselves to be "Christian" have forgotten the teachings of Unconditional Love given to us by the Christ.

I would dearly love to be proved wrong; but it is my firm belief that no established religion today promotes the practice of Unconditional Love as a policy within the entire religion. In addition, it is the Church of my roots, the Christian Church, which has the most to be answerable for; for that religion was established on the teachings of Unconditional Love given by the Christ.

If you still believe that the Church of Jesus Christ has been faithful to those teachings, I would suggest that you read *The Christian Conspiracy*, then ask any Jew, Cathar, Inca, Mayan, Muslin, Wiccan or Witch what their thoughts might be about the Christian practice of Unconditional Love. Although many of those examples are from a period of time before the Reformation, ask some women of Salem or even Michael Serventus whether the Reformation generated a renewed belief in the practice of Unconditional Love.

Although many of the Church will tell you that all of this ancient history has been changed by the Enlightenment, I feel that there were some nineteenth century Africans in the United States and some nineteenth century colonized folk in Africa who might disagree. Even today, there are many "men of the Church" who continue to demonstrate that they do not love practice Unconditional Love as they rail against those whose sexual preference is different than the majority; or against those who question any part of an "Apostle's Creed" which was developed 700 years after the death of the last Apostle; or against those who wish to be considered a Christian without accepting all of the theology developed some 300 to 650 years after the Resurrection. Rejecting all such people demonstrates a love which is conditional. It is not the Unconditional Love which Jesus gave to the Samaritans, and which he taught that all who follow him should give to their enemy.

In my opinion, few religions were established on the basis of Unconditional Love; and none preach the practice of Unconditional Love today.

ISSUES CONCERNING UNCONDITIONAL LOVE

The major issue concerning Unconditional Love is the question of "What is Unconditional Love?" Although the definition of Unconditional Love should be obvious, this Cosmic Concept is so vital to the entire meaning of this book, that it seems worthwhile to discuss some issues which make an acceptable definition virtually impossible. Those issues are: [1] love which is thought to be unconditional, but which is presented with subtle conditions attached; [2] the oft-repeated concept of "hate the sin but love the sinner"; and [3] the need to detach from unacceptable activities.

Love which is subtly conditional

Much love which one might consider to be unconditional, really has subtle conditions attached. Numerous examples could be cited from within the parent-child relationship. A few examples of subtly conditional love might be: "I want you to make good grades"; or "If you love me, you will clean up your room"; or "Your father and I hope that you will become a doctor"; or "When you were raised in a Christian home, how could you think those New Age thoughts?" These are examples which a parent might think would fall into the concept of Unconditional Love, or at least fulfill the modern concept of "tough love." However, all of these, and many others which could be cited, are examples of love which have conditions attached; for even if the conditions were not spoken, the receiver will feel that they were implied. Those to whom such messages are sent will feel that you will love them *only* if they get good grades, or clean up their room, or become a doctor, or attend a church you approve.

Some examples of conditional love are even more subtle. As one example, I would dearly love my wife to answer my questions with a "yes" or "no" rather than giving me her feelings and then letting me guess the answer; but the more I insist on it, the more I am letting her know that I would love her more completely if I could get a direct answer. In that way, I am making my love for her a conditional thing. I don't mean to do that, for I truly love her without any conditions being attached; but this three-dimensional, emotional vehicle in which my soul is incarnated can often betray my desire to practice Unconditional Love.

As another example, I will occasionally have a dream in which I am back with a corporation where the relationship between my boss and me got strained. As a result, I was made a scapegoat and forced to leave. I would like to feel that I have transformed all the feelings of rejection and betrayal which that incident created in me, but occasionally the dream will return. I then know that I have a love for that boss which has conditions attached to it, such as his saying, "I made a mistake," or "You were unjustly accused since it really was my fault." That, of course, will not happen. And so, it is up to me to transform the feelings which the dream represents to me; for when this dream recurs, I know that once more, I have not been completely successful either in the practice of Unconditional Love, or in the detachment from the unacceptable activities of another person.

Among other examples of the subtle addition of conditions to love which could be cited, the most prevalent one is probably that of judgment which implies that we [rather than God] know what is best for another person. However, it is probable that the few examples cited are sufficient to give the reader an idea of the problem.

Hate the Sin but Love the Sinner

On a much less subtle basis, there is the concept prevalent in the Christian Church that one should "hate the sin but love the sinner." To illustrate the problem which such a concept creates in the practice of Unconditional Love, I will go to an extreme by using examples of "totally unacceptable activities," and then modify these extremes with examples of activities which may be acceptable to some, but unacceptable to others. In this section, I will use the term "sin" to communicate. I hope the reader can accept that I am not making a judgment, and that I actually do not believe in the concept of "sin." I am using the word in a communicative sense only.

There have been many historical activities which are totally unacceptable in a humane society. I would suggest that the crimes against humanity committed by the leaders of Nazi Germany would constitute such a "totally unacceptable activity." As a direct result of those unacceptable activities, I would submit that Adolph Hitler and the rest of his gang are among the most hated men in modern history. This is but one example, albeit a horrible one, in which hating the sin led to hating the sinner. I would also suggest that in a human sense, the people of Israel have all the justification needed to continue their attitude of "We shall never forget!" How could anyone forget or forgive an atrocity against an entire people which is as horrible as that of the Holocaust?

There are lesser-known examples of historical activities which are totally unacceptable to a humane society. One of them is particularly offensive to me. In the thirteenth century, the Catholic Church committed genocide as they conducted a crusade against the Cathars, also known as the Albigenses. Each time I think of that episode in history, I develop an anger which almost overwhelms me. That is one reason that the episode against the Cathars was included in *The Christian Conspiracy*. Because of this anger in me, I have a visceral hatred for Pope Innocent III. What a name for a man who sponsored the crusade which generated genocide! It is because of this feeling that I can be sensitive to the hatred which the Israelis feel. It is also another example of how "hating the sin led to hating the sinner."

One of the previewers of *The Christian Conspiracy* has a similar sensitivity. She is presently a witch. She practices no black magic or any other such thing as popularly thought by most people; but nevertheless, after being raised in Judaism followed by a try at fundamental Christianity and Zen Buddhism, she is now a compassionate witch. She suggested that a section on "the Burning Time" be added to the book. This was the period between 1200 and 1700 when many, many people were burned at the stake in order to save their souls. Some historians have reported that as many as nine million people were killed; but the number is probably closer to a few hundred thousand. No one knows the real number, for the records are very incomplete. However, it is a fact of history that a vast number of people were burned at the stake in the "defense of Christian beliefs." It was a part of the history of the Catholic Church which generated as many strong feelings in her as the episode of the Cathars did in me. In fact, despite her Jewish heritage, this episode seemed to have a greater effect on her than did the Holocaust. Because of her suggestion, a section on the persecution of witches by the Christian Church was added. It was a proper addition.

Each of these major events in history has been considered to be unacceptable behavior by many humans. Some humans have generated so much hatred for the "sin," that they have applied their hatred to the "sinner." These are striking examples of the failure to "hate the sin but love the sinner."

But I would suggest that even smaller cases of unacceptable behavior can easily lead to the same result. As one example, in 1979 my wife and I were on a European trip which included stops in Warsaw and Amsterdam. We had been taught about the cleanliness of the Dutch in our high school geography classes many years before; and we were looking forward to our first experience about how a major city could be kept clean. But we had that experience in Warsaw, not in Amsterdam. Even though Warsaw was in a police state, it was a beautiful, clean city in which the people showed a great deal of pride in their environment and in their craft skills. On the other hand, Amsterdam was a pig-sty in which environmental pride seemed woefully lacking. Seemingly, the overly tolerant attitude of the Dutch toward their youth had led to a city which had been trashed. To us, it was behavior which we had a hard time accepting. It was entirely unexpected, and it generated an intolerance toward those who had done it. It is another example in which an unacceptable activity had caused an interference with the Unconditional Love we wanted to feel for all people.

In addition to these examples on a national basis, there are examples of "unacceptable behavior" within almost every family, whether the family will admit it or not. Unfortunately, this unacceptable behavior on the part of some family member has often led to a reduction in the level of love given to that member. In other words, the family has failed in their attempt to "hate the sin but love the sinner." Some examples might be an uncivil attitude toward an adult member of the family by one of the children; or an unacceptable use of alcohol or drugs on the part of any family member; or physical or sexual abuse; or the commission of crimes; or almost any other activity presented in the "catalogue of unacceptable behavior." I would challenge any family member to state that in such situations, they have truly been able to "hate the sin but to love the sinner unconditionally."

The point to be made is that in a human sense, there is great difficulty in practicing Unconditional Love so long as one accepts the belief that one can "hate the sin but love the sinner"; for the hatred of the "sin" and its association with the "sinner" will soon generate a reduction in the love of the one who caused the "sin" or "unacceptable activity." If I were to think that I might love a loved one more if he/she were sober, then I have associated the condition of sobriety on my love for that person and the Unconditional Love I might want to feel for him/her has been damaged. I know that it is extremely difficult for one to give Unconditional Love to an alcoholic member of the family, for the cost to the family in human terms is truly high; but as long as the "hated sin" is associated with the "loved sinner," it will be impossible for the love to be unconditional.

In the extreme example of our time, the same could be said for Adolph Hitler; for it is virtually impossible for any human to give Unconditional Love to Adolph Hitler as long as he is associated with his unacceptable activities. On a humanitarian or a human personality basis, the Holocaust was horrible; and I can truly understand Israel's desire "never to forget." But in either the case of the family alcoholic or the Nazi activities, never to forget is never to forgive. Horrible as an addicted family member is or the Holocaust was, in cosmic terms these are emotional experiences which can be overcome; as can other emotional experiences such as those connected with the genocide of the Cathars, or the "Burning Time" of the witches.

I have tried it both ways; and I believe that Unconditional Love is not possible when you "love the person but hate what he or she does." I have developed the belief that Unconditional Love includes all activities. There is no such thing as giving Unconditional Love when a part of the person you are giving that love to is excluded. Merely by the act of the exclusion, you are placing conditions on the love.

However, I have the firm belief that there is a way to practice Unconditional Love even in the presence of unacceptable activities. It is the subject of the next section.

Detachment from Unacceptable Activities

The point made in the preceding section is that because we are humans who do not practice Unconditional Love, then the hatred of any unacceptable activity will soon lead to a lack of love for the agent of that activity. That is a human reaction. It is almost inherent in our present personality. The point to be made in this section is that the lack of love is generated by our *attachment* to the unacceptable activity, and not by its association to the person who did it.

Do you hate Adolph Hitler, or Pope Innocent III, or any other agent of an unacceptable activity because you know the person as a person and just cannot stand him/her; or do you hate the person because you have become attached to the unacceptable activity which he/she caused? That question really has more importance than you may imagine; for attachment to the hatred of an unacceptable activity can lead to problems on both the human and the nonhuman levels. It can interfere with our physical health, and it can interfere with our relationship with God. It is the attachment to the unacceptable activity which is the problem, not the recognition.

A young social worker whom I recently met is having health problems because she attaches herself to the many child abuse problems she sees in the foster homes which are her responsibility. I contend that her health problems are not caused by her *recognition* of the problems, but by her *attachment* to them. In my opinion, the attachment has led to a human health problem. My advice to her was that she must become detached, or else she will "burn out" at a very young age. I suggested that long periods of quiet meditation in which she did nothing but listen, could lead to the desired detachment. I would never suggest that she deny the recognition of the unacceptable activity; merely that she detach herself from it.

On the nonhuman level, the people of Israel have to recognize the Holocaust, and they have to honor the memory of those who suffered there. To do less would reduce the humanity of those who survived.

But is the *attachment* to that memory reducing the spirituality of those who survived? Is the hatred expressed in "We shall never forget" such an *attachment* that it interferes with the relationship with God on the part of those who practice it? Is the world's *attachment* to the hatred for Hitler something which it can no longer afford? Is the personal *attachment* to any unacceptable activity generating health problems on the human level and preventing a closer personal relationship with God on the nonhuman level? Does such an *attachment* make us repeat and repeat the activity until we finally learn how to detach and to forgive? In asking these questions, I am not making judgments—merely asking the questions.

In the search for Unconditional Love, an attachment to an unacceptable activity will eventually became a condition for love; for the attachment will become a judgment against another. In my opinion, it is impossible to practice Unconditional Love for another person when you have made a personal judgment against that other person. Only when an individual can become *detached* from an unacceptable activity of another can love be given without judgment, and without conditions being attached.

The same is true for the love of God. As mentioned in Chapter 5 of *Part Two*, an inordinate emotion for a material thing can interfere with a closer relationship with God. In the same way, an inordinate emotion for an unacceptable activity which will lead to an absence of love for the agent of that activity, can also interfere with a closer relationship with God. It makes no difference whether the emotion is love, or absence of love, or hate, or even something as "simple" as judgment. **These are blocking emotions in all cases.**

Having examined these issues about Unconditional Love, let us return to the second Cosmic Concept. As you remember, this Concept states that the one God practices *Unconditional Love* for all which S/He created, and requests that all of His/Her creatures and other creations also practice Unconditional Love. This concept is not practiced by any established religion; for the God each of them has defined does not promote the practice of Unconditional Love. In practice, the reward-punishment God of **Judaism** says that if you obey His commandments, then He will make of you a great nation. In practice, the reward-punishment God of **Christianity** says that if you believe in His Son, then you will not perish but will have everlasting life. In practice, the reward-punishment God of **Islam** says that if you accept that there is no other God and if you do good deeds, then you will be in paradise. Each religion will also say that if you do not do these things, then dire things will happen to you.

It seems to me that God could get awfully confused about the conditions that the leaders of the established religions have put on His/Her love. As a few examples, can't you just hear God saying, "Now let me see—do I love that person or do I hate him if he goes into the Holy of Holies?"; or "Do I love the sin and hate the sinner or is it the other way around?"; or "Am I supposed to love him if he kills an unbeliever or do I hate him for committing murder?"

How simple it would be if God were to love us unconditionally. How difficult it would be for us to follow His/Her example. It is easy for us to follow rules and regulations. That is why the established religions produce so many of them. But it is very difficult for us to live as I believe God lives—in an all-encompassing love which is unconditional. Although a completely acceptable definition of Unconditional Love might help, as the issues presented above may indicate, it may be that such a definition is simply beyond our human capability.

Three Guiding Principles of Unconditional Love

Although an acceptable definition for Unconditional Love may be beyond us, it may be possible to develop some guiding principles which might help. The first such principle may be illustrated by imagining a stone which is tossed into a quiet pond such that it makes a ripple which proceeds until it caresses the shore. The stone expects nothing in return for that act, for the ripples are generated freely and without expectation of a reward in return. Such is the first principle of Unconditional Love. It is given freely without expectation of reward. It is the act of one human trying to emulate God's greatest gift of love, a gift which is given freely without expectation of a reward, but possibly with the hope that it will be imitated.

That leads to the second principle of Unconditional Love. Eventually, Unconditional Love, freely given, is returned by imitation. You cannot, throughout eternity, continue to hate one who constantly gives you love freely and without conditions. It is not possible. And so, eventually the Unconditional Love started by one human becomes *mutual* Unconditional Love, for more than one human is involved.

That leads to the third principle of Unconditional Love. Eventually, the Unconditional Love started by one person becomes universal; for the one has become two; the two have become four; the four have become eight; the eight have become sixteen; and on and on until the universe is involved. This may take a while, but it is possible within eternity. And it only needs *one* to start.

The end result of these three guiding principles is Universal, Mutual, Unconditional Love. Oh I know—there could possibly be atrocities along the way which will wipe out the present incarnations of all who practice Unconditional Love; but those souls will return, and eventually, they will win out. Darkness cannot survive the light; and hate cannot outlast love. Within God's eternity, neither Darkness nor Hate is possible.

SUMMARY AND CONCLUSIONS

In this chapter, we have looked at the religions whose original teachers taught the practice of Unconditional Love. There were only two: Christianity and Mohism. Only one of those religions survives today: Christianity. The other ceased to exist, possibly because human nature was not ready at that time to accept the concept of Unconditional Love. But the surviving religion whose original teachings were based on Unconditional Love no longer practices those teachings. Instead, the Church has placed conditions on its love, possibly because it had to do so in order to survive.

In addition, in this chapter we have examined some of the human issues which may restrict the practice of Unconditional Love. One of these issues may be the lack of truly understanding Unconditional Love in human terms. However, it is possible that the three guiding principles might help.

Both of these examinations were made in an attempt to examine the Second Cosmic Concept. As a conclusion to these examinations of the second Cosmic Concept, I will generate one premise and then ask one question.

The premise is:

It is possible to have a world which has no laws if the people of that world were to practice Universal, Mutual, Unconditional Love.

The question is:

If you can accept that premise, and if you can imagine the heaven which such a world would be,

then are you the one who starts it?

A Hymn for the Second Reformation

If the Christian Church could possibly return to its roots by practicing the Unconditional Love originally taught, then a number of new hymns would be needed. Although I have always loved the melody and the beat of "Onward Christian Soldiers," I have never liked the words of that hymn. Some more appropriate words for the Second Reformation are suggested below. They are offered solely in a sense of sharing.

Onward Those Who Love the Christ

Onward those who love the Christ, Now love all you see
Give love to your neighbors, In peace let them be
We are stepping forward, To a love so fine
That we will become the Christ
And with his heart entwine

Chorus: Onward those who love the Christ
Now love all you see
Always love your neighbor
Live in harmony

Love that's Unconditional, Is our solemn vow
Christ said, "Love your neighbor," Why not do it now
Love that's freely given, Is a goal that's good
Let us try to be a part
Of holy brotherhood

Chorus: [Repeat from above]

Christ accepted all who came, With him so can we
All the world's our brother, If it just could be
We will be united, Loving God within
For accepting all who come
Is surely not a sin

Chorus: [Repeat from above]

CHAPTER THREE
THE THIRD COSMIC CONCEPT: ONENESS WITH GOD VIA FREE WILL

The third Cosmic Concept states that it is the Supreme Will that all of God's creations find their way into *oneness* with Him/Her by their own *Free Will*, even though such an effort might take an eternity. There are two basic elements to this Cosmic Concept. The first is that it is God's will that all find their way into *oneness* with Him/Her; and the second is that we do this by our own *Free Will*. The third element which is implicit is that because of human nature, it could take most of us quite a long time before this will happen.

ONENESS WITH GOD

In the religious world of today, there are three major approaches which try to define our association with God. The first approach teaches that certain selected ones must find their way into the presence of God *for the first time,* because some ancestor was once with God, but that ancestor did something which caused him and his descendents to separate from God's presence. The descendents are still separated. This is the story which is presented in the Old Testament as the story of Adam and Eve and the Fall. It is the approach proposed by Judaism, Christianity and Islam. In today's Christianity, the reason for the Fall is defined as "Original Sin."

The second approach teaches that <u>all</u> of us were with God in the beginning, but that we left of our own Free Will in order to evolve through experience; and that through these experiences, we are finding the way to *return* into oneness with Him/Her. By "all of us," this approach does not mean merely the humans who have a consciousness which knows that there is a "God." Instead, it includes all the animals, all the plants, all the rocks, and all the other creations consciousness that there is a God.

In addition to those creations with which we are familiar because we can see them, this approach includes all of those creations of God which are not in three-dimensional form; both those who have not, as yet, experienced three-dimensionality and those who have, but have gone on. Parts of this approach represent the belief system of the more mystical religions such as Hinduism, Cabalistic Judaism and Sufism. The totality of this approach represents the belief system of some of those who are searching for a new and expanded paradigm of beliefs, such as those of the New Pilgrimage [see page 239].

There is a third approach which is accepted by some who belong to the new paradigm belief system. It teaches that all of these entities were with God in the beginning, *and still are*. In this teaching, there is the belief that since God is the ALL, and since all creations are a part of the ALL, then nothing has ever left God on a long-term basis, but has merely take short-term sojourns to gain experience for evolutionary development via transformational events, many of which are merely illusions. This approach fits into the phrase which my good friend Father John W. Groff, Jr. has often written. That phrase says, *"The Journey is one from a place which we never left to a place we have ever been."*

Most belief systems which teach the *return* to oneness with God [i.e. the second approach] believe that this teaching is justified because human beings are an emanation of God. This belief is contrary to the present teachings of many established religions, especially Christianity which teaches in no uncertain terms that we are created by God, and that we contain no emanation from Him.

However, within the Judeo-Christian heritage, this was not

always the case. At the time of Jesus, Judaism believed that an emanation of God existed in all people. As Susan Haskins says in her book *Mary Magdalen: Myth and Metaphor*:

"About two hundred years before the birth of Christ, the rabbis made a significant change in the teachings of Judaism. The early Hebrews had blamed themselves, and only themselves, for any woes which befell them. However, the change was made to attribute to God the source of the <u>Yecer</u>, which they believed was implanted in the "heart' or the "consciousness" of each individual either at his birth or at his conception. The Yecer was therefore not hereditary as the Christians, particularly Augustine, later proposed. As a creation of God, the Yecer was intrinsically good, and it was a source of creative energy; for it had been a part of humankind from the very beginning. However, because it involved appetites, the Yecer could be carried to excess and it therefore had a strong potential for evil, particularly where sexual matters, man's relationship with God, or man's relationships with his fellow man were concerned. It was believed that only by the <u>Law</u> could these strong appetites be curbed."

This understanding of this change in Judaism is important for two major reasons. The first reason is that this change implies that the *Yecer*, [i.e. a "spark" of God] was implanted in every creature as an emanation of God, a theme which was repeated by the Christian Mystic, Meister Eckhart, some 1400 years later. He had a large following, so the Church decided not to oppose him during his lifetime. However, some four days after his death, the Church condemned all of his teachings. The second reason is that the appetites of the human side of this "spark" could be controlled by the <u>Law</u>. As previously described, Jesus Christ replaced the Law with Love. He therefore suggested that any excesses of our humanity could be healed and balanced by Love.

Another point about the *Yecer* which was not important to the Judaism of that day but which is vitally important to us today, is that since this spark of God was not hereditary, then there was absolutely no belief in "original sin" in Judaism at the time of Christ. Original sin is, of course, one of the major teachings which was subsequently developed by the Christian Church. This happened despite the fact that in the entire New Testament, only Paul makes any reference whatsoever to "original sin" being the reason for the "Fall." He does this as a minor point in I Corinthians 15:22. In other words, Jesus never mentions it, and neither do the Apostles who knew him or the Gospel writers who wrote about him.

In the fourth century CE, Augustine leaped on Paul's minor point to make an entire case. Augustine taught that because of our sexual appetites, if humankind were to use its Free Will it would give in to sex at every opportunity and thus forsake God. Further, Augustine said that because of original sin, humankind had not only given up its Free Will, it had given up its position at the right hand of God. In fact, the doctrines of Christianity teach that *only* Jesus Christ was at the right hand of God in the beginning, and that *only* Jesus Christ was emanated from God rather than being created by the Creator from *nothing* as everything else was. This is quite a change from the teachings of Judaism at the time of Jesus. These teachings proclaimed that humans were created from *something* which was used as a part of them. This was the *Yecer*, or an emanation of God. Since these teachings of Judaism were not changed by Jesus, it could be argued that he subscribed to them.

As a result of the concept of original sin, which was not a part of the early Judeo-Christian heritage, the Church makes quite a case for their belief that *only* Jesus Christ would *return* to God, and that the rest of us would get there for the first time. The doctrines which teach this were developed by the early Church Fathers, and not by God and not by the Christ. These activities of the early Church Fathers were addressed in depth in *The Christian Conspiracy*.

As previously mentioned, the second approach proposes that we will *return* to God after having been "away" for a long time. The third approach does not subscribe to the concept of a "return to God," for this approach expresses the thought that we have never left. This approach proposes that since God is the ALL, and since we exist within the ALL of God, then we have never really left Him/Her, but merely have taken a sojourn in order to generate some experiences not available within the all-encompassing, Unconditional Love of God. Examples of such experiences might be the emotion of hating something, or the despair of having nothing, or the trauma of being murdered and dying. This third approach will often suggest that these experiences are illusionary rather than being reality.

I fully understand this approach and accept that it could be valid. However, to me the effect of either of these two approaches on our present personality would be the same. In the case of a long-term return to God [i.e. the second approach], we would want to have our experiences and feel our emotions while still trying to be like God, even though we are in an atmosphere which is very unlike God; and the same would be true in the case of the short sojourn [i.e. the third approach]. In other words, if you accept the concept that we are to *return* to God, then as far as this present personality is concerned, you would act the same whether you had been away from Him/Her for a long time and therefore needed to *return*; or had really never left except for a short, experiential sojourn. It seems to me that even if you accept the belief that you are coming into the presence of God for *the first time* [i.e. the first approach], then you should want to act the same way. You would want to express a God-like activity. In my opinion, the God-like activity which you would want to express would be the practice of Unconditional Love.

Even though the *return* to God is not presently supported by the major Western religions, spending an eternity in the presence of God is. In particular, the reward-punishment religions of the Western world such as Judaism, Christianity and Islam grant such a promise. Some elements of Judaism go further in their belief system in that they believe that the family unit and other such family relationships will be continued throughout eternity. In this belief, they are echoing the sentiments of the Essenes of 2,000 years ago, and the sentiments of today's Mormons.

Christianity's promise of being with God, is justified by the teachings of Jesus when he said: *In my Father's house are many rooms...I go and prepare a place for you...that where I am you may be also* [John 14:2-3]. It is probable that if it were not for this promise, Christianity would not have survived; for the early Christians needed to believe in the promise that their miserable Earthly life would improve when they came into the presence of God.

Islam promises a similar experience of eternity, for in the Koran it is said:

"therefore strive with one another to hasten to virtuous deeds; to Allah is your return, of all of you; and ...you are mortals from among those

whom He has created...and Allah's is the kingdom of the heavens and the earth and what is between them, and to Him is the eventual coming."

It should be noted that since those who follow Allah are created rather than having an emanation from God as a part of them, then the word "return" in the quotation from the Koran is not the same meaning of the word "return" which was presented earlier in this section.

Although the Eastern religions place less emphasis on the existence of an identified God with whom one would spend eternity, it seems to me that being in the oneness which is represented by *Nirvana* presents a similar concept to that of being with God for eternity. In my opinion, this description of *Nirvana* not only is a better description of heaven than anything the Christian Church has ever offered me, it also can be achieved without subscribing to any belief in "original sin."

In respect to finding our way into oneness with God, the existing belief systems have suggested at least three major ways in which that oneness can approached: either as a *first time experience*; or as a return from a *long-term separation*; or as a return from a *short trip*. It is up to the reader to decide which approach is the one to be experienced on his/her unique and individual pathway into that oneness.

FREE WILL

Free Will is arguably the most controversial subject in the characterization of the human species. Some may belittle its importance, but I believe it is of prime importance in understanding the relationship between human and God. As evidence of my belief, there are more references to Free Will in the Index of *The Christian Conspiracy* than any other subject except Excommunication. Excommunication is the Church's punishment to an individual for his/her exercise of Free Will. I included this subject so often because I feel that the attack on Free Will by the Christian Church, particularly by Augustine, represents one of the major alterations which the Church made on the teachings of the Christ.

In most of this book, I have implied that only the human species recognizes the existence of a God who is transcendent [i.e.

preeminent]. Others disagree with that viewpoint and suggest that other species recognize such a God. They will often mention the dolphins or the whales as an example.

As evidence for the existence of God in their lives, the human species will often point to the stability of the family unit, to the orderliness of their society, and to their desire to exist peacefully with their neighbors. Those who support the dolphins and/or whales can easily counter that argument with evidence that these species practice those three elements at least as well as the human species does. Furthermore, if the premise of this book is correct in stating that God is encompassed in Unconditional Love for all, then the competitive, combative human species has to take a second seat to the love expressed by the dolphins not only for their own species, but for other species as well.

In other words, there is evidence that we are not alone in our world in living our lives in a way which might recognize that there is a God.

However, I would contend that the greatest gift of love given to the human species by God was not given to other species, much as S/He loves them. That is the gift of individualized Free Will. The Free Will which I am describing here is not related to a level of intelligence, or to the practice of making mundane choices such as a sheep makes when it decides to eat a certain tuft of grass rather than a leafy bush. I am describing a Free Will which gives us the chance to recognize God's will for our lives, and allows us to freely *choose* to exercise that will as a gift of love and not as a response to fear or to the urging of others. I am describing the ability to make our movement toward God by our choice based on love rather than from fear or in hopes of receiving a reward. Finally, I am describing a Free Will which makes us totally responsible for the results of our own, individual choice of activities. Our responsibility is to God, and to no other leader or institution.

Although some may disagree, I believe that this kind of Free Will may be the only characteristic which makes the human species a unique species on this Earth; and that Earth may be one of the few places in this universe where the experiment with this kind of Free Will is being conducted. Those who teach the existence of other species in other dimensions within our universe will often state that our beautiful Earth is unique within the entire universe in the amount of Free Will given to its inhabitants. They will state that there is more Free Will here, than anyplace else. If that is so, then it is truly a magnificent gift we have been given.

Many of the established religions have not recognized Free Will as a gift, but have taught that it is a human characteristic which must be controlled. Although many examples could be cited which support this viewpoint, and indeed many examples about Christianity were cited in *The Christian Conspiracy*, only two general examples will be mentioned here.

The first is **Islam**, for the very name of the religion means "submission," and the first step in becoming a practicing Muslim is to give total submission to the will of God. If this were to be done as an individualized, loving gift to God, it would represent the type of Free Will described as a magnificent gift in the preceding paragraph. However, the practice of submitting to God often represents coercion on the part of the religious society rather than an individual gift of love. In this way, the applicant has given his Free Will to the religion rather than to a personal movement toward coming into oneness with God. Although the distinction between these approaches may seem to be a minor one, I feel that it is an important one in developing a personal pathway into oneness with God.

Christianity has been the most zealous in its attacks against Free Will, and has continued those attacks throughout its existence. A prime example occurred in the fourth century, when the Church had a conflict with a movement known as "Pelagianism" [see *The Christian Conspiracy*]. As a summary, Pelagius was possibly one of the most moral Christians of his time. He came from Britain to Rome and immediately came to abhor the spiritual sloth and moral laxity of the Roman Christians. He blamed this moral decay on the doctrine of divine grace presented in the *Confessions* of Augustine. In this doctrine, Augustine beseeched God to grant whatever grace His will would allow. Pelagius felt that such an entreaty would lead people to believe that any transgression could be forgiven merely by asking God or the Church to do so. He felt that such a belief would imperil the entire structure of moral law.

Pelagius soon had a large following who believed that <u>all</u> of the commandments should be strictly obeyed. This movement not only proposed a strong moral position, they also proposed that man has the Free Will to choose whether or not he wanted to live this strongly moral life as a Christian devoted to God, and as one who could freely choose to accept God's grace. Augustine and many other early Church Fathers opposed Pelagianism by arguing that man gave up his Free Will when he fell from grace as a result of the original sin. They proposed that man had no say in whether or not he receives God's grace, but that he must, if necessary, be <u>forced</u> to believe that through the Church, and only through the Church, one could receive such a redeeming gift from God.

They won the debate. Pelagius and his followers were excommunicated; and the Church started into a long-lasting campaign to <u>force</u> others to accept the Church as the sole site in which God's grace could be found. This differed from the exercise of an individualized Free Will which would allow the individual to *choose* to accept God and to be responsible for this choice only to God.

Activities which would force compliance to these Augustinian teachings were common in the early Catholic Church, and many devout people were excommunicated for deviations which would be considered minor today. Such activities were not limited to the Catholic Church. In the sixteenth century, the early Protestant leader, John Calvin, was very adamant against the belief in Free Will and had the Swiss state exile those who chose Free Will over predestination. In addition, Calvin indirectly caused the burning at the stake of John Legate and Edward Wightman in England, not only because they preached against the Trinity, but also because they proposed Free Will instead of predestination.

The major point about Free Will is a subtle one; but in my mind it is of prime importance for exploring a pathway into oneness with God. The question is this: do you become one who submits to God's will by coercion; or do you become one whose will coincides with God's will by a Free Will gift of love?

If you <u>submit</u> to God's will because of coercion by society or loved ones, or if you accept God's will because you want a reward or you fear what will happen if you do not accept His/Her will, then you have learned something about God; but you may have learned this through the coercion which made you submit. Consequently, I would suggest that you may not have learned as much about God as you might have thought.

However, if you make the Free Will choice to live a life such that your will and God's will *coincide* at all times through Unconditional Love, then you have learned much more about God, for you have imitated His/Her actions. It seems to me that if God gives us Unconditional Love, then to imitate Him/Her, we must return that love without any conditions being attached.

I am trying to say that there is a difference between doing God's will by submitting to it, and doing God's will because it has become the same as yours via Free Will choice. In the first case, you could alter your pathway to God whenever there was a change in society, or loved ones, or anyone else who pressured you to submit to God; or you could alter your pathway if the rewards you expected from this submission were not received as soon as you might have liked. In the second case, the Way you walk the personal pathway into oneness with God has become synonymous with the Way S/He walks, and therefore cannot be changed.

Although some may think I am inflating a minor difference here, I feel it is a difference of major importance.

COMMENTARY AND CONCLUSION

It is my opinion that to be on the pathway to oneness with God, first you use love to exercise your Free Will choice to be on that pathway; and then you continue on that pathway by learning what God's will is for you and by exercising your Free Will choice to accept that will until it becomes your own will in all instances. Then, and only then in my opinion, you will be on the pathway for *oneness* with God. It might take an eternity of love to have your will coincide with God's will in all instances; but I believe it is well worth the effort; for

**what better way could there be
to spend a fruitful eternity?**

CHAPTER FOUR
THE FOURTH COSMIC CONCEPT: THE UNIQUE PATHWAY

The fourth Cosmic Concept states that the pathway which each creation uses to come into oneness with God, is a *unique* pathway unlike that developed for any other act of creation. This is a concept which is very difficult for the established religions to accept, for it states that each who has been "created in the image of God" is a <u>unique</u> individual; and as such must find a way into oneness with God which differs from that found by any other unique creation of God. No major established religion in the world teaches that; for most teach that there is only *one* way to God—the way which is taught in that particular religion. Even the individual nature of Buddhism has been institutionalized to the extent that the Eightfold path is *the* way to go.

But one's relationship with God is not a mass-produced product. It is not the same for everyone. Instead, the relationship is an individualized one. As was mentioned in the preceding chapter, arguably the greatest gift given by God to those "created in His image" was the gift of *individualized* Free Will. The Free Will portion of this gift was addressed in the preceding chapter. The individualized part of that gift will be addressed in this chapter.

Have you ever heard the advice which states that you should not criticize a person until you have walked a mile in his/her shoes? What that means is that until you have lived *exactly* as another has, then you cannot know exactly what that person has been through. Consequently, how can you criticize him/her? Despite the fact that we are not talking about criticism here, exactly the same principle is involved. If you are not exactly like another person, then how can you have exactly the same personal pathway into oneness with God?

The comparison with the "criticism example" falls somewhat short of what we are really talking about here, for that example applies only to the present life. Of even a greater import is the past.

An illustration might possibly help. I believe that in the beginning, you were created [or possibly emanated] as an individualized soul, different from any other soul which has ever existed. For sake of illustration, let us forget that belief and assume that you were not created as a unique soul, but were identical to 1,000 others. Then you started to experience. I would suggest that the experiences you had in your first life were different than the experience of any other soul who started out identical with you; but for sake of illustration, let us assume that you and 500 of those 1,000 identical souls had exactly the same experiences. An impossibility you say? Of course it is, for to repeat Heracleitus [see page 19], *"All is flow and it is impossible to step into the same river twice."*

However, let us assume that it happened. If it did, then you and half of those 1,000 identical souls were identical after one lifetime. Let us follow that with another incarnation, and again assume that your experiences were exactly identical to half of those who started out identical with you. You are now, after just two lifetimes, identical with only one-fourth of those who started out exactly identical with you. After three lifetimes there would only be one-eighth; then after another lifetime there would be only one-sixteenth or slightly over 6%.

To condense this narrative, if you started out with 1,000 identical souls, and if you had exactly identical experiences with half of those identical souls in a number of consecutive lifetimes, then after only ten lifetimes, less than one person would be identical with you. Since it is difficult to be less than one person, that would mean that no one would be identical with you after only ten lifetimes, even though there were 1,000 souls exactly like you in the beginning.

What we have done in this illustration is to create two

impossible situations. The first impossible situation was that 1,000 carbon copies of your soul were made in the beginning. Then we added the impossible situation that any two souls would have exactly identical experiences in any one lifetime. We made that impossible situation absurd by stating that half of the identical population would again have identical experiences. Even with all this impossibility, after a mere ten lifetimes, no two individuals would be identical. Compound this with the probability that all of us have been involved with literally thousands of incarnations, and you can see the virtual impossibility of any two people being exactly identical.

If no two people are identical in their source and past experiences, then how can literally thousands of people find an identical personal pathway into oneness with God? For even two people to have an identical pathway would require that each had made exactly the same decision each time that a fork would come in their pathway. Like everyone else, there have been many forks along my eternal pathway, possibly millions of them. Each time a decision as to whether to follow my will or God's will for my life was made, that was a fork in my pathway. At each fork, I chose one way or the other. In just this one lifetime with which I am presently so very familiar, I have made thousands of such decisions. It is quite likely that everyone else has made a like number of decisions. When this is taken into perspective, can anyone's pathway be identical to another's?

Yet, the established religions would have us believe that there is only *one* way to find God—the way which they share with you. If anything I have said in the paragraphs above has made sense, then trying to fit everyone onto one pathway is an absurd absurdity. However, as I have previously said and as I will emphasize in the next chapter, time spent in the institution of an established religion is time well spent.

What I believe is involved here is that the institutions such as Christianity, Judaism, Islam, Mormonism, or others, have gathered evidence which says that those who have followed certain steps have found their way to God. Those steps have become recorded for the use of others. Although I do not intend to establish a religion, that is exactly what I am doing in this book. I am putting down ideas or concepts which I believe have helped me to define, for myself, a personal pathway into oneness with God. Much of that pathway was defined from lessons which I accepted while I was within the institution of the established religion of my roots—Christianity. As one example, if I had not learned of the teaching of Unconditional Love by Jesus the Christ, do you think I would have put so much emphasis on it in this book? But the recording of steps which have helped some, soon creates a problem; for those who have recorded these steps have said to themselves, "Well, if I helped those people, then this must be the kind of help which all people need." From that, it is but a short step to the concept that, "This is the *only* way to do it." And from there, it is even a shorter step to, "I will *reject* anyone who does not take exactly these steps."

That has been the sequence which all Western religions have followed. It has led to each one feeling that it has the *only* recipe for finding God. The Eastern religions have been more tolerant, or possibly have had less of a drive to define a recipe for finding God. However, although they have avoided making the intolerant directives made by the Western religions, even the Eastern religions have tried to make strong recommendations for their method to find the Way. There is nothing wrong with making recommendations. Everyone needs help from time to time. However, the threat that if you do not do it a certain way then you will be punished forever, is not the way to make a recommendation. Instead, that is the way to coerce or to control another. It has represented the practice of many of the established religions.

Personally, I am not against the institution of an established religion. I stayed within the shelter and under the restrictive thinking of the religion of my roots for over fifty years. I learned a lot, not only about what I presently accept, but about what I presently reject.

However, in the time since I left that shelter, I have come much closer to a personal God, and much closer to a personal relationship with the Christ who reflects that God to me, than I ever could have achieved while under the sheltered restrictions of the Church. Although I believe it is highly likely that the progress made in the past few years would not have happened without having spent the previous fifty years within the Church, I also believe that it was time for me to leave. I believe that at some point in eternity, each person will arrive at similar decision for the institutionalized religion of his/her choice; for at some point, a unique and individual pathway must be experienced.

The reason for that is rather obvious to me now, although I did not really see it when I was inside the Church. The reason is that I am an *individualized* soul, and not an institutionalized one. I am a solitary figure on the way into oneness with God, and not the member of an army.

When I was much younger, I had to draw on all the love I was given by my family before I could develop the courage to leave that sheltered nest and to step forward to make a living on my own. In the more recent stages of my life, I have had to draw on all the love I was given by the church of my roots before I could develop the courage to leave it and to step forward to find my *individualized* pathway into oneness with God.

There is an additional story which justifies leaving the sheltered confines of the institutionalized Church in order to find your own way. I will present it with the faith that those who can relate to it will accept it; and those who can't relate to it will simply forget that it ever was mentioned. The story is as follows:

Lewis Grizzard was a southern humorist, author and columnist. Although some did not think much of him, others loved him and his work dearly. He died during 1994. In early September of that year, my wife had a meditation in which Lewis Grizzard appeared. He told her that there is much more here [i.e. on the other side] than he ever realized. He showed her a hall which had a series of doors. Each door led into a room. On each door was the name of a religion, e.g. Christianity, Islam, Buddhism, etc. When he would open the door to any room and look in, there would be a wall which indicated that after going only a short distance, you could go no farther. However, when he ascended a stairway at the end of the hallway so that he could look down at each room because none had a ceiling, he could see that there was a lot of space on the other side of the wall.

In other words, there is more to the universe of God then any religion is letting you see from the inside. The only way to see what else is there, is to jump over the wall and reach the outer side. That wall has been placed there by every religion which has asked you to restrict your thoughts in order to accept only that which has been preached from their pulpit, or taught from their lectern.

Don't let anyone or any religion tell you that there is *only one* way to reach God and that they *know exactly* what it is. Part of the reason we are on the journey we are on, is so that we can develop for ourselves just what the final steps of that journey will look like. Draw on everything that anyone wishes to teach you about those who have trod the pathway before you; but don't try to walk in exactly their footsteps. It won't work. You are <u>different</u> than they, and so is your pathway.

The next chapter will make some generalized guidelines about certain milestones or turning points which may be on a personal pathway into oneness with God. They may give you some insight; but remember that even if these milestones are on your pathway, how you get to those milestones and what you do after you leave each of those milestones will be different for you; because you are <u>unique</u>. God threw away the mold when S/He made you; and with the help of Spirit working with soul, the experiences since that beginning have also been different for you than for anyone else, because

***you are unique; you are loved;
and you are of God!***

CHAPTER 5
PERSONAL PATHWAYS

The purpose of Chapter 5 is to indicate how a personal pathway into oneness with God might be experienced by defining various milestones along that pathway. Those milestones are defined by the things we have decided to leave behind. The abandoned things are those which we once worshipped, but which we have decided are no longer worthy of receiving our reverent love and adoration.

In order to understand this concept, there must be a distinction made between love and worship. The word "worship" means *"the reverent love and allegiance accorded to a deity, idol or sacred object."* Reverent love means a love which shows a feeling of *"profound awe and respect."* Deity means *"a God or a divine one."* Sacred means *"that which has been set apart or made holy."* Holy means *"that which is worthy of receiving high esteem or being revered."* Consequently, **worship** is more than just love. It is the adoration of that which has been ***set apart as being worthy of receiving both profound awe and respect.***

In this sense, I can love and even adore my wife, my children or my grandchildren; but I cannot worship them. In the literal meaning of the word "worship," they cannot be worshipped; for they have not been set aside as being worthy of profound awe or respect. I can wonder at the miracle that my wife loves me, or I can stand back in true awe at the miracle that a beautiful, living grandchild has just been born to a daughter who unfortunately had so many still-births; but neither of these miracles gives me the right or even the privilege of holding either my wife or this daughter in awe. If I hold either of them in awe as an person, I soon will be hit with the fact that I have created a "god who has clay feet." This fact would not diminish my love for either of them; but it also would not permit me to worship either of them.

There is a difference between love and worship. We can have love without worship. It is difficult, if not impossible, to worship without having love.

The basic premise of this chapter is that we worship various things along the pathway into oneness with God; and that it is only when we give up the worship of these things that we achieve progress along the Way. By giving up the worship of things along the way, we do not reject them.

As one example, we could worship property and then abandon that worship in order to make progress along the Way without necessarily renouncing or rejecting property. We would merely stop treating it with the awe which it previously demanded from us. I think the perfect example of this was given by Clement of Alexandria, an early Church Bishop who lived in about 200 CE. The poor of Alexandria demanded that he make the Christian rich sell what they had and give the proceeds to the poor. His response was that wealth was a neutral factor in that it could be used either to generate good or evil. He wrote: *The Word does not command us to renounce property but to manage property without inordinate affection.*

This quotation presents an important lesson for two reasons. First, it explains the Parable of the Talents which Jesus taught and which has been given to us in the 25th Chapter of Matthew. It fully explains the anger which Jesus expressed toward those who did not manage property properly. Secondly, it suggests that you can respect something without having an inordinate affection for it. As you abandon the milestone created by the worship of property as if it were your God, you can march on with respect for property and property rights without worshipping either one. The milestone of worshipping property is discussed more thoroughly in the next section.

In this chapter, several objects of worship will be presented and discussed; and then discarded for worship as progress is made on the pathway into oneness with God. As with the other parts of this book, these ideas are presented for consideration and not necessarily for acceptance unless the individual feels that such acceptance would help to make progress along the unique, individual pathway being experienced by him or her.

THE WORSHIP OF MATERIAL THINGS

Some years ago, I was standing at the front door of the headquarters building of the company I worked for. I was chatting with a young man, fresh out of college. I had just offered him a job, and he had accepted. Just then, the Chairman of the Board rode by in his brand new Lincoln, one of the most expensive and respected cars in the world of that time. The young man turned to me and said, "If he had a feather in his armpit and I had that car, we would both be tickled pink!" Whether he realized it or not, that young man had just told me what idol he worshipped. It was a car which was beyond his present ability to afford.

Shortly after that, I was traveling with my boss who was a Senior Vice President of the corporation. We sat in the First Class section of the airplane. It was nice. I then realized that at certain levels of the corporation, you did not have to travel in the back of the airplane. I wanted that privilege so much that I could taste it. It became my idol for worship. Less than a year later, I was granted that perk.

The point is that at certain times during our experiences on the pathway into oneness with God, material things can become such an overwhelming desire that we worship them as if they were our God. We express an inordinate affection for them. We want them so much that we would sacrifice anything to get them. This phenomenon of humanity is not restricted solely to physical things such as a Lincoln or First Class travel. It can apply to emotional things such as the love of another male or female; or the activities of a favorite sports team; or the sublime taste of special foods from many cultures; or even the judgmental evaluation of another's behavior.

As was mentioned in Chapter 2, attachment to the unacceptable behavior of another is a very prevalent idol worshipped by humankind. It is one of the idols which prevents the practice of Unconditional Love.

As prevalent as that example of worship is, there are other examples which could be used to describe the replacement of God by the worship of lesser idols. We simply replace God on our list of priorities with material things such as the ultimate job, house, car or person to love. Anyone who does not admit that this has happened is probably not willing to face that part of him/herself. It is an experience which almost all human beings have had.

There is another experience which many have had. It is the other side of this issue—the side of avoidance instead of having a full experience. Let me give an example. I know of several advocates of the New Age who are so into the spiritual side of things that they not only avoid the human side, they advocate such avoidance on the part of others. As an example, they disdain the thought of taking care of their financial needs in the belief that Spirit will provide all that they need, and they counsel others to do likewise. Although I am trying not to make a judgment here, it does seem to me that such a process not only starts to interfere in the life of another, something which the universal laws say we should not do, but it also neglects the fulfillment of the human side of the equation.

I know that some will think I am on shaky ground here, but I am going to state the belief that we are both divine and human. I know this goes beyond the teachings of many established religions; but it is my belief, nevertheless. When I was doing the needed research for *The Christian Conspiracy*, I was delighted to find that the Church had so overemphasized the divine nature of Jesus Christ during the first two Ecumenical Councils, that they had to hold the next two Councils in order to reestablish his humanity and bring his divine-human sides back into balance. It took four Ecumenical Councils to decide that Jesus was both divine and human.

In my opinion, each of us also is divine and human. We, like the Church of the first two Ecumenical Councils, can so emphasize our divinity that we forget our humanity. In our doing this, we can neglect the needs of our family, loved ones and society in general. In fact, we can so de-emphasize the responsibility to take care of our financial needs, that we start to let our lack of prosperity influence our spirituality. I have seen it happen.

It seems to me that we should handle our human needs in such a way that it does not inhibit our spiritualism and our spiritual growth; and that we should handle our spiritual needs in such a way that it does not inhibit our humanism and our growth as a responsible participant in humanity. In this way, we can have the balance which the Church found it needed for the Christ.

My belief is that material things are not bad so long as having them does not interfere with spiritual progress. I believe that Jesus was saying this when he said, *"Render, therefore to Caesar the things that are Caesar's, and to God the things that are God's."* [Matt. 22:21]. He was implying that the human things are to be devoted to the human activities; whereas the spiritual things are to be devoted to the spiritual activities. He further implied that you should not let either one become so dominate in your activities that you lose the balance between your divinity and your humanity. In this way, material things should not interfere with the divine needs, and spiritual things should not interfere with the material needs. Each should support rather than interfere with the other.

In this context, I have no problem with the person who has the desire to become president of General Motors or even of the United States so badly that he or she rejects everything in the worship and the pursuit of that goal. It is a typical activity of the three lower Chakras; for it presents the positive messages of a good self image and vitality, but also presents the negative messages of insecurity, greed and the desire to have and use power. Although I have no problem with such a desire, I <u>do</u> believe it is the worship of temporal things, and that it is a passing phase which must be left behind on the pathway into oneness with the eternal God, just as the insecurity associated with the first Chakra must be left behind.

I will also say that it is better to have gone through that phase and decided that the worship of God is preferable to the worship of material things, than to have been told by someone that you should avoid that phase and never experience it. Even after having passed through the experience of worshipping material things to the point of realizing that they are not where God is, having material things is not a prohibition of spirituality. It is not that you have it, it is how you got it and how you use it that really count; for if anyone is hurt along the way, it can become a less-than-spiritual experience and have the possibility of interfering with spiritual growth.

I know I have presented controversy in this section and possibly alienated some people; but if by doing so I have helped any person to generate thoughts which define their pathway, then the controversy has had meaning. Possibly another example would help. It is an experience which happened to another person, but I was closely involved.

During the 1970's, a close friend of mine was deservedly being groomed as a possible future president of our company. One of the characteristics of that company was that the leaders were all good golfers and did a lot of business while they entertained on the golf course. Neither my friend nor I were good golfers; for we each had large families of small children with whom we preferred to spend our free time. My friend worried that his lack of golfing skills would be held against him. At a company party one evening, his wife walked up to the president of the company and said, "Mr. ___, you want three things from my husband: [1] you want him to travel for the company; [2] you want him to play golf for the company; [3] and you want him to be married to me. Pick two!"

The pressure to play golf was immediately lessened. The man never became president, but he did become the number two man in that company. He not only received tremendous prosperity from that position, he also raised a fine family and remained married to that brave lady who had used her strength of character to express her feelings. In this case, the appeal of ambition was replaced by the appeal of family, and also of God; for I know him to be a man whose business success was achieved while hurting no other human.

One of the points in using this example is that you can become prosperous by treating your internal competition with respect, by winning out on talent, and by occasionally going against the tide of general opinion. It is not necessary to give up everything which is meaningful to you in the pursuit of business success, or in the pursuit of a goal which is so exclusive that it becomes an object of worship and adoration. As previously stated, it is not what you have which might be held against you in any cosmic evaluation.

Instead, it is how you got it, what you did with it, and whether you gave it inordinate affection or worshipped it to the extent that it interfered with your relationship with God.

We do worship material things. It is a very human reaction. Some have tried to propose that we avoid material things so that they do not become an object of worship. However, the worship of material things is an experience which <u>does</u> happen and which should <u>not</u> be denied; but it also should not represent the final stage. Many feel the desire for worldly goods and fame so strongly and with so much inordinate affection that they choose to repeat life after life seeking <u>only</u> those goals. As Jesus said,

"Therefore be not anxious saying, 'What shall we eat?' or 'What shall we drink?' or What shall we wear?' For the Gentiles seek all these things; and your heavenly Father knows that you need them all. But seek <u>first</u> his kingdom and his righteousness, and all these things <u>shall be yours as well.</u>" [Matt. 6:31-3, underlining is mine].

It almost seems that the ability to handle the human needs is a part of mastering the human side of the divine-human equation. I will fully admit that there is a milestone on my pathway into oneness with God which is labeled, "The Worship of Material Things." It is an experience which I have had, and which I believe has been put in the background. I believe it is a lesson for all to have and for all to learn. However, after having been learned, I believe it should be put in the past. When put in the past, it could possibly mark a milestone on each one's unique and individual pathway into oneness with God.

THE WORSHIP OF GOD AS DEFINED BY HUMANS

Although this thought may be a difficult one for many people to accept, it is my firm belief that all the Gods presented for worship by the established religions are Gods who have been defined by humans. This is not necessarily bad, for we are involved in human communication here; and anything which has been communicated from one human to another has had to be defined by the human doing the communicating.

Let me present an example. Let us suppose that a person walked up to you on the street and said, "The most important thing I can say to you is 'acanaxious,' " I would think that you would be a most unusual person if you did not immediately say something like, "What do you mean by that word?" In his or her next breath, the communicating human would then define what "acanaxious" meant. In this way, a human would have defined something which was unknown to you. In case you are wondering what "acanaxious" means, it doesn't mean anything. It is an artificial word used to make the point that words do not communicate understanding until they have been defined.

In the same way, a God who was unknown to you would have to be defined by a human for you to have any idea what was meant by the word, "God." Consequently, I would submit my belief that the Jehovah of the Old Testament was defined for us by humans; as was the Father of the New Testament; and the Allah of the Koran; and the other Gods of the other established religions. I will illustrate that belief with additional information in a later part of this section.

To develop the major point, I will now repeat a statement I have made many times in my life. That statement is, "I believe that the Holy Scripture presented in the Bible is the inspired word of God." I will also make a statement that I have never made before. That statement is, "I believe that the Holy Scripture presented in the Koran is the inspired word of God." And I could repeat, for the first time in my life, that statement about many works which are considered by a significant number of followers to be the inspired word of God; for if the words were not believed by the followers to be the inspired word of God, then there would be no followers. I believe that this is additional evidence that God has tried, in <u>many</u> ways, to present His/Her message to those whom S/He loves.

However, despite the inspiration given by God to the words originally used, I believe that all Holy Scripture of all religions has been so repeatedly translated, so repeatedly mis-translated, and so subject to the temporal interpretation of words whose meanings change with the times, that any literal use of Holy Scripture must be accepted as being an interpretation of the words of a human being. Because of this, I believe that any human who worships the God presented by any established religion, is worshipping a God who has been defined by humans, even if that God is thoroughly defined in the existing Holy Scripture. I believe that worship of a God defined by humans will continue until God becomes personally experienced through definition by Spirit as described in the next section.

I once belonged to an established religion whose God was defined by humans, and I found nothing wrong with that experience. I also found nothing wrong with having worked very hard to see that the message of that established religion was heard by as many people as possible. As those who have read the previous books in this series may recall, I was raised in a Christian home. I was baptized in a Baptist Church, albeit one which was somewhat more liberal than the churches of the Religious Right which exist today. As a youth, I was active in Church activities. During my late high school and early university years, I toured small rural churches with a gospel quartet. In my later college years, I transferred to the Presbyterian Church, possibly because I found more intellectual stimulation there, or possibly because my Scottish ancestry was starting to assert itself. After receiving my BS degree, I seriously considered entering a leading Presbyterian Seminary, but the US Army got to me before I could make that happen. I first met my wife at a Youth for Christ meeting; and I have taught adult Sunday School in various Presbyterian and Congregational Churches for almost twenty years.

As the reader can readily see, there is much in my background which is normal, conventional, orthodox Christianity. But I have left the Church. As I mentioned in *The Christian Conspiracy*, one of my reasons for leaving was because I became intolerant of the intolerance I found within orthodox Christianity. Despite my having left the Church, any time I walk through the sanctuary of a Christian Church I still feel the comfort of the God who is there. Then I am given a strong message that I must move on.

Even though I have moved on from orthodox Christianity, I have never regretted the time spent in that established religion. When I was there, I learned about the God who was defined by humans. In many ways, my odyssey reminds me of a similar journey taken by John Hick who left the fundamentalism of his youth to became one of the leaders in the modern liberal Christian movement. Professor Hick said that fundamentalism had been a wonderful place to spend his youth because it taught him about God and kept him off the streets.

He then said that despite its charm to the teenager, no one should spend their adulthood there. This was the liberal-Christian side of him speaking out.

The point is that it is not a waste of time to use a part of a lifetime, even a major part of a lifetime, being a part of an established religion. There is much to be learned there; and if anyone wants to have a life of continuing spiritual development, it is preferable that the beginnings of that life be spent within an established religion rather than on the street.

Within the established religions, we do worship Gods who have been defined by humans. In doing so, we are responding to a normal third Chakra message with its positive aspects of peace and emotional rest; but also with its negative message of an emotional, attached love so powerful that it can lead to the control of the ones being loved. In addition, the Gods defined by humans respond to the normal fifth Chakra messages; both the positive message of logic and reason as well as the negative message of being so prejudiced as to see only one viewpoint, such as, "I follow the *only* true God." All of these aspects of both chakras are present in the Gods who have been defined by humans.

Is it correct to state that the Gods of the established religions have been defined, maybe even invented, by humans? Let us examine that hypothesis by looking at the God of Abraham who has been accepted as the God of Judaism, Christianity and Islam.

The first step in defining something is to give it a name. We do this not only for personal identification, but also so that we can communicate to another human being what we are talking about without having to go through the definition every time. Let us suppose that we had not given the name "car" to an object which most of us can identify. If it had no name, then we would probably have to say to our neighbor, "Oh, I see that you have a new metallic enclosed space for people with seats and a steering wheel on the inside and with four wheels, an engine and a transmission on the outside. It surely is nice." That would be kind of silly, wouldn't it? Consequently, we name things so that we can say, "Oh, I see that you have a new car. It surely is nice."

In the same way, we have given God a name, not only for

identification, but also so that we can sense the vibrational sound of His/Her name. The God of the Judeo-Christian heritage was given His names in the Old Testament of our Bible. It was a very tortured process. A large section on this subject was presented in *Christianity and the New Age Religion*. Only a portion of that will be repeated here.

The name given to God in the Old Testament depends on which Bible is being used. The Revised Standard Version [RSV] of the Bible, first authorized in 1870 and constantly revised as the meaning of words change, uses only three words for God. They are: *God, Lord*, and occasionally, *Lord God*. This differs form the King James Version [KJV] of the Bible, first translated from Latin [not from the original Greek or Hebrew] in 1611, and still the favorite of many Christians. The KJV uses many more names for God. In addition to Lord or God, the KJV uses names such as: *Elohim, ha-Elohim, Jehovah [or Yahweh], Jehovah-Elohim, El Shaddai* and others. In this manner, whereas the RSV has simplified the names of God in order to emphasize monotheism [i.e. the belief in only one God], the KJV has followed the Hebrew texts more closely; for Judaism had many names for God.

As an example of how the same text of Holy Scripture might look in this tortured process of giving a name to the Ultimate Source, let us look at Exodus 6:2-3 as presented in the RSV and as presented with the English versions of the names from the Hebrew text. The RSV would say:

"...And God said to Moses, 'I am the Lord. I appeared to Abraham, to Isaac, and to Jacob, as God Almighty, but by my name the Lord I did not make myself known to them.'"

The use of the appropriate Hebrew names in the same text would read:

"...And Elohim spake unto Moses and said unto him, 'I am Jehovah; and I appeared unto Abraham, unto Isaac, and unto Joseph as El Shaddai; but by my name Jehovah, I was not known to them.'"

The simplified words of the RSV do communicate, but some of the flavor seems to have been lost in the process of simplification.

There is something else to discuss in this presentation of how humans have defined the Gods. That is the fact that in its early days,

Judaism was not necessarily monotheistic. Even later, they were monotheistic only in that they proclaimed Yahweh [or Jehovah] as the one god who counts for Israel, and as they equally proclaimed the passionate rejection of all other gods for Israel.

By real definitions, this is not necessarily the practice of monotheism [i.e. there is only one God]; but is more nearly the practice of monolatry [i.e. the acceptance of one God without the denial that there are other Gods]. In a true analysis, the belief that there is only one God for all people [i.e. true monotheism] did not exist among the three religions of Judaism, Christianity and Islam, until proclaimed by Islam. The point is that although all three religions have proclaimed that they follow the same God, the humans of each religion have defined their Gods differently.

In **Judaism**, their God, Jehovah, was defined in the first part of the 20th Chapter of Exodus when Moses conveyed the Ten Commandments to the assembled people. At that point, Moses told the people the following:

"And God spoke all these words, saying, 'I am the Lord your God, who brought you out of the land of Egypt, out of the house of bondage. You shall have no other Gods before me.'"

Therefore, the God of Judaism is the one who had freed them from oppression. This is one of the pleas which many people have made to their Gods. The God which answers this plea is generally the God of choice for the people; for He is the One who has given them significant help during their Earthly lives. Thus, the God of Judaism was defined by Moses, using the words which He had said to him: *I am the One who freed you.*

Although there is a continuum between Judaism and **Christianity** known as the Judeo-Christian heritage [see *Christianity and the New Age Religion*], and although Christianity says that its God is the same God which Judaism had, the humans of Christianity changed the definition of that God. This subject was covered in great detail in *The Christian Conspiracy*. Only a synopsis will be presented here.

The early Church Fathers were very insistent that their God was the same as the God of Judaism. To show this, when Marcion, a respected teacher in the second century Church who had a great following, proposed that the loving Father spoken of by Jesus was not the same as the warlike, vengeful Jehovah of Judaism, the early Church Fathers excommunicated him and his followers.

However, as mentioned previously [see pages 53-4], these early Church Fathers had a problem. It was of their own making, but it was a tremendous problem to them. Their problem was in three parts. First, they decided that since mankind had fallen from God, then it had to be redeemed via atonement [meaning reconciliation with God]. Secondly, they decided that no human, no matter how talented, could be the agent of this atonement. Thirdly, they decided that since Jesus Christ was their agent of atonement, then he had to *be* God.

It took them almost 700 years after the resurrection to finally agree on exactly how Jesus could *be* God without destroying their viewpoint that there was only *one* God. They fit all of this together by defining the God of Christianity as the *Trinity*, or *una substantia—tres personna* [one substance —three persons], a formula first proposed by Tertullian almost 500 years before it was fully accepted by the Church. They did this despite the fact that in the Holy Scriptures, Jesus said that he was not the same as the Father on at least three separate occasions. For anyone who takes the time to study the first 500 years of the Church, there can be no doubt that the humans of the early Church defined the God that Christians worship today. That God is different from the God of Judaism.

The same can be said for those of the **Islamic** faith. Unlike the Jews who claimed that Jehovah is for them alone, and that they are God's only Chosen People, Islam declared that Allah is for *all* people. Unlike the Jews who infer that there are other Gods but that they choose Jehovah for their God, Islam believes that there is no God but God. Unlike the Christians who believe that their Christ is divine, Islam believes that nothing is divine but God *alone*.

In respect to the Islamic God being for all people, the Koran says:

"Surely those who believe and those who are Jews, and the Christians, and the Sabians, whoever believes in Allah and the Last Day and does good, they shall have their reward from their Lord, and there is no fear for them nor shall they grieve." [Surah II, 62]

In respect to there being no division of any sort within their God, the Koran says: *Your God is one God! there is no god but He; He is the Beneficent, the Merciful.* [*Surah* II 163]. The Koran goes on to say: *He, Allah is One. Allah is He on Whom all depend. He begets not, nor is He begotten. And none is like Him* [*Surah* CXII, 1-4]. And finally, the Koran says:

"Certainly they disbelieve who say: Surely Allah is the third person of the Trinity; there is no god but one God, and if they desist not from what they say, a painful chastisement shall befall on those among them who disbelieve." [*Surah* V, 73]

So, we have three major religions claiming that their God is the God of Abraham. However, we have the Jehovah of Judaism being the God who freed His people and who is the God only for them; we have the Father of Christianity being a God who begot a Son and who has three [and only three] persons within His substance; and we have the Allah of Islam being an indivisible God who is for all people. All three definitions refer to the same Ultimate One. All three definitions were generated by humans. As an aside, in practice all three definitions tend to ignore the female side of God's divinity and of God's humanity.

I have no problem with those who accept God as the One who was defined by someone else. I followed that practice for a number of years myself. However, if one is to establish a personal relationship with the God who calls to him or her, then that God must be the One who is known on a personal basis.

Have you been able to feel a personal relationship with another human if you knew that person solely by listening to someone else's description? I haven't. I might have been able to determine whether that person would be the kind I might like by listening to the description; but the ability to have a personal relationship has always seemed to require more than that. I had to know that person myself. It is difficult to know a person if all you have is a description or a definition which was generated by another person.

I believe that learning about God from the words of another is a viable way to define part of the pathway into oneness with God. It satisfies the need for a relationship with a community of believers. It nourishes the delicate and fragile bud of belief when such a nourishment is necessary. It allows the bud of belief to be supported by others of a like belief, until that bud can blossom into a full belief system capable of withstanding attack and standing on its own.

However, I also believe that such an experience presents restrictions which inhibit growth; for the believer is supported by the community of believers only as long as the beliefs are consistent throughout the community. At the time when the God who calls differs from the definitions established by the community, then the community will expel the one who stands alone. At that time, the outcast must find a definition of God from other sources.

The worship of a God defined by humans is a positive experience. It is an experience to be cherished. However, it is also an experience to be left behind as a milestone along the pathway. That may be a very difficult experience for many. It was for me. Some simply will not be able to do it and will spend lifetime after lifetime trying to submit to the definition of God as supplied by others. However, some who wish to trod where no one has trod before will accept the difficult decision to strike out without the comfort of a community of similar believers. Leaving the God defined by others is a difficult experience to put into the past; but when done, it could possibly mark yet another milestone on one's unique and individual pathway into oneness with God.

THE WORSHIP OF GOD
AS DEFINED BY SPIRIT

Among the religions presently considered to be the major, established religions on this Earth, **Christianity** has a number of unique characteristics. Certainly one of them is the belief that the one who inspired the religion in its very beginning is divine in the same sense that God is divine. Judaism does not have that belief about Abraham or Moses; Pariism does not have that belief about Zoroaster; Confucianism does not have that belief about Confucius; Taoism does not have that belief about Lao Tze; Buddhism does not have that belief about the Buddha; Islam does not have that belief about Abraham or Mohammed; and on and on. One has to go back to the early Egyptian, Greek or Roman religions, all of which have had an effect on the practices of Christianity, before one finds a similar belief. Among the major religions of the present world, belief in the divinity of the original leader is a unique characteristic of orthodox Christianity.

There is another characteristic which is unique to Christianity. This one also is a vital part of the orthodox Christian belief system. It is the belief in the Holy Spirit. In orthodox Christianity, the Holy Spirit is one Spirit for all people. This Spirit is the same substance as God, albeit a different person. This Spirit completes the Trinity of the God of Christianity in that there is God the Father, God the Son and God the Holy Spirit [or Ghost]. Other religions have spirits or other celestial beings which make up an important part of their religious practice; but to my knowledge, Christianity is the only religion in which there is *one* Holy Spirit.

The New Testament presents a considerable amount of information about the Holy Spirit. In fact, the word "spirit" is used 344 times in the books of the New Testament. All of these references are important to the Christian faith. I have chosen three as an indication of this importance.

In John 14:25-6, Jesus says:

"These things I have spoken to you, while I am still with you. But the Counselor, the Holy Spirit, whom the Father will send in my name, he will teach you all things, and bring to your remembrance all that I have said to you."

Consequently, the Holy Spirit was to be the follow-up to the Christ as a teacher. In addition, the Holy Spirit was to speak with the voice of both the Father and the Son.

In Acts 2:4, during the day of Pentecost when those who had followed the Christ were gathered together, the Holy Spirit came upon them, for we read: *And they were all filled with the Holy Spirit and began to speak in other tongues, as the Spirit gave them utterance.* In later verses, the mixed-language population of Jerusalem was astonished to be communicated to by these Galileans, each in his own language.

Then in Acts 9:31, we read:

So the church throughout all Judea and Galilee and Samaria had peace and was built up; and walking in the comfort of the Holy Spirit it was multiplied.

Consequently, the Holy Spirit did come to the followers of the Christ after the Christ had left them, just as he had predicted. Further, the Holy Spirit taught, led and gave comfort to those who had followed the Christ.

During all of the years that I spent within the warmth of the Christian Church, I felt the presence of the Holy Spirit. When I would pray, or better yet when I would be quiet and <u>listen</u>, I would feel the presence of this comforting Counselor. It is an experience which I would hope that all could feel.

Then I was faced with a dilemma; for the comfort of the Spirit suddenly became very personal. The major turning point in this personal relationship came after I retired from business. I then had a lot of time on my hands, and I was still healthy and mentally alert. I soon got bored with playing golf whenever I wanted to; and so I asked the ministers of the Church what I could do for them which would occupy my time and energy. The Senior Associate Minister to whom I addressed the question checked with all the church staff, and the response sent back to me was that I should continue to teach Sunday School. My response to that suggestion was that such a chore would occupy two hours each week. Wasn't there something else?

Nothing was proposed. As a consequence, one day I went into a deep meditation. During that quiet time, I asked what I should do with myself. The answer was given with great clarity. I was told that as a service to humanity, I should agree to write three books in which I would be given much help and guidance. I agreed with that proposal, and I have been given a lot of help during the writing of these books. I did not realize when I agreed to this activity that my agreement would lead to my being asked to stop teaching in the Church, an act which then led me to leave the warm comfort of that congregation.

The point of this personal story is that when I asked Spirit for guidance, the direction I was given was a very personal one; and it was one which completely changed the religious direction of the path I had been following for many, many years and possibly many, many lifetimes. My Christianity was starting to become somewhat unorthodox anyway, but my teaching in the Church was always mainstream. In fact, when it was announced to a class whom I had been teaching that I was no longer authorized to teach there, the class protested strongly. Most of the forty adults in attendance stood up and declared that I had taught only mainstream Christianity. Although I appreciated the support, it has made no difference in the direction my life has since taken.

Now I can state the dilemma which I faced. It is one which I believe everyone will eventually face. That dilemma is this: did my personal message come from the one, institutional Holy Spirit available to all Christians as a part of their faith, which decided at this juncture to make its approach a personal one for me; or did my message come from a Spirit which is personal one intended only for me. The choice I made would be an important one. If I decided that there is only one Holy Spirit as defined by the orthodoxy of the Christian Church, then I also had to accept that this institutionalized Spirit was the one which would define the God who calls to me: *viz.* the God as also defined by orthodoxy of the institutionalized Church. If, on the other hand, I accepted that Spirit was personal to me, then I had to accept that I was not the only one who had a personal Spirit.

I will not go into great detail about the debate which I had with whoever calls to me during my personal meditations; for to do so would require another book. Instead, I will merely say that it is now my firm belief that I have a personal Spirit for guidance, and that this Spirit works with many associates to give me the help I need. Some have called this Spirit the Higher Self; others have called it the Oversoul. The name makes no difference. The important belief is that it is a personal Spirit which works with my soul to bring forth the experiences needed for progress along the pathway. This belief was described more fully in the Articles of Faith section of *Christianity and the New Age Religion.*

A belief in a personal Spirit is quite a change in belief for one who had spent a major portion of his life involved with the single, institutionalized Holy Spirit as defined by the humans of the Church. Not only has Spirit become more personalized, the God who calls to me is also a much more personal God than S/He previously was. This is easily understood, for even the Christian Bible states that:

"*...the hour is coming, and now is, when the true worshipers will worship the Father in spirit and truth, for such the Father seeks to worship* *him. God is spirit, and those who worship him must worship in spirit and truth."* [John 4:23-4].

Consequently, the closer one is to a personal relationship with Spirit, the closer one is to a personal relationship with God. In addition, I have felt much more of a personal closeness to the one who held the energy of the Christ than I was ever able to develop within the confines of the Church. The removal of the restricting requirements of the institutionalized, orthodox Church has allowed progress with Spirit which exceeds that which was possible in my previous belief system.

The God who calls to me is no longer defined by the humans of the established institutions. Instead, S/He is a God which develops and dynamically changes as Spirit continues to refine the definitions. It was time for me to proceed to the personal God who calls to me. In no way do I regret having spent the time with the One in whom I previously felt so much love; for there was love in the comfort of that congregation of believers known as the Christian Church. However, it was time for me to move on.

There is now a milestone in my personal pathway into oneness with God which is labeled "The Worship of God as Defined by Humans." It is behind me. I am now at the milestone labeled "The Worship of God as Defined by Spirit." I have had a glimpse, but only a glimpse, of the milestones still to come. They will require additional work before I reach them. There is the possibility that a milestone entitled "The Worship of God as Defined by Spirit" would be a part of each individual's unique and personal pathway into oneness with God; but that is not a decision for me to make for anyone other than myself. Instead, that is a decision for each individual to make for him/herself.

THE ABSORPTION OF UNCONDITIONAL LOVE

The reader may feel that he or she has heard enough about Unconditional Love. However, there is more to cover. In the first place, it is my firm belief that the Kingdom of God is composed of such substance. In addition, it is my firm belief that before oneness with God could possibly be experienced, oneness through the

Unconditional Love of each fellow human being would have to have been practiced. Further, it is my firm belief that Unconditional Love is not to be given lip service—it is to be absorbed to such an extent that no other activity is possible. Finally, it is my firm belief that heaven knows of no reality other than that of Unconditional Love.

In Chapter 2, we addressed the issue that each religion has proposed that love be a part of its practice. For some, it was the love of God. For others, it was the love of fellow man. For yet others, it was the love of nature. For some, it was a compassionate, nurturing love; while for others, it was a love which controls the activities of others, supposedly for their own good.

Despite this profession for love, the love seemed to have *conditions* attached to it. One religion or sect might practice love only for those who believed the doctrines of their faith. Other religions or sects might practice love only for those who were of a certain, preferred type. Other religions might want to love the person while not loving some of the activities of that person.

One of the most remarkable stories of giving Unconditional Love by separating a person from the activities of that person is presented in the fourth chapter of the Gospel of John in the Christian Bible. It is the story about the woman at the well. In this story Jesus approached a woman by himself for "his disciples had gone away into the city to buy food." In that society, it would be very unusual for one who was known as a rabbi or religious teacher to approach a woman who was not his wife unless other people were with him to help protect his honor. Jesus not only approached her, he asked her for a drink of water. This unusual request surprised her, for Jesus was a Jew and she was a woman of Samaria, and "Jews have no dealings with Samaritans." Jesus not only requested water, he spent time with her as he taught her about "living water."

When she understood and asked for the living water, Jesus requested that she "Go, call your husband, and come here." When she replied that she had no husband, Jesus replied that she had had five husbands and that the one she now had was also not her husband. Again, this discussion is very unusual, for in that society, the normal reaction would have been to shout that the woman was an adulteress who should be stoned. Jesus was so respectful of this woman, despite the mores of the society of his day, that later many Samaritans came to him because of the woman's testimony and spent two days with him, again a very unusual thing for a Jew and a Samaritan to do.

The point is that at least three times in this story, Jesus used Unconditional Love to separate the <u>woman</u> from what his society viewed as her unacceptable activities. In the first place, she was a woman and he was alone with her; in the second place she was a Samaritan who was to be avoided by all good Jews; and in the third place, she was an unmarried woman who had lived with several men. All of these unacceptable activities were overlooked by Jesus as he taught her and gave her Unconditional Love.

If we were to live in the imitation of Christ, we would not let any unacceptable activity keep us from giving Unconditional Love to the person who practiced that unacceptable activity. However, it is difficult for human beings to separate or detach the person from his or her activities. In other words, it is not easy to practice Unconditional Love.

Jesus said to love your enemies; but his Church simply could not do this. They failed to detach the activities which were unacceptable to them from the persons who did those activities. As a result, the Christian Church, and all other established religions, have put conditions on their love. Because of these conditions, the men of the established religions have gone forth with the blessing of their religion to kill Jews on their way to the Crusades merely because they were there; and to commit genocide on the Christian Cathars merely because they chose to worship the Christ in their own way outside of the Church; and to have holy wars in which the Protestants kill the Catholics and the Catholics kill the Protestants; and to have holy wars in which the Serbs kill the Croats and the Croats kill the Serbs; and to have other holy wars in which the Muslims kill the Hindus or propose to have the "Mother of all wars" in which Islam would finally triumph by killing off all who would not accept the one true God. None of this represents the practice of Unconditional Love, even though the God who created us all must have requested that his followers practice it.

Will we have oneness with God who is the ALL when we

hate any one of His/Her creations, even emotional creations? Will we be in oneness with God who is ALL when we decide to love any one of His/Her creatures only if they will do "thus and so"? Will we ever approach oneness with the ALL if we do not accept the ALL?

Is there a milestone on the pathway into oneness with God which is labeled "The Absorption of Unconditional Love?" I believe that there is such a milestone on my personal pathway. I have not passed it as yet, but I will try. As to whether such a milestone belongs on the pathway of anyone else is not my decision to make. However, in my small mind which does not understand all of the mysteries of God, I have a difficult time seeing how we can become a part of *everything* if we deny love to *anything*. That may be worth some thought.

THE ABSORPTION OF NOTHINGNESS WHICH IS EVERYTHING

In this section, I have undertaken a difficult problem; for I will be trying to write about *nothing*. The problem might best be illustrated by describing a television program called "Connections" which is presented in our Atlanta area on The Learning Channel. In a recent episode, the narrator was telling about the discovery of air pressure, and was making a connection from that discovery to the development of the altimeter and the barometer which allow airplanes not only to know how high they are flying, but also to know whether or not they are approaching bad weather.

To begin his "Connections," the narrator related how Evangelista Torricelli, an associate of Galileo in Florence Italy in 1643, discovered that a tube closed on one end could be filled with mercury, and then inverted into a dish of mercury. If the tube had been of the right length, then none of the mercury would run into the dish, but would, instead, be held upright in the tube by the pressure of air pushing down on the mercury in the dish. He then discovered that if he walked up a long hill, the mercury would drop, thus showing that the pressure of air becomes reduced at higher altitudes.

However, this presented a problem to the society of Torricelli's day. His results were reported to the pope, as all things were in those days, especially the activities of anyone associated with Galileo. When the results of the experiment were described, the pope is reported to have asked, "What is in the end of the tube when the mercury leaves there." The answer of *nothing* presented a real ecclesiastical problem; for since God was omnipresent [i.e. in all places], there could be no such thing as *nothing*. As a consequence, the pope ordered that there be no more writing or discussing of anything as unfaithful to God as *nothing*.

In today's scientific thinking, there also is no such thing as *nothing*. Even in the best of vacuums, there are always a few molecules of *something* still floating around. To the best of my knowledge, even the best of the human experiments has not created a perfect vacuum, just as the best of human experiments has not, as yet, achieved a temperature of absolute zero, the point where all molecular motion ceases. There have been approaches to a perfect vacuum, just as there have been approaches to absolute zero; but neither has been reached. Consequently, there has always been *something* around, and that *something* has always been in constant motion. In this sense, the seventeenth century pope was right.

However, I have had a glimpse of the *void*. Like God, the void which I experienced is ineffable in that it is beyond the ability of the human mind either to comprehend or to describe. I have no idea how long I was there, because all references to time were absent. There was no light, no color, no sound, no sense of physical feeling, no smell, and nothing else which could interrupt the complete sense of serenity and peace. It was timeless. In addition, there was absolutely <u>no fear</u>. However, since I did feel love, comfort, serenity and other such emotional or spiritual attributes, I cannot claim that there was *nothing* in the void. I will, however, claim that in a human sense, there was a *nothingness* there. I can also state without reservation, that I would go back to that void anytime I was permitted.

As a part of that experience, I had the distinct impression that the void was a part of the life to come after this physical existence has been completed. Like almost every human who has experienced this dense, three-dimensional form, I have wondered if this is all there is. Does all consciousness stop when the heart stops pumping blood? It is a question which many have asked. Like all who have touched into a deep spiritual experience, I have answered that question for myself with a resounding *NO*. There is, in my opinion and in my belief system, much more than this mere physical existence, important though that may be.

Because of my belief system, I have had a great deal of interest in the many "near-death" experiences which have been reported. In fact, I have a close personal friend who feels strongly that he had "passed over," but decided to come back. The description of his experience is similar to that which has been reported by others. Since these experiences offer some demonstration of the probability of an afterlife, I was rather surprised to see an article presented in the *Atlanta Journal/Constitution* edition of March 12, 1994 entitled, "Near-Death gets no faith's blessing" and sub-titled, "Theologians uneasy with tales of hereafter." My surprise was related to the denial of spiritual experiences on the part of those who are trained to lead our spiritual training; but then maybe that attitude should no longer surprise me.

In that same article, a summary of various beliefs about the after-life was given. It is repeated for information and without comment, and with neither concurrence nor disagreement as follows:

Buddhists: Siddhartha Gautama, the Buddha, preached that existence is a continuing cycle of death and rebirth. Every deed and thought produces good or bad karma, which will effect the form of the next life. The state of mind of the person at the moment of death helps determine the state at rebirth.

Catholics: Catholics await a "general judgment" of all souls. The saintly will ascend to heaven; those who die in mortal sin are condemned to hell. Although it is not emphasized, Catholics also recognize purgatory, a time of cleansing after death.

Hindus: When the body dies, the soul continues to live in a different body until *moksha*, or liberation from the life-death cycle is achieved. There are several paths to liberation, including devotion to a personal God, breaking attachments to the material world and choosing an occupation which benefits society.

Jehovah's Witnesses: An oft-quoted belief of Jehovah's Witnesses is that only 144,000 souls will go to heaven. All other good souls will live on in an earthly paradise. Jehovah's Witnesses do not believe in hell, but in eternal death. Everyone who dies remains dead until Armageddon which is the final battle between good and evil. After this, Earth will be restored to its paradise state. During a 1,000 year reign of Christ, God will resurrect people in an orderly fashion.

Jews: The Jewish tradition teaches that there is life after death and that not only Jews go to heaven. A popular analogy is the fetus in the womb who has no idea of what birth will be like. But many Jews believe a legacy of good deeds and commitments in the family and community is all that continues after death.

Mormons: Members of the Church of Jesus Christ of the Latter Day Saints believe human beings exist as spirit children before their mortal existence and continue to exist after death. Mormons do not believe that everyone will be assigned to either heaven or hell, but accept that one's station in the after-life will be determined by obedience to God in mortality. Mormons believe that family relationships can be maintained eternally.

Muslims: Muslims believe that the end of earth will come in a final judgment by Allah, who will call up those still alive and all those who have died, present them with a record of their deeds, and weigh their obedience to God and actions toward their fellow human beings. The faithful will move on to paradise; the unfaithful will be punished with hell.

Protestants: By accepting the Apostle's Creed, Protestants believe in the "resurrection of the body and the life everlasting." However, they often disagree within denominations about whether one goes immediately to heaven or hell or waits until the second coming of Christ for judgment, and whether judgment will come before or after Christ's purported 1,000 year reign on Earth.

Universalists: Although the principles of Unitarian Universalism state clearly that no member "shall be required to subscribe to any particular interpretation of religion, or to any particular religious belief or creed," Universalism accepts the salvation of all, just as the name implies.

Witches or Wiccans: The "old religion" which predates Christianity traditionally teaches about a place after death called "Summerland," a land of never-ending feasting, merrymaking and music. Since many witches believe in reincarnation, they see Summerland as a place of rest, rejuvenation and preparation for the next life. Witches do not accept the idea prevalent in some Eastern religions that reincarnation can include coming back in other life forms as punishment or reward, but believe that reincarnation is an evolutionary path.

As can be seen by these various beliefs, there is almost no indication of the Great Light which most who have had a near-death experience have reported; nor is there any indication of the comforting void which I have glimpsed and which I believe comes after acceptance into the Light. Instead of a comforting void, some of these religions refer only to the discomforting punishment of hell or eternal death. However, in fairness it does seem as if the Catholic description of purgatory as a time of cleansing, could have some relationship to the existence of the comforting void which I am trying to convey.

Despite the lack of confirming reference material from the established religions, I believe that the void not only exists, but that all of importance to cosmic consciousness is present there. In this sense, it is a void only in relation to this present existence which is so familiar to us. It is not a void in the sense of the cosmic or universal consciousness of God. In that sense, it is the *everything*.

I cannot tell you that there is a milestone in my personal pathway labeled "The Absorption of Nothingness Which is Everything" because I have had only a small glimpse of that experience. There is still more work to do before I can fully understand all the implications of such an experience. But I can tell you that the small glimpse I had gave me such an exalted feeling of peace and serenity, that I believe it could only have come from God and could only be a part of His/Her domain. I think there will be a milestone on my personal pathway which contains such a label. As to whether or not such an experience is on your pathway is not for me to determine or decide. That decision is yours to make.

THE SEVEN SEALS

The Revelation to John, The Apocalypse, is the last book of the Christian New Testament. It is completely apocalyptic [i.e. pertaining to prophetic disclosure or revelation] rather than didactic [i.e. morally instructive] or historical [i.e. a telling of events] as most of the New Testament is. The major purpose of The Revelation to John is to predict that the Church will undergo persecution; and the major lessons are to instruct the Church about how to handle this persecution, and to encourage the Church to be steadfast and enduring in all times of persecution.

In this Revelation, mention is made of a scroll which has writing within, but which is sealed on the back with seven seals. The seals are not described in any great detail—they are just there to keep the scroll closed until each is broken. The story of what happens as each of these seven seals is broken is presented in Chapters 5-8. In this story, the point is strongly made that the breaking of the seven seals cannot be done by just anyone; but instead had to be done by the Lamb of God who is also the Lion of the tribe of Judah and the Root of David.

In the story, the breaking of each of the first six seals presents the calamity which will befall the Church, with the sixth seal also predicting that many would wash their clothes in the blood of the Lamb, and would survive the great tribulation. The breaking of the seventh seal introduces seven angels with seven trumpets who repeat the story of tribulation and recovery previously presented by the seven seals, but in greater detail. Later, the stories are repeated, again in greater detail, with seven angels having seven golden bowls filled with the wrath of God.

I have read numerous commentaries and a great amount of other literature which analyzes The Revelation to John. Anyone who was raised in a Church which predicted that dire things would happen if they did not do certain things would be bound to try to understand The Revelation. As a result of that study and a lot of thinking, I have some thoughts about the seven seals which the Church would believe were not orthodox; but which make a great deal of sense to me as symbolism for representing one's personal and unique pathway into oneness with God.

In the first place, it makes little sense to me that a scroll, written by God, would be closed with seals which could be opened by only one individual. Now I realize that this is the message of the Christian Church; *viz.* that Jesus is the *only* way back to God and therefore *only* he could read the words presented by God. However, that has not been my experience. I feel that God has presented His/Her words directly to me many times and in many different ways.

Within the Christian scripture Jesus is reported to have said:
"I am the way, and the truth, and the life; no one comes to the Father but by me. If you had known me, you would have known my Father also; henceforth you know him and have seen him." [John 14:6-7].

I also know that the teachers of the Church have interpreted the "me" of the statement "no one comes to the Father but by <u>me</u>" to refer to the *person* of Jesus Christ. However, because of the use of terms such as "the way," and "known me," it is my belief that Jesus is not referring to his *person*, but to his *teachings*.

As I have said so often in this book, the principal teaching of Jesus Christ is that of Unconditional Love. Consequently, I feel that Jesus was teaching that unless one practices Unconditional Love, he or she does not come to the Father. It is in the times when I have been successful in practicing Unconditional Love that God has come to me [or allowed me to come to Him/Her] most completely. It is my belief that this happens because God is encompassed in Unconditional Love, and that the only way to be a part of Him/Her is also to be encompassed in Unconditional Love.

As a consequence of all of this, I choose to interpret the seven seals of The Revelation as meaning that the words written by God are closed by personal seals which hide these personal words from each of us; and that when each of us becomes the Lamb of God by fulfilling His/Her desire that we practice Unconditional Love, then we can open each of those seals. I further believe that each seal is opened only as we absorb experiences along the pathway into oneness with God.

In the previous sections of this chapter, I have used the term "milestone" to describe the five distinct markings along the pathway which I believe belong on my personal and unique pathway into oneness with God. The term "milestone" has, as one of its definitions, *"An important event or turning point in one's history or career."* That is the meaning which is intended here. It is a change in attitude or belief which is so potent that it can be considered to be a turning point. It is something which, having been passed, no longer needs to be revisited.

As an example, once having experienced an inordinate amount of affection for material things, and having had them, it is natural to search for something else; and once having found that the "something else" is superior to the material things, then it is also natural that the inordinate desire for the material things would cease. It is a turning point in one's pathway into oneness with God. It is a milestone.

As another example, once having experienced the God as

defined by man, and having felt that there was something else, and having found the God defined by Spirit, one would have a tendency never again to worship the God defined by man. Additional examples could be made using the other milestones labeled 'The Absorption of Unconditional Love" or "The Absorption of Nothingness Which is Everything."

In this sense, the milestone markers are really gates, or one-way doors, or even seals to be broken. Once a one-way door has been used, one cannot go backward; and once a seal has been broken, it cannot be repaired. In other words, once the turning point has been made, there is no returning. As far as the pathway into oneness with God is concerned, once having passed a milestone, there is really no desire to return to prior activities.

So, as symbolism for the various milestones on this personal pathway into oneness with God, I would suggest that the breaking of the seven seals can be a way in which each traveler could open a "scroll" in which are written [or heard] the words of God for him or her. Now I know that only five milestones have been presented so far; and so it is now time to present the other two.

As I have said previously, I enjoyed the time spent in the mainstream Christian Church; and I recommend that everyone spend some time in the established religion which appeals to him/her. One reason for that recommendation is that through the offices of those religious establishments, a great deal of service for humanity is performed. Consequently, I would suggest that another milestone along the pathway is when one decides that service to humanity is of more importance than service for self. This is a very normal sixth Chakra reaction in response to the positive message of brotherhood and creative thinking. However, in order to be of true service to humanity, the negative message of the sixth Chakra, that of egotism, must be given up.

I would suggest that a possible place to find the seal which opens the belief that service to humanity is of more importance than service to self, would be after having given up the worship of material things. For me, I needed two additional experiences before I could truly face that seal.

The first experience I needed was that of participation in an established religion; but I do not necessarily believe that is true for everyone, for I have seen many who have given service to humanity without ever having entered the door of a church or a synagogue. I have also seen some who have used the experience of the church to learn how to serve all of humanity; whereas others have used a similar experience to serve only a material-oriented portion of humanity. For a vivid example of this, I would recommend reading the section on the Conquistadors in *The Christian Conspiracy* which describes two men. One was Bartholome de Las Casas, a former conquistador who took Holy Orders and became the greatest proponent of humanity to the native Indians in South America. The other was Dr. Juan Gines de Sepulveda who proposed that it was God's will that the native Indians be exploited for the greater good of God and Spain. In a face-to-face debate which lasted for a month, de Sepulveda won out. To me, one of these men crashed through the seal of service to humanity; whereas the other bounced off that unbroken seal and remained with the God as defined by man, or possibly even with the worship of material things.

The second experience I needed was a fuller understanding of some of the teachings of the Christ, particularly the teaching given in the Parable of the Talents [Matt. 25:14-30]. In synopsis, this parable tells of the master who went on a journey. During his absence, he entrusted his property to his servants. To one, he gave five talents; to another two talents; and to the third, one talent, each according to his ability.

When the master returned, he found that the one with five talents had invested them wisely, and now could give the master ten talents in return; the one with two talents had done likewise, and now could give the master four talents in return; but the one with only one talent had so feared losing it, that he buried it in the ground, and thus could give back to the master only that which had been the master's in the beginning. The master's response was to berate the third servant and to give his talent to the one who had ten talents. Jesus finished by saying:

"For to every one who has, will more be given, and he will have abundance; but from him who has not, even what he has will be taken away."

For years, this teaching bothered me. First it did not seem to indicate the concept of sharing which I had always considered to be a part of Christian teaching. One idea of sharing is the Communist Manifesto of: *From each according to his ability; to each according to his need.* This parable taught just the opposite. Also it did not seem to be an expression of Unconditional Love, because in the parable, Jesus has the master really tearing into the lazy servant.

So, I struggled with this parable until one day in church, a young female minister was being ordained. She was very dear to my wife and me, primarily because of the help she had given our daughter when it was needed. I knew that the Senior Minister did not think she was very talented, and so in his part of the Ordination Service, he said to her, *"What you do with what you have been given is of utmost importance to God."*

All-of-a-sudden, I understood not only the parable, but also what constituted Service to Humanity. There are those who say that they have nothing great to contribute to humanity; but the message does not concern itself with what you have been given, or even with what you do. Instead, it says, "What you do with what you have been given is of utmost importance to God." Some have been given little. Of them, little is expected; but it is expected. Others have been given much, and of them, much is expected. For it is not what you do, but what you do with what you have been given that is important to God.

With this lesson, learned from within the loving congregation of an established religion, I was finally ready to face the seal, or the milestone, labeled, "Service to Humanity." As previously mentioned, my Service to Humanity, at least as it was given to me for this incarnation, was to write three books. Other service to humanity may come later, but at the present time, this work defines the milestone. Even if no one were to read one word of these books, it is important for me to write them. It is a Service to Humanity which was given to me by Spirit.

Since this is a milestone on my pathway, then it may possibly be a milestone on the pathway of others. If it is, then when it is faced, it is a life-changing event, one which once having been experienced, would no longer permit a life in which it was absent. My experience came after I had experienced the adoration of material things and after I had also experienced the love coming from the God defined by man; but I believe it is an experience which could occur at any time along one's unique pathway toward oneness with God.

The final milestone or seal to be described is similar to the one just mentioned, albeit on another level. It bears the label, "Service to Divinity." This is a very normal seventh Chakra response to the positive message of oneness with all and of cosmic consciousness, but a rejection to the negative message of alienation from life because divinity and life go hand-in-hand. As with the milestone just described, Service to Divinity can happen at any time; but to me, it would be doing Divinity a disservice rather than a service if one were to try to serve without having experienced the absorption of Unconditional Love. That is a personal opinion and may not apply to everyone. It may be possible that service to Divinity could occur in the absence of Unconditional Love; but my feeling is that it would not be a major turning point such as it would be in the presence of Unconditional Love.

With the addition of "Service to Humanity" and "Service to Divinity" as milestones, this completes the description of seven milestones which could be on a personal pathway into oneness with God. These have been presented in this section through the symbolism of the seven seals. In using these seals, I am merely using them in a symbolic sense and not saying that this is the true meaning of the seals as presented in The Revelation. However, I will say that this explanation makes more sense to me than any of the many commentaries on The Revelation which I have read. I cannot judge whether it makes sense to you or not. That is a decision which only you can make.

COMMENTARY AND CONCLUSION

This chapter has presented six sections covering seven milestones which I believe are on my personal and unique pathway toward oneness with God. Those seven milestones were:

    1. The Worship of Material Things
    2. The Worship of God as Defined by Man
    3. The Worship of God as Defined by Spirit
    4. The Absorption of Unconditional Love;

    5. The Absorption of Nothingness Which is Everything
    6. Service to Humanity
    7. Service to Divinity

I have had the full experience of some of these milestones, but merely glimpses of others. Although the milestones described here are so general that they may well be on the unique pathway of many people, and although the progression from one milestone to another suggests an innate and objective order, that is not necessarily so for each individual. Again I say that the milestones on your individual and unique pathway into oneness with God are up to you to experience for yourself.

There are three other points to make before closing this chapter. The first point is a major one. This chapter has been presented as if we were completely detached from God and were trying to find our way back to Him/Her. On the basis of our present three-dimensional personality, that is a relevant picture; but in a cosmic sense, it may not be so relevant. In a cosmic sense, it is possible that we have never left God in any meaningful way, and that we are doing what we are doing solely for the experience of it. There are many who believe exactly that, but it is impossible to know whether or not that is a true representation as long as we remain in this three-dimensional personality. Any statements to the contrary are either speculation, or an expression of deep faith.

The second point is also a major one. The information in this chapter is presented as if we were completely separate individuals. That is probably not true even in this present, three-dimensional personality. Our present existence would certainly change if we had no others to interact with; for we are certainly not alone. Of even greater impact is that this is certainly not true in a cosmic sense. If there is a God, and if S/He is the ALL, then in a cosmic sense we are already in oneness not only with Him/Her, but with everyone else; for we are all a part of the ALL. Nevertheless, the way we handle ourselves in all of our activities is important; for the progress of the ALL depends on the progress made by any and all parts of the ALL. In addition, if the four Cosmic Concepts have any validity, then all will not be with God until all have accepted the practice of

Unconditional Love. Consequently, as could be sensed during the discussion of the Parable of the Prodigal Son [see pages 122-3], each one is of vital importance to God.

The third point may not be so major, for it has to do with personal experiences which have led to my present belief system, a system which differs greatly from the belief system I had when I joined the Christian Church over fifty years ago. Although there are many stories I could relate which have helped along the way, I have chosen to present only six episodes, each of which has a specific message to relate. Those episodes are presented in Appendix C. To finish this part of the book, I will repeat only a few paraphrased sentences from the last episode. They are as follows:

During a meditation at Palenque in the Yucatan during the Fall of 1993, I was given a gift when I heard a choir of voices saying, "You are coming home." About one year later, while on vacation on Martha's Vineyard, I heard an old record which presented Hal Holbrook as Mark Twain. For reasons recorded in Appendix C, it reminded me of the time at Palenque. And so, on Martha's Vineyard that night, I excused myself, went to the bedroom, took out my ledger and wrote, "And so I say to you, I am God's ship, Dave Moore, long out of Mount Hope, West Virginia, loaded with God's love for all, and headed for home!"

To all who have shared the thoughts of this chapter, and who will share the personal experiences presented in Appendix C, I would like to say that it has been good having you travel along my pathway with me. I would like to add that I hope you also are filled with God's love, and that you also are Going Home.

GOD BLESS!

POSTLUDE: A SUMMATION OF A FEW BELIEFS

It seems hardly fair to leave the reader without a summation of where all the beliefs presented in this book could lead. With that thought in mind, this Postlude has been added to present a few beliefs in a concise format. In advance, it must be stated that these beliefs are ones which I have accepted for myself during the last quarter of my present incarnation. Consequently, they all start out with the words, "I BELIEVE."

These are beliefs which I will share with anyone, but which I will demand that no one accept. They are presented merely for consideration. In advance, it must also be stated that it is much easier to have these beliefs, than it is to practice them consistently.

There are eight beliefs presented in this Postlude. The first five of these are spiritual beliefs. As such, they may be generally applicable. They are presented for general consideration and possible acceptance.

The sixth belief is a personal one. I will share my belief in Christ with anyone; but unlike many of the others who follow the Christ, I will not force this belief on another person. I present it solely in an attitude of sharing.

The seventh belief is one which is intended for humankind. As I am certain that anyone who has read this book will attest, I believe it is a very important belief for humankind.

The eighth belief is presented to show compassion for God, for I feel that it is important to return some of the compassion which S/He feels for us.

BELIEF ONE:
I BELIEVE THERE IS AN ETERNITY

It is quite possible that this belief is so universally accepted that everyone will say, "Of course there is an eternity." And yet, how do you prove the existence of eternity? The definition of eternity is *"The totality of time without beginning or end."* If time never ends, then how do you prove it?

Eternity is not a simple concept to grasp. In many ways it is like the definition of God, for it is beyond the comprehension of the human mind. In *The Christian Conspiracy*, I presented a few pages on the concepts of *Time* and *Space*. I think there has been more feedback on these concepts than on any other concept in the entire book. This description of Time and Space certainly seemed to open some minds. As a consequence, I decided to include most of those concepts in Chapter 4, *Part One* of this work [see pages 72-5].

As one illustration of those concepts, if the physical age of our Earth were to be compressed into one year, then Christ would appear on Earth in the last 16 seconds of that year. In other words, Earth would have existed for all of January, February, March and the other months until the final seconds of the last minute of the last hour of the last day of December before Christ would appear. Yet, parts of the physical universe are believed to be five times as old as Earth itself; and God has been in all of those parts for all of that time and even longer; for the existence of the physical universe is but a tiny portion of God's eternity.

This analysis of Time led to the conclusion that Jesus Christ could not be the only messenger ever sent from God to "those created in His/Her image," because God certainly would not have been idle or non-caring for all of that time.

In addition, there is the eternity of Space. Possibly Space does end and thus does not represent an eternity in the sense that Time does; but at any rate Space is still a totality which, again, is beyond human comprehension.

And so, I will say that eternity is not an easy concept to accept. But once having accepted even a glimpse of eternity, can one worry about temporal things? I spent a major portion of my life convinced that the consciousness we call "human" has been around for only 10-30,000 years; and that the civilization which we call "humanity" has been around for only about 4,000 years. I was convinced of those thoughts because the biology and the history books said so. I no longer accept what those books say, for I am convinced that humans and humanity have been on Earth for much, much longer than that.

In addition, I spent a major portion of my present life convinced that we humans are in physical form only once. I was convinced of that because the man in the pulpit said so. I no longer accept what he said to me, for I believe that parts of this human personality have had many, many involvements in the activities of humanity over a long period of time.

In giving up those prior beliefs, I have been presented with a glimpse of eternity. I wish I had not wasted so much time with the prior concepts; because the small glimpses of eternity which I have been privileged to see have been more fascinating than anything the previously restricted thinking had ever offered me.

It is truly difficult to accept the concept of eternity and not merely pay lip service to it by using phraseology such as "they [i.e. the martyrs] came to life and reigned with Christ a thousand years" [Revelation 20:4]. A knowledgeable teacher has said that 1,000 of our years equals one-third of a cosmic second. This means that a cosmic year equals 95 billion of our years, meaning that the universe has been in existence for only about 4.5 cosmic hours. And yet, even a cosmic year is not an eternity.

Other biblical phrases about eternity which may be familiar to you are: "...may have eternal life."[John 3:15]; or "Thou art a priest forever..." [Hebrews 5:6]; or the like. I accepted those phrases for many years before having even the slightest thought about what eternity really meant. Since then, I have been given a glimpse of the eternity as generated by my thoughts and meditations. As a result, a lot of additional things have started to be revealed to me. As one example, I no longer accept that coincidences are an accident.

So, the first belief which I would like you to consider is a belief in eternity.

BELIEF TWO:
I BELIEVE IN CALMNESS
WHICH LEADS TO DETACHMENT

Again, I can hear an exclamation from the reader which might be something like, "Well of course we should be calm. All religions teach us that!" But I guess there is calmness, and then there is the calmness which permits enough detachment that one can *listen*.

Let me give a small example. Earlier in this book I talked about the noise which is generated within the Church as it goes about its services. In mainstream Christianity to which I once subscribed, we want to *hear* things, almost to the point of being entertained by noise. In most of the Church services which I used to attend, there would be a "minute of silent prayer" during which the mental messages around you would tend to say, "Let's get this over with so I can hear some more noise." And then when the "noise" would resume, the mental messages would be, "Let's move the 20 minute sermon along, preacher. I've got a roast in the oven"; or "I've got a football game to watch!"

I used to think that the sermons were too short; but maybe that was because we had a preacher who could give marvelous messages if one would only be calm and listen. Possibly with these mental messages being sent out from the congregation and being heard by me during the latter days I spent within the Church, the reader can understand my astonishment when someone not of the Church suggested that meditation for an hour was really too short a time. The Christian Church would suggest a "minute of silent prayer" and the audience would get restless. How about an hour of meditation?

Then I tried it. I will admit that the first few minutes were rough; but once having got past them, I was truly amazed when told that the hour was over; and I truly was amazed at where I had been and what I had done. I had become calm, an attribute which we simply do not understand in this society of ours; and I had become detached enough from the daily activities that I could <u>listen</u>. Many have suggested that the mind must become 90% calm before truth can enter. I cannot comment on the arithmetic; but I can recommend the concept.

So, the second belief which I would like you to consider is a belief in calmness, and in detachment.

BELIEF THREE:
I BELIEVE IN UNCONDITIONAL LOVE

Again, I have to think that any religious person reading these words will say, "Of course I believe in love. My religion teaches me that one of its purposes is to promote love." But I would suggest that most religions teach conditional love rather than Unconditional Love.

Jesus taught Unconditional Love, even to the extent of loving your enemies; but the Church which bears his name rejects and condemns to eternal damnation those who do not believe as they do. Islam will love those who love Allah, but will fight anyone who believes that Jesus is God. Other examples could be given; for in almost every case, the love taught by established religions is that of conditional love. That is the way that established religions got established. They were established on the condition that you believed as they did. Consequently, it is only logical that the established religions would sponsor a Love which has conditions attached to it.

I believe in Unconditional Love. I have this belief despite the difficulty of practicing it while encased in this three-dimensional, emotion-laden body. I also believe that if Unconditional Love were practiced by all, this Earth would be a heaven. Finally, I believe that Unconditional Love cannot be practiced until or unless some level of detachment is experienced.

So, the third belief which I would like you to consider is a belief in Unconditional Love.

BELIEF FOUR:
I BELIEVE IN THE VOID

It is probable that we have now found a belief which is <u>not</u> obvious. I can now hear the reader saying, "What in heaven's name is the void?" I have had a hard time answering that question, either in person or on the previous pages of this book. This difficulty arises because the void is very close to being beyond human comprehension. The three beliefs of eternity, calmness and Unconditional Love may stretch the extent of human comprehension; but this one takes it

to the breaking point. I will try to explain the wonder of it by saying:
I have been there only once, but I believe that it is real;
I loved it and want to return; and
I have talked with others who say the same.

I cannot tell you how long I spent in the void because time does not seem to exist there. The total meditation lasted for more than an hour; but since the void has no reference to time such as sounds, colors, smells or the like, then again, time as we know it simply does not exist there. My three-dimension mentality says that the time was very short; but I can say that the experience of nothingness so encompassed me that it seemed "an eternity" before I returned.

The other people who are personal friends and have shared their experience with me, also were there for a relatively short time as we measure time. Some teachers of the New Age state that they can remember being in the void for many thousands of years. I know that the concept of the void will seem incredible to some who have rational minds; but I also have a rational mind, and I will state that it is real. It is truly there.

So, the fourth belief which I would like you to consider is a belief in the void.

BELIEF FIVE:
I BELIEVE IN GOD

Now we are probably back to an accepted belief. In a recent survey, it was stated that 90% of the people surveyed believe that there is a God.

However, the God which I am trying to convey in this section is a God who created ALL and who is ALL. Therefore, what we would consider to be evil in human terms, is not a thing of evil in terms of the Cosmic God of ALL. That definition of God may be difficult for some to accept.

In addition, I am trying to convey a God who sees more than just this Earth, for S/He was around for a long time before this Earth existed. I am trying to convey a God who loves those created in His/Her own image so much, that S/He has attempted many times, with many messengers, to send His/Her messages to them. I am trying to convey a God who is beyond the pronouns which are available in our language and for whom I, therefore, have to make up pronouns in order to avoid offending anyone; for as much as our female population needs their Goddesses for identity, and as much as our male population objects to God being anything other than the Father, God is beyond those petty practices of our human comprehension.

Further, I am trying to convey a God who is beyond the void; He is the ALL beyond the veil of nothingness. I am trying to convey a God who cannot be described or defined by using human terms. I am trying to convey a God who cannot be proved to be factual, because if God were a proven fact, then belief would not be needed. I am trying to convey a God of belief.

So, the fifth belief which I would like you to consider is a <u>belief</u> in God.

BELIEF SIX:
I BELIEVE IN CHRIST

This one is the personal belief previously mentioned. It is personal because I have personally chosen to try to live life in imitation of the Christ, whereas others may chose another model as the one who reflects God to them. Since God is beyond our present comprehension, we need someone or something to reflect to us the God whom we accept, but whom we cannot comprehend. I have chosen the Christ to generate this personal reflection to me.

To explain this choice, I will have to repeat a section from *The Christian Conspiracy*. For those who have already read these words, I will not apologize for repeating them. Instead, I will say that maybe these words bear repeating. They are from pages 220-221 of that book.

"The major understanding which I am trying to transmit is that God is represented to us by something else, by the reflection of God which is made in the activities and the stance of another. In the case of the Christ, if you accept the beliefs of Jesus and what he stands for, then you are a Christian and have the Father as your God. If another appeals, then another pathway is open to you.

"In his magnificent book, *Jesus Before Christianity*, Albert Nolan described the God who would be reflected by Jesus Christ. The following words are not his, for they have been changed to fit the context of this work. However, the sense of the words is similar.

"If you see God in Jesus Christ, then the God that you see is a God:
1. *who is tolerant of others rather than being intolerant of their beliefs;*
2. *who serves the needs of others rather than being served by them;*
3. *who is without rank in the world rather than ruling the world;*
4. *who proposes love rather than fear or blind obedience;*
5. *who chooses to be associated with people of compassion rather than of power;*
6. *who liberates humankind rather than enslaving it to dogmas;*
7. *who practices Unconditional Love for all rather than accepting only those who think as he does.*

If that is the picture of God to you, then your God is more human and more thoroughly humane than any human being. He is the God who has been pictured by what Jesus Christ stood for, and not necessarily by what the Church has stood for. If that is the picture of God to you, then you are blessed, whatever the Church may say. You are with the 'Most Radiant One.' "

After repeating that section from a previous book, let me state that if it were not for a belief in the God who calls to me, I might be considered a Buddhist; for much of what I have become as a human being is reflected in their practices rather than in the practices of the Christian Church. However, the God who calls to me is reflected more in the human and divine activities of the Christ, rather than those of the Buddha.

Consequently, even though as explained in *The Christian Conspiracy* those reflections are not necessarily represented by the activities of the Christian Church, I consider myself to be a Christian, possibly of the New Age or of the New Pilgrimage, rather than of the Church.

BELIEF SEVEN:
I BELIEVE IN UNCONDITIONAL LOVE
FOR HUMAN ACTIVITIES

Although Unconditional Love is generally considered to be a spiritual attribute, I submit that it can also bring forth the best in human beings. I love the quote recently presented which says, "We are not human beings having a spiritual experience; we are spiritual beings having a human experience." Consequently, I feel that all spiritual things should be applied to all of the human activities wherever and whenever possible. Can you imagine what the world would be like if Unconditional Love were its only law? Can you believe that it might be possible? I can!

BELIEF EIGHT:
I BELIEVE THAT GOD MUST HAVE FELT BOTH PAIN AND PRIDE AS S/HE WATCHED HIS/HER CHILDREN DEPART.

If you are a parent, how did you feel as you watched your children leave home to go out on their own? These feelings may first have occurred when you left your small one at a summer camp, knowing that at night, he or she would go to bed without your presence. Or it might have been when you dropped him or her at the college dorm, and then you slowly drove away as you kept glancing back at the rapidly diminishing figure in your rear-view mirror. Or it might have been when you watched your son or daughter get married and knew that their primary devotion would henceforth be to someone else.

Whatever memory you may have about the time of separation, I feel certain that you can remember the feeling not only of pain, but also of pride as you said to yourself, "Well, I have done all I can to prepare them for this. I hope it was enough." And so, with a mixture of pride and pain, you watched those who were "created in your own image" set off to find their own experiences.

If you can remember those emotions, then try to understand how God must have felt, knowing that humankind was leaving Him/Her in order to experience evolutionary development on their own. S/He must have felt not only a great deal of pain in the separation, but also pride in the fact that it was happening. S/He must have hoped that those "created in His/Her own image" could handle it.

Just as parents wait patiently and with great expectations to hear some word from their child, or just as parents wait eagerly for a visit by their child, S/He must have the same feelings about us; else why would the Christ have given us the Parable of the Prodigal Son as a part of his teachings? God must be waiting eagerly to hear about our progress along the Way; and must be waiting patiently as we attempt to find our way into oneness with Him/Her. At least, that is my belief.

With these reflections on belief, I leave you to find the individual pathway to oneness with God which is meant for you. I wish you well as you experience your journey.

SO BE IT!

APPENDIXES

APPENDIX A: ADDITIONAL NOTES FROM THE AUTHOR

In an earlier draft of this work, these Notes were included in the front of the book. They have been moved here to facilitate the reading of the first part of the book. The Notes are:

1. The term "New Age" is used in this book. This term is objected to by many in the movement; and alternate names have been suggested. I particularly like "New Paradigm Pioneers" or "New Paradigm Pilgrims" which were suggested by an ordained Presbyterian minister in north Georgia. I would like to shorten those names to "New Pilgrimage" in order to designate those pioneers who have left the restrictive thinking of the established religions, but have not accepted the restrictive thinking of the cult movements which are often associated with the term "New Age."

To many people, the term "New Age" automatically presents a picture of the cult worship of an individual person on Earth. As explained in *Christianity and the New Age Religion*, that is as far as it can be from the belief system which could be called "New Pilgrimage," a system which has complete freedom from any mind control, even the type which is practiced by the established religions. Consequently, I do not like the name "New Age" because it creates a false impression in my writings. However, since no one would understand what I would mean by "New Pilgrimage," I will continue to use "New Age" as a name which communicates. I will continue to use it until a name which is more appropriate, more accepted or more descriptive is developed.

2. In this book, I might use the words he, him, himself and the like when I mean them to designate a human. I know that some are offended by this practice because they consider it to be sexist. I have attempted to modify this habit; but since this was the way I was taught to write, I sometimes may slip back into those old habits. I do not intend my use of the masculine pronouns to be sexist, and I do not in any way intend it to imply superiority; for that is about as far from my true belief as it is possible to get. If there is any offense, it is unintentional and I apologize.

As mentioned in the earlier Notes from the Author, I have used S/He as a pronoun for God. In addition, I have often used him/her as a pronoun for a person. It is a difficult way to write and does seem to make the reading more difficult. Nevertheless, it is an attempt to show my understanding to those who are concerned about such things.

3. In this book, as in previous books, the abbreviations BCE [Before Common Era] and CE [Common Era] and are used in place of BC and AD to designate those years as being before [BCE] or after [CE] the year commonly accepted throughout most parts of the world as being year 0. I do this for a reason to which I was first alerted by Bishop Spong, the Episcopal Bishop of Newark. Bishop Spong has written many books on religious subjects. Some parts of his writing present an erudite explanation of the sources of Christian tradition; whereas other parts of his writing present pure speculation. I enjoy his writing very much, even the speculative part. Bishop Spong decided to use the designations of BCE and CE because he feels that it is pure arrogance to indicate to our non-Christian friends that we do not believe that they can tell time by requiring them to say "in the year of our Lord" [the translation of AD]. I agree with him.

4. In this book, I have used the phrase "restrictive teachings" or the like several times. I mean that phrase to mean the teachings presented by any established religion which the follower of that religion <u>must</u> accept. I do not mean for this phrase to bemean those teachings. As a father, I know that I had to give restrictive teachings to my children until they could think for themselves. Sometimes those restrictions worked, and some times they did not. The Church Fathers or other religious leaders have done the same thing. They have developed teachings for their adherents which restrict what the followers can believe.

I believe that it is better to have restrictive teachings than to have no teachings at all; for it is a way to "get the kids in off of the streets and let them know that there is a God." However, it is my personal belief that at some time, the restrictions must be removed so that each individual can find the way into oneness with God intended for him/her alone. That is the reason for giving this book the sub-title *Our Song of Freedom*. After having removed the restrictive teachings of the Christian Church from myself, I have found the freedom to find the personal God meant for me.

5. This is not an escape novel or a book to be read in any sort of light-hearted manner. Instead, it is a book which was written to transmit understanding. I have tried to make it as readable as possible, but the material is, at times, weighty stuff.

6. At this point, I would like to share an experience I had during a deep meditation in early September, 1994. Those who have read the biography which was presented in the second book and which is repeated in this book, know that I have a Ph.D. in Chemistry, and that I spent my industrial career in the chemical and paper industries. Much of that career was spent in developing chemicals which purify water from prior pollution; and I feel positive about a career which used chemicals to prevent rather than to cause pollution. Because of that career, I understand how chemicals are produced. I feel certain that is why the meditation presented me with an example of producing chemicals as a way of teaching me about religion.

In the meditation, I was shown that despite my knowledge about chemistry, I simply could not tell what was happening inside a piece of chemical equipment [e.g. a chemical reactor] merely by looking at the outside. Instead, I had to know what had been put into the reactor and what conditions were present in the internal part of the reactor in order to understand what was going on. Trying to understand what is happening merely by looking at the outside of a chemical reactor is somewhat analogous to trying to understand a religion merely by reading the writings produced by that religion. To really understand the religion, it is necessary to understand what the society was like at the time those writings were developed, and what the character and the training of the author had been like. Merely taking the writings at face value could be as misleading as merely looking at the outside of a chemical reactor.

In addition, I was shown that a chemical reactor was a generic thing out of which a variety of chemicals could be produced, depending on what was put in, what conditions were used, etc. In fact, the same reactor might be used in one period of time to make one chemical, and used to make an entirely different chemical at another time. In one sense, the chemical reactor could be said to be evolving toward a new system of usage. The same is true for a religion. It evolves toward a new system of beliefs. It isn't the same thing at all times.

However, just as the original use of the chemical reactor is possibly the most effective use of that equipment, the original teachings of a religion are probably those which are nearest to the truth which it was trying to express in the beginning.

It is because of this understanding that I suggest that each follower of the Christ try to understand what the teachings were before they were altered by the early Church Fathers, particularly those teachings which were developed during the fourth-sixth centuries. This suggestion was my principal reason for writing *The Christian Conspiracy*. It is also the principle reason for writing this book in which there is some indication of how our belief systems might expand, and where we might take them from here.

7. As a follow-up to the preceding paragraph, people have always had a tendency to look at something from the outside, gain some small insight about what they see, and then act as if they know exactly what things are like on the inside. Some may feel that I have done that in this book when I talk about religions with which I do not have a life-long association. If that impression has been given, I apologize; for I do not really feel as if I know what a Muslim or Buddhist or Confucianist really feels about his/her religion.

There are three stories I will relate to show how people have had this tendency and how misleading a view from the outside can be. The first story is the old one about the seven blind men who wanted to know what an elephant was like. The first grabbed a leg, and exclaimed that an elephant was like a tree. The second grabbed an ear, and instantly "knew" that an elephant was exactly like a fan. And on it went, each blind man feeling that he knew just what an elephant was like; but since no one had "seen" the complete picture, then no one was completely correct.

The second story is a personal one. In the Spring of 1995, I was traveling to Rome and Turkey with a group of friends. While waiting to go into a men's room in a restaurant in Rome, a man in the line behind me asked if I were from the United States. When I replied that I was, he stated in a very Germanic accent that he had visited my country and that "it is very flat and very wet." When I asked him where he had visited, he replied, "New Orleans." I kept a straight face when I was with him, but later, we all had a good laugh. Sometime, I would like to show him the Rockies and Death Valley to see if he would continue to have the same impression of the United States.

The last story has to do with religion. It is the quote from Mohandas Gandhi which has previously been used [see pages 162-3], but in this case it has been expanded and slightly paraphrased. In this slightly paraphrased form, it says, "All religions are true. However, they have been interpreted, and sometimes misinterpreted by humans who are less-than-perfect. Consequently, imperfections have crept into all religions. Sometimes when we look at those religions from the outside, we see the imperfections rather than the truths."

If we can learn to understand these three stories, then possibly the adherents of one religion will not take so many potshots at the belief systems of another person in the future.

8. Although some of the material in this book is truly weighty stuff, the words in this book are not the ultimate answer to anything. In fact, I have been introduced to energies and to concepts which are far beyond anything described in this book. Those energies are so advanced, that if those created in the image of God had accepted them and worked with them in the very beginning, reincarnation might never have been needed. Instead, the Personal Pathway to God [i.e. the third Cosmic Concept] would have been immediately assured. However, so few of God's creatures accepted these energies, that reincarnation became the only way through which the third Cosmic Concept could have been achieved. That is the reason why reincarnation has been mentioned so often in all three books.

9. Finally, I again want to emphasize that these thoughts of mine are for your consideration in developing thoughts of your own. In *no way* am I trying to dictate that you *must* accept them!

APPENDIX B
CREATION MYTHS
FROM AROUND THE WORLD

In this Appendix, a number of creation myths from around the world are presented. This is done to show that religions other than those described in the text of this work have developed creation stories which may show relevance to the first Cosmic Concept. The first Cosmic Concept stated that there is One God who created *all things*, and all of the things which S/He created are *good*. It is up to the reader to decide whether these creation myths show relevance.

Many of these stories are paraphrases of the stories presented by Virginia Hamilton. Her book is listed in the Bibliography. Although most of the creation stories and their corresponding analysis will be presented in one paragraph, a few of the longer ones have been divided. The source of each creation story will be given in **bold** print.

The **Krono people of New Guinea** have a legend which states that Sa, or Death, came first and made a world of mud. God visited Sa, and saw that everything in Sa's kingdom was dirty and dark. And so, God made the mud into a solid material which we now know as Earth. And then he made plants and animals to live on Earth. And then God took Sa's daughter and with her he populated the Earth with people; but all was still dark. And so God used the rooster and the tou-tou to make the light of day with the sun. And when the sun went to sleep, he made the stars and the moon so that the Earth would not again be dark, and so that the people would be comforted. But since God had taken Sa's only daughter without paying the bride-price, then God did wrong; and thus Death has a call on any of God's children whenever he wishes. Consequently, although almost all that God did was good, he did one wrong thing and thus Death can win out over God's children.

In the **Banks Islands, north of the New Hebrides in Melanesia**, the Sun always existed and was the father who, with Quatgoro the huge stone who was the mother, generated twelve sons. Quat, the major son of the Sun, then made humans from a tree. One of his brothers imitated this development, but then he decided to bury his humans. While Quat's humans lived, the buried ones rotted, thus introducing death. To help his living humans, Quat made all the plants and the animals, but his greatest achievement was to make night, which generated the need for sleep, and the need for the birds who awaken the living humans from sleep. Thus, all the good things came from Quat. They include all the plants and animals of the Earth, all the birds of the air, the night and its accompanying sleep, and the day and the work which is possible only because of the night and the sleep which was brought by Quat. Consequently, all that was good was brought by the God, Quat, the major son of the Sun. All that was not good was introduced by one of Quat's brothers.

In **China**, it was believed that in the beginning, the universe was in the shape of a hen's egg. The inside of the egg contained *no thing*, inside of which there was Phan Ku who had not yet been born. When Phan Ku was born, he was the Great Creator who created the Earth, separated the sky [yang] from the Earth [yin], chiseled out the earth's rivers and valleys, and created the mountains. He placed the stars and the moon in the night sky and the sun in the day sky. He made the great seas and placed them where they now are. When Phan Ku died, after 18,000 years, the world was completed. His skull made the dome of the sky. Soil was made from his body. Rocks were made from his bones. All plant life was made from his hair. Thunder and lightening were the sound of his voice. The wind was his breath. Rain was made from his sweat. The fleas of his hair made all of humankind. Only after Phan Ku vanished were the bad things introduced such as pain and suffering. Thus, by losing their living God, humanity lost its creator which means that in His absence, humankind suffers forever.

The **Blackfoot Native Americans** tell the story of the "Old Man" who came from the south, and as he traveled north, he created the birds, the animals, the plants, the prairies, the mountains, the timber and the brushlands. In one part of his journeys, after he had grown tired of being alone, he created a mother and her child out of clay. He buried them and returned each day to see the changes which had occurred. At the end of the fourth day, they had become people; and so the Old Man bade them to walk with him to the river. The woman asked if they would live forever; and the Old man admitted that he hadn't thought about that. And so he took a buffalo chip and said that if it floated on the river, then people would die;

but they would die only for four days, and four days after they die, they would live again. However, if the buffalo chip sank, then people would live forever. The chip floated. However, the woman was not willing to accept the decision of the Old Man, and so she suggested that a stone be used and that if it floated, people would live forever. However, if the stone sank, people would feel sorry for one another and they must die. The stone sank, and so people must die because they were not willing to accept the decisions of God in their lives.

There is a lot of Judeo-Christian theology in this simple, but beautiful story. There is the background of God's creation, followed by humankind's decision not to accept what God had offered them. As a consequence, God's vision for man has been spoiled. This story echoes the Garden of Eden story, even though it comes from an entirely different source. It also echoes the Christian belief that after three days of death and burial, a resurrection will occur on the fourth day. This belief came from people who, according to written history, could not have known of the Christian story of the Resurrection.

There are many **Russian** legends which have the God, Ulgen, creating man as his companion, and then creating the Earth in which they can dwell. Finally, man creates woman as his companion, but needs Ulgen to breath life into her. This tale echoes the story in Genesis 2:7 which states, "then the Lord God formed man of dust from the ground, and breathed into his nostrils the breath of life." This happened even though the Russian creation story was an ancient tale, told long before Christianity entered Russia.

The **Maidu Indians of California** have a story which begins when there was only darkness and water. The turtle then comes down from the north on a raft searching for land, but there is none. Then "Earth Starter" comes from the sky. In conjunction with the efforts of the turtle, Earth Starter creates the land; but since it was still dark, Earth Starter brought the sun who was Earth Starter's sister. He then asked the stars to come out, and then created the great oak tree under which he rested after his many labors. Then Earth Starter asked the birds to go into the air, and he took some mud out of which he made the first deer. Then he made all of the animals, and told the coyote that he now would make man and woman which he did out of red earth and water. The coyote suggested that the people should have paws just as he did, but Earth Starter said that they would have real hands, just like he did so that when they were chased by bears, they could climb trees. As the people multiplied, Earth Starter visited them less and less; but that was all right, because he had made life easy for them. The fruits were easy to find, and no one had to be sick or to die. However, they did grow old, and so Earth Starter told them that when they got old, they merely had to dive down in the water of the lake and when they rose, they would be young again. The part about diving down into the water of the lake in order to be young again is very much like the Christian baptism, in which one is reborn by the water. After telling the people how they could regain their youth, then Earth Starter went away in the night. He went up above, somewhat as Jesus ascended.

The **Hurons, a Native American tribe of the East**, tell a story almost identical to this story of Earth Starter, although their "Earth Starter" is a divine woman.

The **Australian aborigines** tell the story of Karora. It starts when there was only darkness over the Earth and Karora created first the bandicoots [great rats] as food, and then gave birth to many sons as people. However, since there were not enough bandicoots to feed all the sons who were created, then most of the sons were destroyed in a great flood of honey. The flood of honey is somewhat like the great flood in which the people of the Earth were destroyed during the time of Noah. This implies that what is created by God must be perfect, or it will be destroyed.

The **Lonzi people of Zambia** tell of Nyambi who lived on Earth with his wife and made all the birds, the animals and the fishes and then climbed to the sky on a spider's thread where he now reigns and appears each day as the sun. Consequently, Nyambi created all things then went to the sky. Sound familiar?

The **Yoruba people of Nigeria** talk about Olorum, the Supreme Being who created the solid land on an Earth which was only water. It took him four days to do this. Then he sent the first people from heaven and breathed life into them. The thought that God "breathes life into those created in His image" as is repeated in many Creation stories, even that of the Jew or the Christian.

The **Maya of Guatemala** have an extraordinary story of creation in four parts. In the beginning, there was no sound and nothing which could make a sound. They was only darkness and the silent water of the calm sea. Yet within this dark night and calm sea, there was Maker and there was the Feathered Serpent. These two called into the Heart of Sky where God lived. The three, God, the Maker and the Feathered Serpent, brought their thoughts together, and from these thoughts came words which were so powerful and clear that whatever they said came to be. In this way *the Word* was formed. The Word said "Earth" and earth was created. The Word said "mountains and valleys" and merely by the saying, these were created. In this way all the wild animals were made. This was the First Creation.

Then God said, "Say Our names, but the deer, the panthers, and the serpents could not form the words to say Our names; and so God decided to begin again. He decided to leave the wild animals in the forest where they would kill and be killed, where they would stay and serve because they could not talk and praise their God.

And so, this ended the First Creation and the Word was tried again. This time the Word made the human form, but it was damp and watery and did not look like Them who had made it. It made no sense when it tried to talk. Since it would just get wetter, it was allowed to melt into the watery sea. This ended the Second Creation.

For the Third Creation, the Word decided to make human out of a wood carving. These humans could talk and praise God; they could stand up and walk; they looked like people and they could multiply; but they had no hearts, no minds and no memories of the Maker. Although they were the first people who could cover the Earth, they were merely the model for humankind because they were too wooden. And so God made a great flood to destroy them. All were destroyed except a few who escaped to the trees as monkeys. They are all that is left of the Third Creation which produced wooden dummies that could not think.

Then the Maker said that morning is coming for the people of the Earth. The sun, the moon and the stars are coming soon, and the Word thought and thought about what they could use as a source of human flesh. As they thought, four animals came to them: the mountain cat, the coyote, the little parrot and the crow. These four animals were from the Broken Place where the white and the yellow corn were plentiful. The Word then had the thought that the white and the yellow corn could be used to make the bodies of human beings, with water used as blood. These materials would flesh out the formed and shaped people, the Final Creation. Maker and the Feathered Serpent said that they would use ground corn to build the bodies, and water with fat to make the blood and flesh.

The resulting four humans were never born of mother and had no father. Instead, they were shaped by the Word of God. They were human. They walked, and talked and worked and listened and gave thanks to the Maker. This was the Fourth and Final Creation. However, these humans could see through rocks and trees and people. The Maker thought that they had gone too far, and so they took a little back and allowed them only to see what was near them. In this way they would be satisfied with sowing and reaping and having children. Thus, because they were to be humans and not Gods, they were made to lose their complete knowing of all things.

They knew a few things, but they did not have complete knowledge like the Maker and the Feathered Serpent who were the Heart of Earth. They knew God who was the Heart of Sky. In this manner, through Four Creations the Word was used to form all things, including humankind who would be above all which had been created before the Final Creation, but would be below the Gods. It would seem that anyone who reads this story with its creation by the Word, and its fall from the full knowledge of God, will recognize that it contains a number of elements which Christians have previously thought belonged to them alone.

The **Tahitians of the Society Islands** have creation myths which are identical to the **Samoans**, two thousand miles to the West. These identical creation myths teach that the Supreme Being lives in an egg. This Supreme Being [Ta-aroa in the Society Islands and Tangaroa in Samoa] is the source of all things, and the egg acts as the incubator in which all things are formed.

In **Egyptian** mythology, Ra was the first to come into being. His father was Nun, the waters. From Ra's mouth all things were created. First was the earth, then the ground, then the creeping things, then air and then moisture. Then came the lesser Gods who came from Ra and who rule the Earth and the Moon with Ra, the sun-God.

In **Greek** mythology, first there was Nothing, followed by Earth so the gods would have a place to stand. Then came Tatarus, the underworld and Eros, love. Out of Nothing came darkest Night and Er-e-bos, another part of the underworld who gave birth to Day and Space. Earth brought forth Heaven and the Sea, followed by the mountains which were the home of the Gods.

There are many other Creation Stories which could be related, but these give enough of a feel for the belief that throughout the world, the Creation Stories have many similar elements, even though history records no meetings of the various people who developed these similar stories. It kind of makes you do some thinking, doesn't it?

There is one more point to make before closing this Appendix. That point was developed in a recent book by a Christian minister. In his excellent book, *Earthspirit, A Handbook for Nurturing Ecological Christianity*, Michael Dowd, a minister of the United Church of Christ, makes a very interesting point about the Creation stories which came from the Western tradition *vs.* those which came from the Native American cultures. He says that since the Western Creation stories gave humans dominion over the Earth, we could allow ourselves the opportunity to use the resources of the Earth in order to explore and to develop science. In this way, we could understand more about the Earth and therefore, if we let ourselves, could come more into the consciousness of the Earth. However, since the Native Americans Creation stories made humans a part of the Earth, then they could not explore what the new mysteries of the Earth could be, but merely had to accept the Earth as they found it. This meant that their science, or their understanding of the consciousness of the Earth, could not grow, but could only remain rather stagnant.

In his request that Christianity take a more ecological viewpoint of the Earth, Reverend Dowd makes the point that there is a middle ground between these two Creation theologies which would allow us to understand evolution without destroying that which gives us this understanding. In other words, he requests that we learn from our study of the Earth, but while doing so, we respect the Earth and not destroy it while doing this study.

As a Christian who spent a fair amount of his working life in the science of minimizing the effects of civilian and industrial pollution, I support his request. In this way, we could learn something from the Native Americans, and they could learn from us. Each society has something to offer. Neither society has its act together exactly the way that the Prelude to this book would suggest; for one chose to evolve by hurting mother Earth, while the other chose not to evolve. There is a balance between these contrasting viewpoints which would be preferable to that proposed by either one alone.

APPENDIX C: PERSONAL STEPS ALONG THE PATHWAY

As those who have read the books of this series will recognize, I feel that the "New Paradigm" kind of "New Age" [see page 239] represents a step toward oneness with God which goes beyond the established religions with their restrictive teachings and their need for conformity. This Appendix will present some personal experiences as I have walked on my unique pathway into oneness with God as a part of this new belief system. Out of the many events which could be reported, I have selected six episodes, all of which happened while on spiritual journeys conducted by Dr. Norma Milanovich. Her book, co-authored with Linda Myers, will describe these journeys in depth. It will be published in 1996.

This is the first time that these stories have been shared. They may generate skepticism on the part of the reader; but I am convinced that they hold truth—at least for me and for those who walk a similar pathway.

Despite my willingness to share, I have some reluctance in reporting these stories. One of the parts of the New Age with which I do not resonate is the "Show and Tell" aspect in which teachers ask their students to share meditation experiences, both for the support which it creates and for the confirmation it gives when relatively identical experiences are related. The part which I do not like is the "can you top this" aspect. This happens when the results of one person's meditation become so expansive that they generate a competitive urge on the part of another person who then tries to show what great meditative experiences he/she has had. That is not the purpose of these meditative experiences. The real purpose is to teach love; and if that is not done, then the experience is not a truly meaningful one. Consequently, my reluctance to report these episodes is the fear that some will accept these metaphysical experiences as the end result of the meditation—when they most certainly are not. The end result of any meditation is to experience love. That is the total *raison d'être* of meditation.

Two stories might help to illustrate this lesson. The first story was supplied by Father John W. Groff, Jr., for whom I feel a deep level of love, not only for his help and encouragement, but for his suggestion that these personal experiences of mine were so meaningful that they might be considered by some to be worthwhile for their own sake. He knows that I do not feel that way, but I needed his gentle and loving nudge to set the record straight. The second story is from the teachings of St. Paul.

In the first story, three yogis, each the student of a different spiritual master, chanced to meet while on a pilgrimage. As they shared their evening meal and contemplated the meaning of the divine presence, one student looked at the other two and stated that his master was so great that he had attained the *Siddhi*, and therefore could levitate, to which the other two responded in unison, "Ahhh." After a suitable pause, the second student announced that his master was such a high being that he had attained the *Siddhi* of bi-location, to which the other two also gave a respectful, "Ahhh." When all eyes turned to the third student, fully expecting him to continue in this great game of spiritual one-upmanship, he simply said, "My teacher knows how to love." The response was an awed silence, for when love is present, no words are necessary.

The second story is reported in the 13th Chapter of 1 Corinthians in which St. Paul teaches:

"If I speak in the tongues of man and of angels, but have not love, I am a noisy gong or a clanging cymbal. And if I have prophetic powers, and understand all mysteries and all knowledge, and if I have all faith, so as to move mountains, but have not love, I am nothing. If I give away all I have, and if I deliver my body to be burned, but have not love, I gain nothing. Love is patient and kind; love is not jealous or boastful; it is not arrogant or rude. Love does not insist on its own way; it is not irritable or resentful; it does not rejoice at wrong, but rejoices in the right. Love bears all things, believes all things, hopes all things, endures all things. Love never ends; as for prophecies, they will pass away; as for tongues, they will cease; as for knowledge, it will pass away. For our knowledge is imperfect and our prophecy is imperfect; but when the perfect comes, the imperfect will pass away. When I was a child, I spoke like a child, I thought like a child, I reasoned like a child; when I became a man, I gave up childish ways. For now we see in a mirror dimly, but then [i.e. later] face to face. Now I know in part; then I shall understand fully, even as I have been fully understood. So faith, hope, love abide, these three; but the greatest of these is love."

The moral of these two stories is that the only experience worthy of our seeking is the experience of Love and Love does not have to be sought at all—only opened to; for Love is what we are.

And so I will share six metaphysical experiences, not in the belief that they are important in themselves, but in the hope that through the experience of opening yourself to the possibility that they did happen, you can remove the restrictions that bind you, and in this way open yourself to the Love that is you.

A FEW INDICATIONS OF PAST LIVES

This book is being written in late 1994 and 1995. Some 25 years ago, my wife introduced me to a man who has since had quite an influence in my life. His name was William David. Recently he has been given a new name, Elias DeMohan. This spiritual name has the potential to serve him through a great part of his adventures still to come.

I will not state that Elias awakened me, for I do not believe that one can be awakened by anyone other than one's self, or at least one's higher self. However, when the time came for the awakening to occur, much of what I had discussed with Elias started to fit into its proper slot.

I like Elias very much. We have talked about many things, including the belief that each individual who exists in this physical plane has existed here in many previous incarnations. In addition, we discussed the belief that each has existed in other locations within the physical and the etheric universe; and that few, if any, souls had originated on Earth. Instead, they have come here to gain an experience which can be found only rarely in other parts of the universe. The experience which is so prevalent here is that of feeling *emotions* in a dense, three-dimensional, physical body. It is a fascinating experience.

To accept a belief in reincarnation, one must, of course, accept the belief that past lives did occur; but accepting a belief does not make it factual. Belief and fact are not meant to co-exist. When the fact of anything becomes established, then one does not need to have the belief. To establish that past lives have occurred as a fact would be similar to establishing that an afterlife does exist as a fact. An experiment which could prove either would be a very difficult experiment to design, an even more difficult one to conduct, and probably an impossible one to analyze or reproduce. Nevertheless, I believe in each.

Despite the difficulty of proving the reality of past lives, I believe that in the fall of 1993, I had an experience which gave several indications that past lives really did happen.

At the time of this experience, I was involved with thirty-three other human beings in a spiritual journey to the Yucatan. During that journey, we visited a number of the sacred sites in the Yucatan including Tikal, Tulum, Coba, Chitzen-Itza, and Palenque. I felt that one of my specific purposes for this trip was to get in contact with a soul fragment of mine named Oh-Ma-Nah who had lived in a country named Obadia, an ancient civilization in South America. In that incarnation of my soul, Oh-Ma-Nah had performed some rather spectacular feats of sharing knowledge with others. He did this despite opposition on the part of the leaders of Obadia; for they did not want information to be shared with the people of the country. However, since his efforts did not continue to be practiced after his physical death, Oh-Ma-Nah felt that his life had been such a failure that he did not wish to return to the Monad. I felt the need to contact him and convince him to return. I felt that the Yucatan would be the proper place because before we left the States, every time I had tried to visualize the Yucatan during meditation, I had been constantly pulled further south toward a place in South America where I knew Obadia had existed.

Since I had visited the Yucatan only about 14 months prior to this trip, when we arrived at Tulum I did not feel the need to explore the site as so many of my fellow travelers did. Consequently, I went to a spot overlooking the ocean to the East. I found a comfortable seat on a rock, and I sat down to meditate about Oh-Ma-Nah. During this meditation, for the first time in many, many attempts, I was allowed to see Oh-Ma-Nah's face. He was a handsome, vibrant youth with dark, curly hair. I strongly felt that he had been a previous part of me. During the meditation, we talked, and I had the distinct feeling that he was ready to return to the Monad. I feel strongly that he did that, for since that time I have not been bothered by the "lost" feeling I used to get each time I would think of him. Instead, I feel a great sense of joy. I feel that he is now back where he belongs. The belief that he can be with the Monad while I am in physical form supports the belief system of the "Third Viewpoint of Reincarnation," which was presented on pages 88-93.

It was with a great deal of joy that I finished the meditation with a parting word to Oh-Ma-Nah. When I opened my eyes, I saw a Coke can jammed between two pieces of rock just to the right of where I was sitting. My immediate reaction was that the can had been put there in hate, and that I had to remove it as an act of love. The can was really jammed down, and I couldn't budge it. Then a shadow fell over me. It was one of the other tour members whom I will call Ann [not her real name]. I said, "Ann, I have to get this can up as an act of love" and just then, the can was released as if someone had pushed it up from below. In that way, I got that piece of trash away from that sacred site.

Then I looked up at Ann and realized that she was falling apart. She was crying with great sobs and shaking as if she were truly going to break into pieces. I got up and started to hug her and soothe her and tell her that everything was all right. I have held many people when they cried, and I have cried deeply myself; but these were the deepest sobs I have ever heard or felt. They were truly coming all the way from her toenails. I tried to get a focus on what was happening, but all I could see was a deep red color and a leg. I tried to get her to transmute that deep red color into a light pink, and then to a light blue, then to a silver and then to a gold. This seemed to have a calming effect on her emotions; and later, she told me that she could remember seeing the silver and the gold.

The sun was quite hot, so we went over to some shade where I kept saying soothing words to her. She remained silent, almost comatose. After a while, she spoke a few words which indicated that she felt better. Since it was time to get back to the bus, we started to walk there. It was about half a mile. We got within about 10 yards of the bus when Ann collapsed. The healers came out of the bus to help her, and I left her in more capable hands than my own. After some time, Ann was able to get on the bus where she sat next to a person who has great psychic gifts. I will call this person "Jean" [not her real name].

When the bus arrived at our hotel, I had to pass Ann and Jean as I got off the bus. Ann was simply beaming with a beautiful smile. I took her hand and said, "Welcome back." I had no doubt that she had returned to us from what must have been an arduous journey to some other time or place.

Jean said that she wanted to talk with me later. When she did, she said that she had seen the entire story. She said that prior to their present incarnation, four people had made a contract to help Ann through her very traumatic experience because she could neither face nor transmute this experience by herself. The four people, all of whom were on this particular trip, had agreed to be at a specific place at a specific time in order to open a vortex for Ann which would permit her to relive a past life experience and, with our help, to transmute it. The transmutation was needed because in a previous existence at that site, Ann had been a member of a very peaceful tribe which had been massacred by a neighboring, fearsome, war-like tribe. At that time, one of the present-day people had been her uncle. Another had been the sister of her lover who was there as a substitute for the lover. The lover could not come because it would have been too traumatic for Ann. I had been the High Mayan Priest of the village and of the tribe. The fourth person was required to ground the energy of the transmutation which he did by remaining back at the hotel, sick as a dog, while he grounded all of the energy we were expending during the transmutation.

Ann's particular experience which had to be transmuted occurred because the conquering tribe slaughtered Ann's lover in front of her eyes while he was defending her family instead of his own. The rest of the tribe also was slaughtered—all but Ann who was kept as a prize. She was exhibited and abused for a long period of time. Finally, she obtained a knife and committed suicide by slashing her leg. I told Jean that the story fit with all that I had seen, particularly the vivid red color of blood plus the leg. Jean then said that I had been able to transmute my particular experience at this site as had all of the other participants, but that Ann could not because of the trauma involved. She needed our help.

By the next day, Ann's aura shone. It remained radiant for the rest of the ten day journey. It was as if a tremendous burden had been lifted. In fact, Ann was a great help to the others who encountered traumatic experiences at Chitzen-Itza the next day when thirteen of the thirty-four member company experienced past life trauma at this site of high Mayan sacrifice. It was a heavy experience for all of us, and all were grateful for the prior-day's experience at Tulum in preparation for Chitzen-Itza.

I suppose you are now starting to wonder how such an experience could be more than just a slight, psychic-led indication of the existence of past lives. Well, the story isn't over yet. Ann returned to her home after the ten day trip to the Yucatan was over; but I continued on for another twenty days, first to Peru and Bolivia with another group of thirty-four people, and then to Easter Island with yet another group. Consequently, it was another three weeks before I got back to my home. The experiences at each subsequent site were rather great, and I located another soul fragment when we were in Peru. My only reason for mentioning this is to state that the next two segments of the trip were so full of my personal experiences that I really did not think of Ann again.

After getting back home, Ann returned to my mind as some unfinished business. I had a hard time understanding what was unfinished, because she had certainly seemed to be a happy person the last time I saw her. However, the feeling just would not go away, and so I went into a deep meditation about her. I then saw the one who had been her lover in that previous life. I will call him John. He was someone I knew very well. I had to ask myself how I was ever going to handle this.

At Christmas time, I received a nice note from Ann. This gave me a reason to write back and suggest that she attend the *Conclave of Michael*, a meeting of some 800 Lightworkers which was held in Banff, Canada during March, 1994. I did this because I knew John would be at that convention. However, she could not get there. I was still in a quandary, because to make a direct suggestion that they meet could be considered to be interfering in the lives of other individuals; and a chance meeting was unlikely, because one lived in the deep Southwest and the other in the deep Southeast, almost a continent apart.

By mid-summer, 1994, the pressure was getting heavy. I had the strong feeling that these two should meet, but I did not know how to do it without causing interference. In meditation one day, I asked how I should handle this and received the strong suggestion that I send Ann a copy of my new book [*The Christian Conspiracy*] and in a very simple letter, tell her that I had seen her on the inner planes with John, and that I felt she should meet him to exchange experiences. Ann responded with thanks for the book, and a statement that she would love to meet John.

In the spring of 1995, Ann, Jean and I, along with 33 others, were on a spiritual journey to Rome and Turkey. I told Jean that I believed I knew who the "missing person from the Tulum drama" was. She immediately told me who he was, thus confirming my intuition. Jean urged me to tell Ann the full story about John. The next day, during a bus ride, I told Ann the entire story, and showed her a group picture from which she immediately picked out John. She asked me to tell John about the situation, for John knew absolutely nothing about it.

On the last day of that spiritual journey, the group had a successful meditation at the base of Mount Ararat. We then parted company.

I came home. About two days later, I told John the entire story and showed him a picture of Ann with which he felt a closeness. He then told me that he and a few friends had just returned from a vacation in the Caribbean. The ten days there had been a great deal of fun and laughter for him—all except for one short period of intense discomfort. That day was when the group toured Tulum. John said that within five minutes of entering the site, he felt a very heavy pressure bearing down on him, and he became nauseous for some totally unknown reason. He had to leave the site. Within 15 minutes of leaving, he was fine again. No one else in the group had the same experience. John had been at Tulum on the same day we had been at Mount Ararat; and he had his reaction at Tulum without ever having been told that Ann even existed!

At the time of this writing, Ann and John have not met, but they are planning to. It will be interesting to see what develops. The similar reaction each had at Tulum [18 months apart], and the fact that neither knew about the other at the time they had those reactions, is fascinating to me.

Some may not consider this to be much of an indication for the reality of past lives—but I do.

A PROOF OF HUMAN TELEPATHY

Of all the gifts which God has given to us, possibly one of the most startling is that of being able to communicate with another person through telepathy. It is interesting to note that although there have been many cases of telepathy recorded, few have been recorded while doing work other than that which was a part of God's work; and those which have been done outside of God's work have often proved to be fraudulent. I believe that a trip which I participated in during the fall of 1994 was a trip which served God's purpose. During that trip, an extraordinary fact of telepathy occurred. I submit it as proof that telepathy can occur.

The trip in question was a trip to Maui. This trip was done with a group of thirty-four people who were to hold the energy for the group of twenty-five other people who were going to China and Tibet. As a part of the purpose for this trip, the Maui group was to receive symbols and coding while at Maui, and was to transfer these symbols and coding to the Earth from whence the information would be received by the group in the Far East. This transfer, using human spiritual capacity, was necessary because the energies preventing direct spiritual communication to Tibet were strong.

The two groups, the group in Maui and the group in the Far East, would have frequent contact through the spiritual plane. In particular, the contact from one "soul mate" in Maui to his/her counterpart in China/Tibet would be intense and frequent. The contact between the soul mates would be initiated by a group of seven symbols which would be exchanged at a combined group meeting in Los Angeles prior to one group's leaving for Maui, and the other group's leaving for China/Tibet.

Although the trip was not going to occur until late September, instructions were issued in July that each participant in the combined journey would meditate daily in order to receive three symbols. This meditation would be as practice for two subsequent activities: the receiving of seven pertinent symbols which would be received "three days before leaving on the journey," and the activity in Maui and China/Tibet during which a multitude of symbols and other codings were to be received and transmitted.

The day "three days before leaving on the journey," was Friday,

Appendix C: Personal Stories

September 24, 1994. Consequently, on that date, I meditated and immediately was given seven symbols, four of which were symbols which contained the pyramid in one form or another. I then asked to whom these symbols were to be given. The answer was Peter [not his real name], a friend in Albuquerque, half a continent away from Atlanta. Although I was a little surprised, I was pleased because the symbols seemed to be so appropriate for him. I then sat down and wrote Peter the following letter, dated September 24, 1994:

"My dear Peter:

"I have to assume that today, Friday, is the "three days before the journey" which Kuthumi mentioned in the instructions received in July. Anyway, today is the day I chose to develop the seven symbols by which I will communicate with my "soul mate." By the time you read this letter, I will already have given them to you on a card. This letter is merely some background information.

"You should know that I developed these seven symbols before I asked who was the person to whom I would give them. I then asked the question and got your name. I have to admit that I broke out laughing, first with the complete surprise of it and then with the joy of it. I had fully expected someone with whom this present personality of mine had seemed to establish a deeper sense of camaraderie, but that is how our ego sometimes gets in the way of spirit, isn't it? On a spiritual level, I grew instantly comfortable for three major reasons.

"First, I have been receiving the symbol of the pyramid almost every time I meditated on the daily three symbols. I often would get so frustrated that I would think, "Oh no, not again!"; but those old pyramids just kept coming. Many times I did not choose the pyramid as one of the three daily symbols, primarily because I would have to choose only three out of the hundreds of symbols I would be given each day, often in a dynamic, changing sense rather than as a set, single symbol. Nevertheless, as you review the daily symbols, a copy of which I have enclosed, you will see that the pyramid is repeated often and in many different forms. Of course, since you are working so closely with pyramidal structures in your daily work, these symbols seem particularly appropriate for you.

"Secondly, I was immediately told that you and I had been builders together many times. I feel certain that we were together at the Egyptian pyramids, but I was not shown that particular lifetime or lifetimes. However, I was shown our working together on the cathedral at Chartres. The scene was very specific and was instant confirmation of our association in the past, and of our need to associate in this present venture.

"Finally, with one exception the symbols are very appropriate for you. In fact, there is no other individual that I know on this Earth to whom six of the seven specific symbols could be so appropriate. The exception is the five-pointed star which is one of the seven symbols I have given you. In the daily meditations, I received the five-pointed star almost as frequently as I received the pyramid. I also received the cross many times and in many different forms, but I think that was more for me than for you, because the cross does not appear in the final seven symbols which I have given you. In respect to the five pointed star, many times I tried to convert it to the six pointed star for balance, but each time I did that, the message would come back, "No, the star is five pointed. The lotus is six-pointed." And you will note that the six-pointed lotus is on your symbol for destiny. I rarely saw the six-pointed star, and when I did, it would immediately have its corners rounded off to become the lotus. This may not be to your personality's liking [in this present life, Peter is of Jewish descent], but it is what I was given, and I was given this long before I knew you would be the recipient.

"Anyway, my brother, I thought I would share these few thoughts with you. I thought you might have an interest in the background and in the set of daily symbols. We will continue to be in communication. Go on your very important journey with all the Love and Light I can send to you—and go with God!"

I also wrote a letter which described the seven symbols in intimate detail, all oriented around what I knew about Peter.

The spiritual journey for each group began at the group meeting in Los Angeles on Monday, September 26, 1994. At that meeting, the method of picking the "soul mates" was drastically changed from what I had expected. Instead of my presenting the seven symbols to the person I had chosen, the procedure was to have each person in the China/Tibet group choose one person from the Maui group to whom he/she would give his/her symbols. Since there were more going to Maui than to China/Tibet, this would mean that there would be some Maui people not chosen as a "soul mate." In order to have the choosing proceed in an orderly manner, the China/Tibet group lined up on one side of the large room in which we met, while the Maui group lined up on the other side. The choosing was to start from the far left of the China/Tibet group.

I counted down the line and realized that Peter would be the twenty-second person to make a choice. I personally knew eighteen of the people who would choose before Peter, and I had become personally very close to many of them as a result of previous spiritual journeys. I truly did not believe that I would last until Peter had the chance to choose. However, one-by-one the China/Tibet people chose. I was still left when Peter's turn came. He left his side of the room at a rather deliberate pace; and at the half-way mark, he looked straight at me, and with a big grin on his face, he ran forward and we hugged.

As we walked to the center of the circle, I pulled the letter addressed to him out of my pocket and asked him how long he had known that we would be connected on this trip. He answered that for some time he had been getting my name, and that he had mentioned this to his wife. I told him that I had not asked until last Friday, and that when I was given his name I laughed first with surprise and then with joy. I then ran upstairs to share this news with my wife. I also told him that the symbols fit him perfectly, since most were pyramidal in form. He then gave me the seven symbols which he had been given for me, and all of them were pyramids. We both agreed that all of this was rather fantastic.

As can be noted in the letter which I had written the previous Friday, I had apologized for presenting Peter with a five-pointed star. Later, after he had read my letter, he came to me and said, "David, don't you remember that this was the way we recognized each other when we were in the School of Pythagoras?" I admitted that I had forgotten that, because our experiences there had been during an incarnation of almost 2600 years ago! He also said that the five-pointed star was a symbol for the rose, and that the rose was a very important part of the trip to China and Tibet. When Peter told me about the Pythagorean School, I told him about a person I knew in Atlanta who also had been a part of that school, and whom I had also seen working with me on the Cathedral at Chartres. I said to Peter that he and I had been together many times in the past and he agreed.

Although the reader of this story may not appreciate how improbable the selection of Peter and me as "soul mates" would be without divine or at least spiritual intervention, those who know all of the people who traveled on these journeys would have to express surprise. Whether they are surprised or not, it is a matter of fact that Peter chose me, and I chose him, and we both got the message to do this from a source which was outside of ourselves. Some may doubt that this is telepathy and might want to pass it off as a mere "coincidence." If so, I would suggest that they review the spiritual "phenomenon of coincidence" [see pages 107-13].

Whether this experience fits within "coincidence" or "telepathy," I feel that this is one of the most dramatic examples of how minds can communicate over space which has ever been documented. I believe it presents the truth that telepathy between humans can happen; but maybe only if they have help, and maybe only when they are doing God's work.

AN ANCIENT RITUAL REVISITED

During the week of Passover and Easter in the Spring of 1994, I was touring Israel with another group of 34 people. Five very intense personal experiences were given to me during the twelve days of this journey. All were meaningful to me. Two of them may be meaningful to the reader. One of these is presented in this section; the other in the next section.

In order to conduct our spiritual ceremonies, two individuals from the group had been designated Spiritual Masters. It was their job to design the appropriate ceremonies and to lead the rest of the group as they conducted these ceremonies. Sometimes, the ceremonies were so meaningful, that a short description of them would be given during a meeting on the evening before the ceremony was to be conducted.

Very early in the week, we had such a meeting during which the next day's ceremony was outlined. During this presentation, we were asked to recite the "Kadosh." We were presented with the words, "Kadosh, Kadosh, Kadosh, Adonai, Shevayot," and were asked to repeat these words three times as a verbal chant.

After the meeting ended, I was very uneasy. It seemed to me that something was not right. The discomfort simply would not go away. Consequently, before going to sleep, I stated my discomfort and told those who help me that if there were any explanation for this discomfort, or any reason that I should understand more about the Kadosh, then I would be receptive. With that commitment, I went to sleep. By 4:00 AM when I looked at the time, I knew a lot more than I did when I went to sleep. In essence, I had been shown the entire "Kadosh Ceremony" as it had originally been presented more than 3,000 years before. It was quite a ceremony. The next few paragraphs will attempt to describe this ceremony in the detail with which it was presented to me.

The Kadosh Ceremony was originally developed as a hymn of praise for the Ark of the Covenant [see Exodus, especially Chapters 25 and 26 for background on this Ark]. The ceremony was developed as soon as the Ark had been constructed. It was to be used as the ceremony for moving the Ark from one sacred site to another. I was told that the reason I had felt the discomfort on the previous evening, was because the word Kadosh was to be used <u>four</u> times in each chant, and the chant was to be sung [not spoken] four times. Anyone who had participated in the original ceremony would, therefore, feel as if it were incomplete if it did not follow this format.

To begin this ceremony of dedication and praise, eight priests would come forward. Two priests, an inner and an outer priest, would stand at each corner of the Ark facing outward. The outward facing was symbolic of the belief that the God who was represented by the Ark was meant to radiate from the Ark to all four corners of the world. The ceremony would begin by the outer priests turning a quarter turn to their left while the inner priests turned a quarter turn to their right. While singing "Kadosh" [meaning "Holy"] three times, the priests would take three steps sized so that each priest would arrive at the next corner of the Ark which was two and one half cubits long and one and a half cubits wide. When at the next corner, all eight priests would turn inward to face the Ark and sing the next part of the chant which is "Kadosh Adonai Shevayot," meaning "Holy Lord God of the Hosts [or of All]."

This movement from one corner to another would be done four times, with the outer priests going counter-clockwise around the Ark while the inner priests were going clockwise. The symbology of having two priests at each corner was to represent that more than one people were to pay homage to the Ark. The symbology of having the priests go in different directions around the Ark was that the peoples of the Earth would be separated in their adoration of God, but eventually would again be together as they had been at the beginning. This symbology would happen after the full chant had been sung four times, thus returning the priests to their original positions.

After the eight priests had returned to their original positions, they were then permitted to pick up the Ark and to move it to its next sacred site. Not only were the words of this ceremony sacred, for those who understand numerology, the numbers also are sacred, among which are the seal of seven and the number thirty-three.

I felt comfortable with this general message to humanity, because it stated to me that the messages which God had given to the people who generated the Ark were not meant to be reserved only for those people; but were, instead, to be spread outward to the four corners of the Earth for the benefit of all people. It was only later that the priests converted those gifts in such a way that they were presented only to God's "Chosen People." The priests and leaders did this as they established the Laws under which the Chosen People were expected to live.

I also felt a great sense of comfort and acceptance, because I was told that my personality in a previous incarnation had helped develop the ceremony as a member of the priestly tribe of Levi. In a later incarnation, the personality was a member of the tribe of Judah in order to help convert the Law created by the priests into the Love created by God. This happened during the time in history when the tribe of Judah was the only large tribe left among the twelve tribes of Israel; for ten tribes had been lost when the Northern Kingdom was conquered in about 740 BCE, and the only surviving tribe besides Judah, the tribe of Benjamin, was a relatively small one.

I awoke with a great sense of personal peace. Later, when I described my experience to the Spiritual Masters, they readily accepted the changes as feeling right; and the one who was the spiritual leader for the entire journey came up to me and said, "I wondered who would bring the singing chant in. I knew last night that it was not to be spoken."

Later that morning, a very successful ceremony resulted. It felt very familiar. It should feel familiar, for we had revisited an ancient ritual.

A GIFT ON EASTER MORNING

After the reprieve of the ancient ritual on Wednesday morning of the Passover-Easter Week of Jerusalem in 1994, the tour continued to many nearby sites including Masada, Jericho and the old city of Jerusalem. On Friday, Good Friday to the Christian world, it was a dreary, wet day in Jerusalem. As a follower of the Christ, I guess I expected that; but I also expected Easter morning to be bright. It was.

I awoke at 5:40 AM on Easter Sunday morning. There was no alarm clock—just the knowledge that it was now time to get up. It was still dark as I looked out of my window in the Mount Zion Hotel, but fortunately my window faced East; and I could easily see the beginning of the streaks of morning light in the far east. The sky was completely clear, the stars were unbelievably bright, the moon was a half-moon and a bright star dominated the sky away from the sunrise. The birds were singing as if they were choirs of angels. The day was glorious, both in its physical and in its etheric being. With the exception of the angelic choir of birds, the morning was very quiet. I felt completely at peace.

As the sunrise started up over the hills to the East, it began with a symphony of beautiful reds and oranges. Then a most extraordinary thing happened. The last color, just before the sun broke its contact with the hills, was a deep purple. It was a broad band of purple which circled the area of sunrise and stayed there until the sun broke completely free.

My first instinct was that the laws of physics had been repealed, because that is not the way things are supposed to be. Purple simply should not be the last color before sunrise. It almost seemed as if the laws of light had been turned upside down, and as if the rainbow had been reshuffled; for purple, the color with the shortest wavelength in the visible spectrum was adjacent to red, the color with the longest wavelength.

Later, I started to mention this broad band of purple to another member of the group and she confirmed it before I mentioned it. She also confirmed that there were no clouds in the sky so that we were not seeing a reflection of clouds in some unexplained manner. When I explained the counter-physics of having purple next to the sun, her eyes got wide in wonder. It seemed to both of us that on this Easter Morning, the rainbow had been reversed with the royal purple of Christ the King immediately preceding the rising of the sun.

On Easter evening, we had a long meeting during which we shared the experiences which we, as individuals, had been having. During part of the meeting, we discussed what progress we felt we were making in our attempt to reunite the twelve tribes of Israel. I decided to tell my story about how the royal purple band of color had appeared during the sunrise on Easter morning. I did so, and then said that in my opinion, this had been a sign that the twelve tribes had been united under the royal purple mantle of Christ the King. There was support from others of the group, both on the fact that the royal purple mantle had appeared, and that it symbolized an important message which each could interpret as he or she saw fit.

The next morning, one very psychic member of the group asked Lord Sananda, the present name of the one who had been known as Jesus Christ during his Earthly incarnation, to tell her what the message meant. She was told that "brother Dave" had seen the mantle correctly and had interpreted it well, but not completely.

He went on to say how pleased the hierarchy was with the work which all of us had done on Saturday, the day before Easter. He said that because of this work, the gift of the royal purple mantle had been sent with the message that there would be no more grief for Israel, but only joy for the times which would come. He further said that the 2000 year reign of St. Germain in the Office of the Christ was heralded by the message of the royal purple mantle. St. Germain is believed by many to be the one who presently holds the seventh Ray [purple-violet] for this Earth and who will become the holder of the Office of the Christ in the Aquarian Age, just as Lord Sananda held this Office during the Piscean Age.

It was a very positive message which Lord Sananda gave us. As I listened to it, I felt humble as I gave thanks for the Gift on Easter Morning.

THE STATUES SPEAK

In the fall of 1993, a continuation of the trip which started in the Yucatan with one group of 34 people found me first in Bolivia and Peru with a different group of 34 people, and finally at Easter Island with still a third group of the same number.

If the Yucatan were to represent *violence* such as we found at Chitzen-Itza followed by the full essence of *peace* such as we found at Palenque; and if Peru were to represent the *magic* of Machu Picchu; then Easter Island would represent the *reverence* or *respect* of humanity to its mother. From the moment my feet hit the ground of Easter Island, I strongly felt reverence for that sacred site. And the reverence was not limited to the statues. The entire island generated a feeling of reverence in me for all the time I was there.

As one of the exercises during our time on the Island, we were to find seven statues which spoke to us in one way or another. In our tours to the various sites on the Island, I had no trouble finding my seven statues. The first was "joyful spirit"; the second, "wisdom"; the third, "authority"; the fourth, "solitude"; the fifth, "humility"; the sixth, "pride"; and the seventh was "pain." I mention these attributes because that is what each statue had said to me as I viewed it. Since there are 848 statues on Easter Island as well as several thousand rocks each of which has a name, it is interesting that only these seven statues spoke directly to me as an aspect of myself. After finding these seven, I mentioned to a friend that I was surprised when none of my statues represented "compassion" or "love" to me. She replied that if you carefully balance and blend all that was given [i.e. joyful spirit, wisdom, authority, solitude, humility, pride and pain] then you would end up with "compassionate love." She just might be right!

But despite the wonder of these messages, that is not the occasion when the statue spoke to me. That experience happened on the last day of ceremonies on the Island. In mid-morning of that day, an English psychic for whom I feel great affection, approached me and asked if I had spent any time with the statue on the left. I answered that I had not, because the fourth one from the left was one of my statues [it was "humility"], and I had spent all of my time there. My English friend then said that she had been told that there was a special message from that statue waiting for one specific person from this group, and that she had approached eight people without getting the message which had been given to her. She said that the message was encoded in numbers. I agreed that I would spend some time with that particular statue, which I did. I then came back to her and said that I had received no numbers, but then described to her what I had received. She said, "Yes, that is the same message which I received. So you are the one. I would work on that if I were you."

What I had seen was a series of purple-violet arrows of the directional kind [i.e. not the killing kind of arrow] which led to a kneeling figure entirely covered with a glistening white robe. I assumed that this figure was the Christ, although his face was hidden by the robe which covered him completely. That was exactly the scene which my English friend had seen.

That afternoon, during a personal meditation at another site, I went to work on the message. What it said to me was, "I am Saint Germain as you would have guessed from the color of the arrows. I am here to tell you that I can show you the direction, but if you want to speak to God, you must *become the essence of the Christ Consciousness*. The face of the kneeling figure was hidden to you so that you would not associate it with any one Christ, but would accept that it represents the Christ Consciousness. Again, I can show you the way, but I cannot assume the essence of the Christ Consciousness for you. You must *become the Christ Consciousness yourself* if you wish to speak to God. With this knowledge, when you are talking to your Christian friends, you can tell them that I am a guide and not a God. You can also explain to them the meaning of the Bible verses which say: *'No one comes to the Father but by me,'* and *'I and the Father are one.'* " I sensed that he meant these references to mean, *"No one comes to the Father unless they become the Christ Consciousness"*; and *"The Christ Consciousness and the Father are one."*

The next day, when we had some free time, I walked back to the statue to check the interpretation. I got a resounding "Yes" when I asked if I had it right. I then asked if there were anything to add. I was given another scene. I saw a nice, small Christian church in the valley. A big hand reached down under the church and lifted it to the top of the nearest mountain. I said, "Do you want me to try to help elevate the Christian Church?" and the answer again was a loud "Yes."

The next day I again went back to the statue for another confirmation. This time I was with a young, male American friend. Again I went to the statue, not only to recheck the interpretation of both messages, but also to ask if I had permission to share the story with others. I again was told that the interpretations were correct. I was further told that I could share the story. I therefore shared the story with my young friend. I am now sharing the story with you.

And that is all there is to that!

A MESSAGE ABOUT THE FUTURE

The trip to the Yucatan in the Fall of 1993 which has previously been mentioned, had the sacred city of Palenque as its final site. After a morning ceremony which I led, many of us followed the protocol which would allow us to visit the Temple of the Sacred Symbols, a Temple which exists only on the etheric realm at the present time. To do this, we had previously been instructed to find a comfortable spot, and to start into our deep meditation precisely at 10:00 AM.

At the appointed time, I was seated in a quiet, comfortable spot at the Temple of the Sun, a physical Temple which exists at Palenque. I followed the protocol for accepting the invitation to the etheric Temple, and I got there. I followed the golden road which led up to the great doorway. The doorway was highly carved in dark wood, then it slowly became gilded until it turned into a great carved door of solid gold. I asked that I be allowed to enter, and I was granted that wish. I entered into a great hall, where I was introduced to the Divine Director. He led me out a back door where I saw a large mountain. On the top of this large mountain was a great edifice. I was transported to that building through the air, and when inside, I was cascaded and showered with thousands of golden symbols. It was a virtual shower out of which I could pick no individual symbol

. When I asked what all of this meant, which I felt I was allowed to do, the Divine Director said, "You are coming home"; which was followed first by 10 voices, then by 100 voices, then by 1000 voices, all saying, "You are coming home." The voice choir was certainly beautiful! Any time that I read the notes covering this visitation, I again hear the choir of many voices singing, "You are coming home." I usually feel tears of joy when I re-read those notes. I again feel those tears as I type these words. The words were given to me at a spot I call the "Peace of Palenque."

Almost exactly one year later, my sister and I and our spouses were at Martha's Vineyard for a short vacation. While there, we listened to an old LP record on which Hal Holbrook gave his stage presentation of Mark Twain. At the very end of that presentation, he tells the story of a man who had a small boat which sailed the near-inland waters of New England and made deliveries among the offshore islands. When this man would see a big ship, he would climb into the rigging of his small ship and say, "Ahoy! What ship goes there." The large ship would reply, "The great steamer North America, 142 days out of New Delhi, India, loaded with a great load of spices and headed for home." Then after telling about the response from the man on the little boat, Hal Holbrook would say, "And so I say to you that I am God's ship, Mark Twain, 70 years out of Hannible Missouri, and headed for home. Good night to all."

To me, this heart-warming statement immediately presented the picture which I had seen at Palenque. Again, I heard the choir; and so, on Martha's Vineyard that night, I excused myself, went to the bedroom, took out my ledger and wrote, "And so I say to you, I am God's ship, Dave Moore, long out of Mount Hope, West Virginia, loaded with God's love for all, and headed for home!"

To all who have shared these personal experiences along the pathway with me, I will say that I hope you also are filled with God's love, and that you also are Going Home. With God's blessing for all of us, I will see <u>all</u> of you there!

<u>GOD</u> <u>BLESS</u>*!*

BIBLIOGRAPHY

*I. BOOKS CITED IN THIS WORK
OR USED AS SPECIFIC REFERENCE MATERIAL*

Bailey, Alice A., *Initiation, Human and Solar*, copyright 1951 by Lucis Trust, published by Lucis Publishing Company, New York.

Bailey, Alice A., *The Rays and the Initiations*, copyright 1960 by Lucis Trust, published by Lucis Publishing Company, New York.

Ballou, Robert O., Editor, *The Portable World Bible*, copyright 1944 by the editor, copyright renewed 1972 again by the editor, published by Penguin Books, USA, Inc., 375 Hudson Street, New York, NY 10014.

Campbell, Joseph, *The Masks of God: Occidental Mythology*, copyright 1964 by the author, published by Viking Penguin Inc., 40 West 23rd Street, New York NY 10010.

Campbell, Joseph, *The Masks of God: Oriental Mythology*, copyright 1962 by the author, published by Viking Penguin Inc., 40 West 23rd Street, New York NY 10010.

Dowd, Michael, *Earthspirit, A Handbook for Nurturing Ecological Christianity*, copyright 1991 by the author, published by Twenty-Third Publications, 185 Willow Street, P. O. Box 180, Mystic, CT 06355.

Fideler, David, *Jesus Christ, Sun of God*, copyright 1993 by the author, published by The Theosophical Publishing House, P. O. Box 270, Wheaton, IL 60189-0270.

Furst, Jeffrey, Editor, *Edgar Cayce's Story of Jesus*, copyright 1968 by the Edgar Cayce Foundation, published by The Berkley Publishing Group, 200 Madison Ave., New York, NY 10016.

Grattan, Brian, *Mahatma I & II, The I AM Presence*, copyright 1994 by Light Technology Publishing, P. O. Box 1526, Sedona, AZ 86339.

Haskins, Susan, *Mary Magdalen, Myth and Metaphor*, copyright 1993 by the author, published by HarperCollins Publishers, 10 East 53rd Street, New York, NY 10022.

Hall, Manly P., *Twelve World Teachers*, copyright 1965 by The Philosopphical Research Society, 3910 Los Feliz Blvd., Los Angeles, CA 90027.

Hamilton, Virginia, *In the Beginning, Creation Stories from Around the*

World, copyright 1988 by the author, published by Harcourt Brace Jovanovich, San Diego, New York, London.

Paulson, Genevieve Lewis, *Kundalini and the Chakras*, copyright 1991 by the author, published by Llewellyn Publications, P. O. Box 64383, St. Paul, MN, 55164-0383

Prophet, Mark L. and Elizabeth Claire, *Lords of the Seven Rays*, copyright 1986 by Summit University Press, Box A, Livingston, MT 59047-1390.

Sanders, E. P., *The Historical Figure of Jesus*, copyright 1993 by the author, published by the Penguin Group, 375 Hudson St., New York, NY 10014.

Thiering, Barbara, *Jesus and the Riddle of the Dead Sea Scrolls*, copyright 1992 by the author, published by HarperCollins Publishers, 10 East 53rd Street, New York, NY 10022.

Viladesau, Richard and **Massa**, Mark, S.J., Editors, *World Religions, A Sourcebook for Students of Christian Theology*, copyright 1994 by the editors, published by Paulist Press, 997 Macarthur Blvd., Mahwah, NJ 07430.

Williamson, George Hunt, *Secret places of the Lion*, copyright 1958 by the author, First Quality Paperback Edition published 1983 by Destiny Books, 377 Park Ave. South, New York, NY 10016.

II. GENERAL REFERENCE RESOURCES

New Catholic Encyclopedia, copyright 1967 by the Catholic University of America, Washington, DC. Library of Congress Catalog Card Number 66-22292, published by the McGraw-Hill Book Company, New York.

The Dictionary used for definitions was *The American Heritage Dictionary of the English Language*, published by the American Heritage Publishing Company and Houghton Mifflin Company, New York, copyright 1973.

The New Encyclopaedia Britannica, 15th Edition, copyright 1987.

The Oxford Companion to the Bible, edited by Bruce M. Metzger and Michael D. Coogan, copyright 1993 by Oxford University Press, Inc., published by Oxford University Press, Inc., 200 Madison Ave., New York, NY 10016.

Unless otherwise noted, all Bible references are from the *Revised Standard Version* published by the American Bible Society, New York and copyrighted 1980 [Old Testament] and 1973 [New Testament] by the Division of Christian Education of the National Council of the Churches of Christ in the USA.

III. OTHER REFERENCE RESOURCES

A number of other books and reference materials were used during the writing of *The Christian Conspiracy* and thus became subliminal reference sources for this book. In addition to the books mentioned here, there are over fifty reference books presented in the Bibliography of *The Christian Conspiracy*.

INDEX

Notes: Major Index References are in **bold** type.
Index notation "[Bib.]" means the author's book is listed in the Bibliography [see pages 269-70].

Abraham or Father Abraham, 26, 27, 28, 29, 45, 46, 50, 73, 131, 150, 164, 204, 208, 209
Angels, 56, 83, 103, 112, 221
Aquinas, Thomas, 20
Aramaic, 63, 108, 109, 111, 120
Arius or Arianism, 45, 138
Athanasius, 54
Atlanta Constitution-Journal, 21, 166, 218-9
Atonement, 4, 53, 54, 207
Augustine, 20, 65, 80, 81, 82, 147, 181-2, 186
Book of Mormon, The, 27, 28, 31
Buddha, 12, 26, **37-39,** 42, 47, 52, 60, 68, 134, 158, 209, 218, 236
Buddhists or Buddhism, 52, 56, 58, 59, 62, 65, 113, **133-5,** 139-40, **157-8,** 161, 218
Calvin, John, 138, 187
Cathars, 81, 170, 172, 215
Catholic Encyclopedia, The New, 19, 20, 66, 77, 78, 152
Catholic or Roman Catholic, 23, 121, 138, 215, 218
Celestine Prophecy, The, 112, 113
Chakra or Chakras, 64, 65, **114-116,** 124, 199, 204, 223, 226
Christ Consciousness, 4, 5, 7, 47, 67, 68, **266-7**
Christian Conspiracy, The, 9, 45, 46, 54, 68, 85, 109, 121, 141, 184, 185, 198, 203, 206, 224, **235-6,** 242, 257

Christianity, 52, 55, 58, 60, 62, 64, **130, 137-8,** 147, **151-4,** 161, 162, **163, 164, 165-8,** 185, 206-7, 209
Christianity and the New Age Religion, 9, 18, 22, 67, 68, 122, 134, 206, 212, 239
Clement of Alexandria, 80, 196
Coincidence, **107-113,** 124
Commandment, The Great, 42-3, 63, 154
Commandments, Ten, 32, 33, 43, 55, 61, 150, 151, 206
Conclave of Michael, 257
Confucius or Confucianism, **39-42,** 47, 51, 56, 58, 59, 62, 65, 69, **135-6,** 139-40, **158-60,** 209
Cosmic Concept, First, 10, 11, **127-44**
Cosmic Concept, Fourth, 10, **189-94**
Cosmic Concept, Second, 10, 11, **145-177**
Cosmic Concept, Third, 10, 12, **179-188**
Cosmic Concepts, Four, 3, 10, 13
Creation Story or Stories, 6, 118, **127-144, 244-50**
Deism, 134
DeMohan, Elias [William David], 110, 111, 253
Dimensionality, **97-103,** 124
Eckhart, Meister, 47, 121, 181
Ecumenical Councils, 20, 21, 42, 45, 79, 130, 198
Encyclopaedia Britannica, The New, 35, 37, 66
Epedocles, 147
Eratus,Thomas [Thomas Luber], 21
Erdman, Dr. Charles R., 30
Esoteric Thoughts, **65-69**
Fideler, David [Bib.], 19, 120
Francis of Assisi, 47
Free Will, 1, 10, 15, 87, 94, 113, 123, **184-88,** 189
Freemasonry, 27, 28
Gandhi, Mohandas, 47, 157, **162-3,** 242-3
Graham, Billy, 103, 165
Grattan, Brian [Bib.], 67, 68
Great Initiates, The, 28, 33, 66
Grizzard, Lewis, 193
Groff, Father John, W. Jr., 5, 64, 180, 252

Index

Hamilton, Virginia [Bib.], 244
Haskins, Susan [Bib.], 163-4, 180-1
Hate Sin/Love Sinner, 165, **169-173**
Heisenberg Uncertainty Principle, 22, 121, 122
Heracleitus, 19, 190
Hick, Professor John, 203
Hindu or Hinduism, 23, 121, **131-3, 139-40, 155-7,** 218
Hitler, Adolph, 170, 172, 173
Holocaust, 170, 172, 174
Holy Spirit, 53, **209-213**
Homosexuality, 57, 141
Ineffable, 17, 18, 22
Islam, 50, 55, 56, 58, 59, 62, 65, **130-1, 138-9, 154-5,** 157, **164,** 185, 207-8, 219
Jehovah's Witnesses, 218-9
Jesus Christ, 12, **42-44,** 53, 63, 64, 66, 67, 70, 76, 78, 113, 201, 236
Josephus, 75
Judaism, 36, 50, 55, 57, 59, 61, 65, 87, **130, 137, 149-51,** 162, **164,** 206, 219
Keys of Enoch, The, 28, 31, 66, 67
Koran, 46, 82, 131, 154, 162, 183, 202, 207-8
Lao Tze or Taoism, **39-42,** 47, 52, 56, 58, 59, 62, 65, **135-6, 139-40, 160,** 209
Letter to the Hebrews, The, **27-30,** 231
Marcion or Marcionism, 81, 139, 206
Martyr, Justin, 79
Maximus of Tyre, 19
Melchizedek, **26-33,** 35, 38, 42, 46, 47, 67, 68, 69
Melchizedek, Drunvalo, 112, 113
Messengers from God, 12-3, **25-48**
Milgrom, Jacob, 57
Mohhamad, 12, **44-46,** 209
Mohism, **159-60,** 161
Monad, 25, 26, 81, **86-89,** 91, 92, 93, 95, 254
Monogenes, 54, 68
Mormons, 31, 183, 219

Moses, 18, 20, 31, **32-34,** 35, 36, 39, 42, 47, 69, 148, 150, 205, 206, 209
Muslims [See Islam]
Myths, **127-8**
New Age, 4, 62, 198, 236, 239, 251
Nirvana, 133, 158, 184
Numbers, Thoughts about, **117-120,** 125
Office of the Christ, **66-8,** 265
Omnipotent, 15, 20, 22, 69, 99, 129, 142, 154
Oneness with God, **179-84**
Order of Melchizedek, **27-30**
Origen, 55, 68, 80
Original Sin, **181-2,** 184
Pain, Suffering and Evil, **140-143**
Parables, 66, 122-123, 196, 224-5, 228
Pelagius and Pelagianism, 186
Pierre Teilhard de Chardin, 47
Plato, 147
Pope Innocent III, 170, 173
Pope John, 23rd, 47
Primary Cause, Creator or Mover, 52, 58, 105, 108, 111, 120, 124, 141
Protestants, 138, 215, 219
Psalms, Imprecatory, **165-167**
Quetzacoatl, 47
Reincarnation, **71-96**
Revelation of John, 220-2, 226, 231
Samaritans, 14, **50-1,** 61, 64, 153, 168, 214-5
Second Reformation, Prayer and Hymn for, **8, 178**
Seven Deadly Sins, **162-3**
Song of Solomon, 149
Space, **72-75,** 230
Taoism [see Lao Tze]
Thermodynamics [and Kinetics], **103-107,** 124
Thiering, Barbara [Bib.], 95
Time, **72-75**, 105, 230
Traits [of the soul], **89-93**

Transcendent, 22-3, 120-1,132, 184
Transformational events, 23, 106, 107
Unacceptable Activities, **173-5**
Unchanging, **23**
Unconditional Love, 1, 44, 48, **63-65,** 122, 143, **145-179, 213-216,** 222, 228, **233, 237**
Universalists, 219
Urantia Book, The, 28, 31, 32, 38, 40, 42, 66
Virgin Birth, 13
Winfrey, Oprah, 79
Witch, 141, 170-1, 172, 219
Xenophanes, 19
Yahweh [or Jehovah], 18, 19, 50, 130, 137, 139, 205, 206
Zoroaster or Zoroasterism, 12, **34-37,** 68, 87, 113, **128-30, 136-7, 148-9,** 209

In the Summer of 1993,
Christianity and the New Age Religion
A Bridge Toward Mutual Understanding
was published to rave reviews.

** A very important book for Christians, for New Agers,
and especially for Christian New Agers!*
** A solid work, the most enlightening synthesis
of Christianity and the New Age around!*
** Will become a classic, guiding many Christians and New Agers
into greater understanding of our changing belief system!*

**The purpose of this book
is to teach both Christians and
the New Pioneer element of the New Age
that once they start to learn from each other,
they can travel together
toward Integrated Spirituality!**

For ordering information, see the next page

Then in the Fall of 1994
The Christian Conspiracy
received even greater praise and sales by telling
*How the Teachings of Christ
Have Been Altered by Christians*

* This is the book Christians have been waiting for!
** The book challenges the Christian world to reform itself,
but to do so as loving individuals who return to the
original teachings of the Christ!*
** This Earth-shattering book distinguishes
Christ from Christianity, and in this way explains
how the Church became so intolerant of other's viewpoints!*

**The purpose of this book is to show
what teachings came from the Early Church Fathers
rather than from the Christ.
Most people in the pews today
are following Augustine, Tertullian, Athanasius and Jerome
rather than the Christ, but they don't know it!**

Now, in the Fall of 1995 comes
A Personal Pathway to God
which sings
Our Song of Freedom

by answering the major question
posed by the first two books which is:
Where do we go from here?

Initial responses from previewers have been enthusiastic!
Some of those responses are presented on
the second and third pages of this book.

The purpose of this book
is to show that humans in all of the world's major religions
have placed restrictions on
the teachings originally presented by the messenger
sent from God. By doing this, they have
inhibited spiritual growth. Full spiritual growth
is a personal matter between an individual and his/her God!

Ordering Information

In the table below, **CNA** represents *Christianity and the New Age Religion*; **TCC** represents *The Christian Conspiracy*; and **PPG** represents *A Personal Pathway to God*.

Book	Retail Price	Pages	Total Delivered Price [one location]		
			1 book	5 book pkg.	20 book pkg.
CNA	$12.95	244	$14.00	$39.00	$140.00
TCC	14.95	360	16.00	45.00	165.00
PPG	13.95	288	15.00	42.00	155.00

To order, please send check or money order to:

**PENDULUM PLUS PRESS
3232 COBB PARKWAY, SUITE 414
ATLANTA, GA 30339**

About the Author

L. David Moore was born in the early 1930s. In 1953, he received a BS in Chemistry from West Virginia University. Later, he received an MS in Polymer Chemistry from the University of Akron; and a Ph.D. in Organic Chemistry from Purdue University.

During an early part of his 30 year business career, he directed technology for the world's leading speciality chemical company, one which specialized in creating remedies for environmental problems. Later, he became Group Vice President and Director of a Fortune 300 company; then Executive Vice President in charge of all operations of a Fortune 50 company where he directed sales of over $3 billion and the activities of some 25,000 employees; and finally, President of Interchem Corp., a company described in a leading chemical journal as one "whose sales have galloped forward impressively." After Interchem was sold, Dr. Moore "retired" to writing books and lecturing.

Dave and his wife Jan have been devotedly married since the mid-1950s. They presently live in Atlanta, GA. They have four children and two grandchildren.

As described in all three books, Dr. Moore has had a lifelong, abiding interest in religious activities. Lately, those interests have included reading many religious works, writing and lecturing on religious subjects, and taking spiritual journeys to the many parts of the world he has read about, an activity which has greatly increased his love for his fellow human. As a result of the time spent on those trips and spent in reading, writing and lecturing, his golf game has deteriorated beyond recognition.